Violence Against Women

Other Books in the Current Controversies Series:

Violence Against Women

James D. Torr, *Book Editor*
Karin L. Swisher, *Assistant Editor*

David Bender, *Publisher*
Bruno Leone, *Executive Editor*

Bonnie Szumski, *Editorial Director*
Brenda Stalcup, *Managing Editor*
Scott Barbour, *Senior Editor*

CURRENT CONTROVERSIES

Library of Congress Cataloging-in-Publication Data

Violence against women / James D. Torr, book editor; Karin L. Swisher, assistant editor.
    p. cm. — (Current controversies)
    Includes bibliographical references and index.
    ISBN 0-7377-0014-9 (pbk. : alk. paper). — ISBN 0-7377-0015-7 (lib. : alk. paper)
    1. Women—Crimes against—United States. 2. Women—Crimes against—United States—Prevention. 3. Wife abuse—United States. 4. Abused women—United States. 5. Rape—United States. 6. Acquaintance rape—United States. I. Torr, James D., 1974– . II. Swisher, Karin, 1966– . III. Series.
HV6250.4.W65V554   1999
362.88'082'0973—dc21
                                       98-35007
                                         CIP

Cover Photo: Ron Chapple/FPG International LLC

©1999 by Greenhaven Press, Inc., PO Box 289009, San Diego, CA 92198-9009
Printed in the U.S.A.

Every effort has been made to trace the owners of copyrighted material.

Contents

factors and minimize statistics that show that violence against women is the more serious problem. Men should work together to curb violence, not pretend it is a myth.

No: The Problem of Violence Against Women Has Been Exaggerated

Chapter 2: What Causes Violence Against Women?

Chapter 3: Are Current Criminal Justice Approaches to Domestic Violence Effective?

Yes: Laws to Fight Violence Against Women Are Necessary

message that intimate abuse is a serious crime. The VAWA is an appropriate government response to the intolerably high levels of violence against women in the United States.

for judges, prosecutors, and probation officers, and innovative sentencing of abusers. To better serve victims, the legal system should institute more training for judges and prosecutors and clearer guidelines for handling domestic violence cases.

Foreword

By definition, controversies are "discussions of questions in which opposing opinions clash" (Webster's Twentieth Century Dictionary Unabridged). Few would deny that controversies are a pervasive part of the human condition and exist on virtually every level of human enterprise. Controversies transpire between individuals and among groups, within nations and between nations. Controversies supply the grist necessary for progress by providing challenges and challengers to the status quo. They also create atmospheres where strife and warfare can flourish. A world without controversies would be a peaceful world; but it also would be, by and large, static and prosaic.

The Series' Purpose

The purpose of the Current Controversies series is to explore many of the social, political, and economic controversies dominating the national and international scenes today. Titles selected for inclusion in the series are highly focused and specific. For example, from the larger category of criminal justice, Current Controversies deals with specific topics such as police brutality, gun control, white collar crime, and others. The debates in Current Controversies also are presented in a useful, timeless fashion. Articles and book excerpts included in each title are selected if they contribute valuable, long-range ideas to the overall debate. And wherever possible, current information is enhanced with historical documents and other relevant materials. Thus, while individual titles are current in focus, every effort is made to ensure that they will not become quickly outdated. Books in the Current Controversies series will remain important resources for librarians, teachers, and students for many years.

In addition to keeping the titles focused and specific, great care is taken in the editorial format of each book in the series. Book introductions and chapter prefaces are offered to provide background material for readers. Chapters are organized around several key questions that are answered with diverse opinions representing all points on the political spectrum. Materials in each chapter include opinions in which authors clearly disagree as well as alternative opinions in which authors may agree on a broader issue but disagree on the possible solutions. In this way, the content of each volume in Current Controversies mirrors the mosaic of opinions encountered in society. Readers will quickly realize that there are many viable answers to these complex issues. By questioning each author's conclusions, students and casual readers can begin to develop the critical thinking skills so important to evaluating opinionated material.

Current Controversies is also ideal for controlled research. Each anthology in the series is composed of primary sources taken from a wide gamut of informational categories including periodicals, newspapers, books, United States and foreign government documents, and the publications of private and public organizations. Readers will find factual support for reports, debates, and research papers covering all areas of important issues. In addition, an annotated table of contents, an index, a book and periodical bibliography, and a list of organizations to contact are included in each book to expedite further research.

Perhaps more than ever before in history, people are confronted with diverse and contradictory information. During the Persian Gulf War, for example, the public was not only treated to minute-to-minute coverage of the war, it was also inundated with critiques of the coverage and countless analyses of the factors motivating U.S. involvement. Being able to sort through the plethora of opinions accompanying today's major issues, and to draw one's own conclusions, can be a complicated and frustrating struggle. It is the editors' hope that Current Controversies will help readers with this struggle.

Greenhaven Press anthologies primarily consist of previously published material taken from a variety of sources, including periodicals, books, scholarly journals, newspapers, government documents, and position papers from private and public organizations. These original sources are often edited for length and to ensure their accessibility for a young adult audience. The anthology editors also change the original titles of these works in order to clearly present the main thesis of each viewpoint and to explicitly indicate the opinion presented in the viewpoint. These alterations are made in consideration of both the reading and comprehension levels of a young adult audience. Every effort is made to ensure that Greenhaven Press accurately reflects the original intent of the authors included in this anthology.

"Because much domestic violence goes unreported, estimates of the true extent of such violence remain controversial."

Introduction

Police reports state that on New Year's Day, 1989, O.J. Simpson allegedly kicked and struck his wife, Nicole Brown Simpson, while screaming, "I'll kill you!" In 1994, the prosecution used these reports and other evidence to portray O.J. Simpson, on trial for the murders of Nicole Brown Simpson and Ron Goldman, as a wife batterer—thus focusing the national spotlight on what women's advocate Charlotte Bunch calls "the most pervasive violation of human rights in the world today."

During the court proceedings attorney Gloria Allred described the O.J. Simpson trial as being "to the domestic abuse issue what Anita Hill was to sexual harassment. . . . It forces the nation to debate." And so it did: The Family Violence Prevention Fund reports that "there was a dramatic increase in both television and print coverage of domestic violence in the months following O.J. Simpson's arrest and the subsequent revelations of his abuse towards his ex-wife." According to the Women's International Network, "With her bruises captured in photographs and her fear echoing on a 911 audiotape even after her death, Nicole Brown Simpson has unleashed a wave of support for battered women and firmly anchored domestic violence in the American psyche as a problem that must be dealt with."

Battered women's advocates say the attention was long overdue. The Bureau of Justice Statistics (BJS) reports that about 30 percent of women murdered since 1976 were killed by their male intimate partners, and estimates of the number of women killed by their abusers each year range between 1,500 and 6,000. The Department of Health and Human Services reports that as many as 4 million women are beaten by their male partners each year, and some women's advocates claim figures of 18 million or more.

Partly because estimates vary so much, some critics have questioned whether the extent of violence against women has been exaggerated. *Washington Post* columnist Armin A. Brott, analyzing the sources of these data, charges that the truth about domestic violence has been "maimed almost beyond recognition by the irresponsible use of statistics." He puts the number of women battered each year in the hundreds of thousands rather than the millions. Psychologist Douglas E. Mould points to one women's group's fact sheet on domestic violence as representative of what he calls "distortions . . . accomplished with the illusion of integrity." The fact sheet states that "at least" 1.8 million American women are beaten in their homes each year; the study from which that figure was taken reported a figure of "almost" 1.8 million abused women.

The often-cited study in question, a survey of over two thousand couples, was conducted by Murray Straus and Richard Gelles of the Family Research Laboratory at the University of New Hampshire, and its results were first published in 1977. Straus and Gelles followed up this study with a survey of six thousand couples in 1985. Projecting their findings onto the national population of married and cohabiting couples, they estimate that between two and four million women are battered each year, a figure frequently quoted by domestic violence awareness advocates.

However, the same study by Straus and Gelles also found that approximately 100,000 men are battered in the United States each year. Male victims of battering account for roughly 5 percent of police domestic violence reports. Men's advocates cite these and other statistics, such as the fact that the majority of child homicides are committed by mothers, as evidence that violence is not solely a male behavior. Writer Philip W. Cook claims that "women hit first at about the same rate as men do, and women claim that self-defense was not the reason for the overwhelming majority of attacks on their mates." Cook and others charge that women's advocates ignore the problem of battered men for fear that it will discredit the perception of domestic violence as a women's issue. Columnist John Leo sums up this belief:

> Feminist studies of partner violence rarely ask about assaults by women, and when they do, they ask only about self-defense. Journalists, in turn, stick quite close to the feminist-approved studies for fear of being considered "soft" on male violence. The result is badly skewed reporting of domestic violence as purely a gender issue. It isn't.

Domestic violence may not be purely a problem for women, but it does affect them disproportionately. After all, in 95 percent of police reports males are the perpetrators of abuse. The Straus and Gelles study found that, although violence may often be mutual, women are more likely to be injured by it. The BJS National Crime Victimization Survey consistently reports that women experience more than 10 times as many incidents of violence committed by an intimate as men do. Moreover, while Richard Gelles, who is now director of the Family Violence Research Program at the University of Rhode Island, remains a prominent advocate of raising awareness about female violence, he insists that "the most brutal, terrorizing and continuing patterns of harmful intimate violence are carried out primarily by men."

Because much domestic violence goes unreported, estimates of the true extent of such violence remain controversial. The BJS does report an apparent gender split in the violence that is reported: One study found that, of women treated in hospital emergency rooms for violent injuries inflicted by another person, 36.8 percent of the injuries were inflicted by a husband or boyfriend. Wives and girlfriends accounted for only 4.5 percent of men's injuries. However, Cook says that men may not report being abused for fear of ridicule, and Gelles notes that "battered men face considerable difficulty (and some cruel jokes) because any discussion of the problem of battered men is typically considered politically incorrect."

After the revelations about the possible abuse that Nicole Brown Simpson suffered, statistics on male violence were repeatedly cited by advocates attempting to raise awareness about violence against women. Many critics, such as John Leo, accused feminists of exaggerating the numbers to support "the feminist theory of violence as patriarchy-in-action, with its dark view of men and marriage."

Others reject the idea that the purpose of these figures is to portray men in a negative sense. According to author Ben Wadham: "The fact that most research on domestic violence reports predominately male violence against women is not a personalised attack on men, but a representation of the real safety issues which women and men face from real violence." And Cook concludes that the figures on battered men show that "domestic violence is a human problem, not a gender problem."

Still others believe the debate over statistics is misplaced. The National Organization for Women, responding to charges that feminists minimize female violence and exaggerate the extent of violence against women, states:

> The real issue—that domestic violence is prevalent despite years of efforts to establish intervention programs—often gets lost as our eyes glaze over and our minds boggle at the effort to provide credible numbers. . . . Findings on issues such as drugs and alcohol, homicides and AIDS are imprecise despite years of study and enormous investments of research resources. Yet few people question that these are serious social problems. We want to stop the suffering of the thousands of women who have to live with the consequences of these very troubling statistics, not debate the statistics themselves.

The statistics on violence against women are among the issues debated in *Violence Against Women: Current Controversies.* Other topics discussed in this anthology include the causes of, the criminal justice response to, and other possible solutions to violence against women.

Chapter 1

Is Violence Against Women a Serious Problem?

Chapter Preface

The discussion in the media over the seriousness of violence against women—most often meaning domestic violence, rape, and acquaintance rape—frequently devolves into a debate over competing statistics. Many social scientists and women's organizations, among others, contend that statistics from the FBI and research studies show that violence is frequent, harmful, and perpetrated against women. Ann Jones, author of *Women Who Kill* and *Next Time She'll Be Dead*, presents some of these findings. Writing about domestic violence, she concludes that

> more than half the women assaulted are injured, and at least 25 percent of them seek medical treatment. . . . Of women requiring emergency surgery, one in five was battered, according to one study; one in two, according to another. Battering accounts for half of all cases of alcoholism in women. It accounts for half of all rapes of women over age thirty. . . . Battering is a cause of one quarter of suicide attempts by all women, and one half of suicide attempts by black women.

Jones and other advocates conclude that such statistics show both the magnitude and the gravity of the problem of violence against women. Ida Castro of the Women's Division of the U.S. Department of Labor says of domestic violence, "It's an epidemic which is profoundly affecting our communities and workplaces."

Others are not so certain. Although they denounce violence against women, many critics contend that feminists and other advocates for women have ignored, inflated, and manipulated statistics to make the problem appear more serious than it really is. Their motive, the critics argue, is to gain sympathy from the courts and to ensure continued public funding. According to these critics, studies done by longtime researchers Murray Straus and Richard Gelles, among others, show that *women* initiate violence more often than do men and that men suffer higher rates of domestic abuse than do women. Phil Cook, author of *Abused Men: The Hidden Side of Domestic Violence*, maintains that

> by their own admission in the surveys, women hit first at about the same rate as men do, and women report that self-defense was not the reason for the overwhelming majority of their attacks on their mates. About half of all incidents of violence are onesided; the rest is mutual combat.

By ignoring contradictory statistics such as these, these critics contend, feminists ignore a major portion of the problem of domestic violence and by doing so hamper efforts to find solutions to the problem. According to syndicated columnist John Leo, "Feminist researchers keep churning out work that fits feminist theory, while independent researchers keep finding equality in the use of violence."

The number of incidents of violence against women that occur each year and the question over who initiates that violence are among the topics debated in the following chapter. Perhaps the only point on which all agree is that violence is universally harmful.

Violence Against Women Is a Serious Problem

by Ann Jones

About the author: *Ann Jones is a contributor to the monthly women's maga-zine* Cosmopolitan *and the author of* Next Time She'll Be Dead: Battering and How to Stop It.

"He's f—ing going nuts," Nicole Brown Simpson told a police dispatcher on October 25, 1993. Eight months later, after O.J. Simpson was arrested for the murder of his ex-wife and her friend Ronald Goldman in the Brentwood section of Los Angeles, that 911 call was played and replayed on television and radio, plunging startled Americans into the midst of a typical terrifying incident of what we lamely call *domestic* violence. Previously, both O.J. Simpson and Joseph Russo, vice president of the Hertz Corporation, which retained Simpson as its spokesman even after he pleaded no contest to assaulting Nicole in 1989, had described O.J.'s wife beating as a private "family matter" of no significance.

The press calls Simpson the most famous American ever charged with mur-der, but he's certainly not the first celebrity to be a batterer, or even to be impli-cated in homicide. Certainly, the list from the sports world alone is a long one that includes boxer Sugar Ray Leonard; baseball star Darryl Strawberry; former University of Alabama basketball coach Wimp Sanderson; former heavyweight champ Mike Tyson, cited by then-wife Robin Givens and subsequently con-victed of raping Miss Black Rhode Island; California Angels pitcher Donnie Moore, who shot and wounded his estranged wife, Tonya, before killing himself in 1989; and Philadelphia Eagles defensive lineman Blenda Gay, stabbed to death in 1976 by his battered wife, Roxanne, who said she acted in self-defense.

The list of entertainers named as batterers is also lengthy and star-studded. Tina Turner reported in her autobiography that husband Ike abused her for years. Ali MacGraw described the violent assaults of Steve McQueen. Sheila Ryan sued her then-husband, James Caan, in 1980, alleging that he'd beaten her. Madonna was roughed up by Sean Penn, and Daryl Hannah by Jackson Browne.

Reprinted from Ann Jones, "Still Going On Out There: Women Beaten Senseless by Men," *Cosmopolitan*, September 1, 1994, courtesy of *Cosmopolitan* magazine.

Such incidents make titillating copy for scandal sheets and tabloid TV. And they continue to be commonplace—as all-American as football—precisely because so many people still think of battering as, in O.J.'s words, "no big deal." But when America listened last June to that 911 tape, eavesdropping on the private, violent raging of the man publicly known as the cool, affable Juice, anyone could hear that what Nicole Brown was up against was a very big deal indeed. For the first time, Americans could hear for themselves the terror that millions of women live with every day.

> *"These days, . . . there seems to be no safe haven."*

That terror begins with seemingly ordinary offenses. Take this list of complaints logged in a single week by the security office of one small institution. One woman harassed by unwanted attention from a man. One woman annoyed at finding obscene photographs in her desk. Two women annoyed by obscene phone calls from men. One woman sexually assaulted in her living quarters by a male acquaintance. One woman stalked by a man in violation of a restraining order.

Routine offenses? You bet. And they're increasingly common—not just because women are disgusted with such behavior and reporting it more often but because these days there's more and worse to report.

What makes this particular list of complaints noteworthy is that it comes from the security office at a small New England college. The sort of place where old stone buildings surround a quadrangle shaded by ancient trees. The sort of place where parents who can afford it send their daughters to be safe from the dangers of the outside world, safe from violence and violent men.

These days, however, there seems to be no safe haven. Not in exclusive Brentwood. Not even on the picture-perfect college campus. Because violence, which has always struck women of every social class and race, seems now to be aimed increasingly at the young.

Last year, at Mount Holyoke—the oldest women's college in the country—the student newspaper carried the front-page headline DOMESTIC VIOLENCE ON THE RISE. Reported cases were increasing all across the country, according to student reporter Gretchen Hitchner, and on the Mount Holyoke campus as well. "There are five or six students on campus who have obtained stay-away orders," Hitchner noted.

Beyond the boundaries of the campus, the statistics grew much worse. Statewide in Massachusetts in 1991, a woman was murdered by a current or former husband or boyfriend every twenty days. By 1993, such a murder occurred once every eight days. Among the dead: Tara Hartnett, a twenty-one-year-old senior psychology major at the nearby University of Massachusetts at Amherst. In February 1993, Hartnett had obtained a restraining order against James Cyr Jr., her former boyfriend and the father of her eleven-month-old daughter. In March, when Hartnett's roommates were away on spring break,

Cyr broke in, stabbed Hartnett, set the house on fire, and left her to die of smoke inhalation.

Incidents like the murder of Tara Hartnett happen all the time. Every day, some four or five women die in the United States at the hands of their current or former husbands or boyfriends. Annually, an estimated two million wives alone are beaten by their husbands. Yet recently, feminists who call attention to these crimes have been taking a lot of heat for perpetuating the image of women as victims. Critics charge that "victim feminists" exaggerate the dangers women face in male violence. Katie Roiphe, for one, suggests in her book, *The Morning After*, that many alleged cases of date rape involve nothing more than second thoughts by daylight after bad sex the night before. Battering, according to the critics, is nothing any woman with moderate self-esteem and a bus token can't escape. What prevents women from exercising their full female power and strength, some say, is not male violence but the fear of violence, induced by fuddy-duddy feminists who see all women as victims.

Could it be true that the apparent crime wave against women, on campus and off, is only a delusion of paranoid radical feminists? Is it real violence that keeps women down or only feminists' hysterical perceptions that hamper us?

In Canada, where the same questions were raised, Statistics Canada, a governmental information-gathering agency, determined to find out by interviewing 12,300 women nationwide in the most comprehensive study of violence against women ever undertaken. The results were worse than expected. They showed violence against women to be far more common than earlier, smaller-scale studies had indicated. They revealed that more than half of Canadian women (51 percent) had been physically or sexually assaulted at least once in their adult lives. And more than half of those said they'd been attacked by dates, boyfriends, husbands, family members, or other men familiar to them. One in ten Canadian women, or one million, had been attacked in the past year.

> **"Annually, an estimated two million wives alone are beaten by their husbands."**

These figures apply only to Canada, but there is every indication that women in the United States are no safer from attack. To be sure, battering is now the single leading cause of injury to women in this country. Nationwide, a million women every year visit physicians and hospital emergency rooms for treatment of battering injuries. Countless others keep their injuries secret, hidden— whether out of sheer terror, humiliation, or shame. The *Journal of the American Medical Association* reports that 8 percent of obstetrical patients are battered during pregnancy, while a March of Dimes study names battering during pregnancy the leading cause of birth defects and infant mortality.

Survivors confirm that a man often begins to batter during a woman's first pregnancy, when she is most vulnerable and least able to pack up and move.

Take Marie's(*) husband, a lawyer who beat her so severely during her seventh month that she went into labor. He then ripped out the phone, locked her in a second-floor bedroom, and left the house. She barely survived, and the son she bore that day has always been frail.

Carol miscarried after her husband knocked her down and kicked her repeatedly in the belly. He threatened to kill her if she tried to leave. When she became pregnant again, he beat her again, saying, "I'm going to kill that baby and you too." Instead, she killed him with his own gun and was sentenced to twenty years in prison, where she bore her child and gave it up for adoption.

Jean left her husband after he repeatedly punched her in the stomach while she was pregnant. Later, when her daughter was diagnosed with epilepsy, the doctor asked if Jean had suffered a fall or an accident of any kind during pregnancy. Now that her daughter is in college and still suffering seizures, Jean says, "I only lived with that man for a year, but he casts his shadow over every day of my life and my child's too."

Millions of women live with such consequences of male violence, but it's not surprising that many choose another way out. Battering is cited as a contributing factor in a quarter of all suicide attempts by women and half of all suicide attempts by black women. At least 50 percent of homeless women and children in America are in flight from male violence. Some years ago, the FBI reported that in the United States, a man beats a woman every eighteen seconds. By 1989, the figure was fifteen seconds. Now, it's twelve.

Some people take those facts and statistics at face value to mean that male violence is on the rise, while others argue that what's increasing is merely the reporting of violence. But no matter how you interpret the numbers, it's clear that male violence is not going down.

As crime statistics go, homicide figures are most likely to be accurate, for the simple reason that homicides produce corpses, which are hard to hide and easy to count. Homicide figures all across the country—like those in Massachusetts—indicate so clearly that violence against women is on the rise, some sociologists have coined a new term for the crime: femicide. The FBI estimates that every year, men in this country murder over fourteen hundred wives and girl-

> *"No matter how you interpret the numbers, it's clear that male violence is not going down."*

friends. The conclusion is inescapable: Male violence against women is real—and it is widespread.

Such violence was once thought to be the plague solely of married women, but battering, like date rape, is affecting young, single women more and more. In its recent study, Statistics Canada found that a disproportionate number of women reporting physical or sexual assault were young, those aged eighteen to twenty-four being more than twice as likely as older women to report violence in the year preceding the study; 27 percent of them had been attacked in the previous twelve months.

In the United States, the first study of premarital abuse, conducted in 1985, reported that one in five college students was the victim of "physical aggression," ranging from slapping and hitting to "more life-threatening violence." When Sarah, for one, was offered a ride home from a fraternity party by a young man who'd had too much to drink, she turned him down and advised him not to drive. He waited for her outside and beat her up—to "teach the bitch a lesson," he said.

Susan went home for her first break from college and told her high-school sweetheart that she wanted to date on campus. In response, he pulled out clumps of her hair, broke her arm, and deliberately drove her car into a tree.

> *"The conclusion is inescapable: Male violence against women is real— and it is widespread."*

After Bonnie broke up with a possessive student she'd been dating at college, he sneaked into her home at night and smashed in her head with a hatchet. Typically, men like this feel they're entitled to get their way, by any means necessary. Resorting to violence seems justified to them. They think they've done nothing wrong—or at least no more than she asked for.

Even high-school boys are acting out the macho myth. A study of white, middle-class juniors and seniors found roughly one in four had some experience with dating violence. In another study, one in three teenage girls reported being subjected to physical violence by a date. After reviewing many such studies of high-school and college students, Barrie Levy, author of *In Love and In Danger: A Teen's Guide to Breaking Free of Abusive Relationships*, reports that "an average of 28 percent of the students experienced violence in a dating relationship. That is more than one in every four students." Male counselors who work with wife beaters confirm that many older batterers first began to use violence against their dates as teens.

Which doesn't mean violence against young women is just kid stuff. According to the FBI, 21 percent of women murdered in America are between the ages of fifteen and twenty-four. Recently, a high-school boy in Texas shot his girlfriend for being "unfaithful," and for good measure, he killed her best friend too. Barbara Arrighi, who has witnessed increased date rape and battering and stalking among college students as assistant director of public safety at Mount Holyoke College, bluntly sums up the situation: "Anyone who doesn't believe America has a serious problem with violence against young women is living in La-La Land."

Some who've studied dating violence say young women may be more vulnerable to male aggression because they believe so innocently in true love. Schooled by romance novels and rock videos, which typically mingle sex and violence, they're more likely to mistake jealousy, possessiveness, control, and even physical or sexual assault, for passion and commitment. Consider the case of Kristin Lardner, who was twenty-one in 1992 when her ex-boyfriend, Michael Cartier, gunned her down on a Boston street, then later shot himself. Lardner had been terrified of Cartier, whom she'd dated for only two months, having done just what abused women are supposed to do the first time he hit her: She stopped dating him. And when he subsequently followed her, knocked her down in the street, and kicked her unconscious, she got a restraining order against him. But even after Lardner was murdered, her best friend and roommate still bought the romantic view of Michael Cartier's violence. She told reporters that Lardner had "cared" about Cartier, and "she was the only one who ever did. That's what pushed him over the edge . . . when he lost her."

Young men, too, buy into this romantic scenario. One of Cartier's male friends commented after the murder: "He loved her a lot, and it was probably a crime of passion. He was in love. He didn't do it because he was nuts."

But Cartier's former girlfriend, Rose Ryan, also talked to reporters, and what she had to say put Cartier's so-called love in a new light. She had cared about Cartier too, she said, and for months had tried to make him happy with love and

> *"Anyone who doesn't believe America has a serious problem with violence against young women is living in La-La Land."*

kindness and Christmas presents, even after he started to abuse her. It didn't work. Finally, after he attacked her with scissors, she brought assault charges against him and got him jailed for six months. Then, after Cartier murdered Kristin Lardner, Rose Ryan spoke about his brand of lovemaking. "After he hit me several times in the head," she said, "he started to cry. He'd say, 'I'm so sorry. I always hit people I love.' And the clincher: 'My mother, she never loved me. You're the only one.'"

It's a familiar part of the batterer's control technique, that message. And the awful truth is that it often works, appealing at once to a woman's compassion and her power, snaring her in a web of love and violence as the two contradictory concepts become inextricably entwined. Not only does it lead some women to reinterpret a boyfriend's violent behavior as passion, it leads some—like Rose Ryan for a while—to forgive and try to help a batterer change. Attorney Lynne Gold-Bikin, founder of the American Bar Association's Committee on Domestic Violence and head of the ABA's family-law section, recently pointed out on ABC's *This Week With David Brinkley* that many married women subjected to abuse don't walk out at once "because they don't want the marriage to end; they want him to stop beating them." But in the end, as the story of Kristin Lardner shows, even a woman who tolerates no violence at all is not safe from it.

It's likely, then, that young women—even young women in love—get battered for the same reason older women get battered. Namely, they have minds of their own. They want to do what they want. Battered women are often mistakenly thought of as passive or helpless because some of them look that way after they've been beaten into submission and made hostage to terror. Their inability to escape is the result of battering, not its cause. According to one study, three out of four battering victims are actually single or separated women trying to break free of men who won't let them go. They are not merely victims; they are the resistance. But they are almost entirely on their own.

How can women be helped to get free of this violence? That's the question survivors of battering and their advocates have been grappling with for twenty years. And they've made history—the first organization of crime victims united to rescue other victims and prevent further crimes. Although still so overburdened that more must be turned away than taken in, battered-women's shelters have provided safe haven over the years for millions of women and their children and undoubtedly have saved thousands of lives.

In addition, the battered-women's movement has brought battering out of the private household and into the spotlight of public debate. There, it has raised a much harder question: How can men be made to stop their violence? To that end, the battered-women's movement has pushed for—and won—big changes in legislation, public policy, and law enforcement. Currently, Congress is considering a crime bill that encompasses the Violence Against Women Act, which considers male violence against women a violation of civil rights and provides a wide range of legal remedies.

Still, much remains to be done. What's especially needed now, say the advocates, is a national campaign to go after the men at fault. Experts such as Susan Schechter, author of *Women and Male Violence*, say that men continue using violence to get their way because they can. Nobody stops them. There's no reason for a man who uses violence to change his behavior unless he begins to suffer some real consequences, some punishment that drives home strong social and legal prohibitions against battering. In the short run, the most effective way to protect women and children, save lives, and cut down violence is to treat assault as the crime it is—to arrest batterers and send them to jail.

> *"Even men convicted of near-fatal attacks on their girlfriends or wives are likely to draw light sentences or be released on probation."*

Usually, that's not what happens. Right now, most batterers suffer no social or legal consequences for their criminal behavior. Although police in most states and localities are now authorized to arrest batterers, many police departments still don't enforce the law, as Nicole Brown Simpson's repeated ineffectual calls to 911 illustrate. (As Lynne Gold-Bikin reported on the Brinkley show, back in 1976, when she founded the Committee on Domestic Violence, many of the police "were beating their wives, and they thought it was perfectly acceptable." Many still do.) If police do make arrests, prosecutors commonly fail to prosecute. And if batterers are convicted, judges often release them—or worse, order them into marital counseling with the woman they've assaulted. Many men are required to attend only a few weekly sessions of a therapeutic support group, where they show-and-tell with other batterers, after which their crime is erased from the record books. (Counselors like David Adams, who lead such groups, are the first to say therapy alone doesn't work.) One 1991 study found that among assaultive men arrested, prosecuted, convicted, and sentenced, fewer than 1 percent served any time in jail. The average batterer taken into custody by police is held less than two hours. He is free to walk away—to laugh at his victim and at the police as well.

> *"We must try to defend the constitutional right that belongs to all women— the right to be free from bodily harm."*

Even men convicted of near-fatal attacks on their girlfriends or wives are likely to draw light sentences or be released on probation with plenty of opportunity to finish the job. Witness the husband of Bernadette Barnes, who shot her in the head while she slept, served three months for the offense, and was released to threaten her again. Desperate, Bernadette hired a man to kill her husband. Convicted of murder and conspiracy to murder, she was sentenced to life in prison.

In Michigan, policeman Clarence Ratliff shot and killed his estranged wife, Judge Carol Irons, the youngest woman ever appointed to the Michigan bench. When fellow police officers tried to arrest him, he squeezed off a few wild shots before surrendering. For killing his wife, Ratliff got ten to fifteen years; for shooting at the cops, two life terms plus some additional shorter terms for using a firearm.

In the scales of American justice, it's hard to deny that men weigh more than women.

We can do better, say the advocates. We must try to defend the constitutional right that belongs to all women—the right to be free from bodily harm. And this is where an alert college can set a good example for the rest of society. While public officials often seem to accept violence against women as an inevitable social problem, colleges can't afford to. They're obliged to keep their students safe. As Mount Holyoke's Barbara Arrighi says, "We've had to work at safety, but as a closed, self-contained system, we have advantages over the big world. If one of our students is victimized, she finds a whole slew of helpers available right away—campus and city police, medical services, housing authorities, counselors, chaplains, academic deans. We'll ban offenders from the campus under trespass orders. We'll make arrests. We'll connect her to the county prosecutor's victim/witness-assistance program. We'll go to court with her. We'll help her get a protective order or file a civil complaint. We take these things seriously, we don't try to pin the blame on her, and we don't fool around." The approach that Arrighi describes is, of course, the way the system ought to work in every community.

As things stand now, however, it's still up to women to make the system respond—and it requires time, money, courage, and determination to get a result that looks like justice.

Take the case of Stephanie Cain. A college student, she had dated Elton "Tony" Ekstrom III for nine months. Then, during the course of one hour on the night of April 28, 1991, he beat her up, punching and kicking her repeatedly, leaving her with a fractured nose and a face nearly unrecognizable to those who saw her immediately after the attack. Subsequently, she said, she lost confidence and felt mistrustful of people. She suffered seizures and had to drop out of college. Major surgery to reconstruct her nose permanently altered her appearance.

Ekstrom was arrested and charged with assault and battery with a dangerous weapon: his foot. But Stephanie Cain wasn't permitted to tell her story in court, for Ekstrom never went to trial. Instead, he was allowed to plead guilty to a reduced charge of assault and battery. The judge gave him a two-year suspended sentence, and Ekstrom walked away—still thinking he'd done nothing wrong.

That result upset Stephanie Cain. Worried that Ekstrom might do the same thing to another woman, she decided to sue him for the damage he'd done. In December 1992, when she was back in college finishing her degree, she finally got her day in court. "The best part," she said, "was looking right at him, knowing I wasn't afraid of him anymore." After hearing her story, the jury awarded Cain and her parents $153,000 in damages for her injuries, medical expenses, and emotional distress. At last, Ekstrom was to pay a price for his criminal act, a civil-court jury having compensated Cain for a crime the criminal court had failed to punish. "Every time I look in the mirror," Cain said, "I'm reminded of what happened. There's no reason he should just forget it."

The victory Stephanie Cain won was a victory for all women. But it shouldn't have been that hard. And she shouldn't have had to fight for justice all by herself.

(*)In the interest of privacy, some names have been changed.

Domestic Violence Is a Serious Problem for Women

by Aimee Lee Ball

About the author: *Aimee Lee Ball is a contributor to* Harper's Bazaar, *a magazine for women.*

We're all amnesiacs, is what we are. O. J. Simpson has confirmed this. Our horror on hearing Nicole Brown Simpson's frantic calls to 911 came just six months after newspaper heiress Anne Scripps Douglas was beaten to death by her husband in the genteel suburb of Bronxville, NY, and six years after we apparently forgot about Hedda Nussbaum, the Greenwich Village book editor who allowed a lawyer named Joel Steinberg to disfigure her and kill their adopted child. Three years before that, we witnessed the resignation of John Fedders, the chief enforcement officer of the Securities and Exchange Commission, after he acknowledged that he'd broken his wife's eardrum and blackened her eyes. We return, over and over, to the conceit that the very successful, the very educated, and the very rich have no place in the annals of domestic violence.

"The truth that everybody seems to stumble over is that wife abuse cuts across social class," says Richard J. Gelles, Ph.D., director of the Family Violence Research Program at the University of Rhode Island. "People are shocked that it happens to an upper-class woman. They think there must be a reason, some pathology in her life. She must be a flirtatious slut or married to a psychopath. It happens because the husband is overly invested in controlling his wife. We call it lack of boundaries. He doesn't know where his life ends and hers begins. That's an important part of marital violence—the enmeshment and dependence that the two people have. She doesn't see herself as having a life independent of him, and his identity is completely tied up in his ability to control this woman—even if he's a prominent doctor, a pillar of the community. What's important is what the world looks like from his eyes."

Reprinted from Aimee Lee Ball, "The Faces of Abuse," *Harper's Bazaar*, November 1, 1994, courtesy of *Harper's Bazaar*.

Every 16 Seconds

The FBI reports that two million American women are beaten each year—one every 16 seconds—and the U.S. Surgeon General ranked abuse by husbands and partners as the leading cause of injury to women ages 15 to 44. The 1993 Commonwealth Fund Survey of Women's Health puts the numbers even higher: 3.9 million women were physically abused and 20.7 million were verbally or emotionally abused by their spouse or partner within the past year. (Any survey done by telephone may grossly underestimate the problem, since a pollster has no way of knowing if the abuser is standing right there by the phone, coloring the response.) A study done by Gelles found that the incidence of violence did decrease exponentially as wealth increased. But still, nearly 20 out of every 1000 women with incomes over $40,000 reported severe violence. That's a lot of Park Avenue abuse.

How does this go on virtually unchallenged? There's a clue in one classic experiment: The participants were ostensibly waiting for a class to begin, in a room with a telephone nearby, when a fight between a man and a woman was staged out in the hall. When it sounded as if the woman was being attacked by a stranger—she was shouting, "Who are you? Why are you doing this?"—everyone rushed to the phone to get help. When it was clear that she knew her assailant—her shouts were, "Bill, why are you doing this?"—nobody lifted a finger.

> *"The U.S. Surgeon General ranked abuse by husbands and partners as the leading cause of injury to women ages 15 to 44."*

"We've been taught to believe it's a private matter," says Jacquelyn Campbell, Ph.D., a researcher in domestic violence at Johns Hopkins University School of Nursing. "In 11 states it is not even illegal to rape your wife." The English common law, on which our legal system is based, actually sanctioned this "zone of privacy" with the early-19th-century Rule of Thumb, stipulating that a man could not beat his wife with a stick that was wider than his thumb. It was not until 1977 that New York State made wife beating a crime. In some states, a man who strikes a stranger is committing a felony, but a man who attacks his wife is committing only a misdemeanor.

It's much easier to predict which man will be abusive than which woman will be his victim. He probably saw his father do the same thing. "But there are no consistent risk factors for women—not education, not finances, not even if they were raised by an abusive father," says Campbell. "Men tend to replicate their fathers' behavior, but women do not replicate their mothers'." Our collective societal shock when the abuser is wealthy or successful seems naive, since, as Campbell remarks, "You see this profile played out in the biographies of our most admired businessmen. They're aggressive and controlling. They step on other people. They get to say what happens in every aspect of their lives. They boss their secretaries and minions. This is the profile of a man who thinks he ought to be in charge at home. Oftentimes the middle-class abuser isn't physically violent very often, and never in a place where it will show. He has a whole scenario of excuses and explanations, as we all do when we do something rotten: 'Yes, I lost my temper, and I did push her, but I don't know how she ended up with a broken jaw.' And the more middle class she is, the less support she gets from friends and neighbors. Her family is more horrified. She becomes more ashamed, more isolated."

Post-Traumatic Stress

There's a war-zone term that makes an unexpected appearance in the chronicles of domestic violence: "post-traumatic stress." Lots of former victims reported flashbacks on hearing of Nicole Brown Simpson's litany of abuse. "Nicole was every battered woman's nightmare," says Lenore Walker, Ph.D., a clinical and forensic psychologist who is the chairwoman of a task force on violence in the family for the American Psychological Association. Walker actually advises women to call a man's former wife or girlfriend, because the behavior is so well disguised; and if he abused her, he is going to abuse the next woman. "Batterers look like everybody else," she says, "and you don't see their violence in the courtship period. They demonstrate only kind, nurturing, Prince Charming behavior. We want a man to listen to us, and batterers get it right. If you're doing a big presentation at work, he calls you in the morning and asks, 'How do you feel?' and he calls five minutes before the meeting to say, 'You're going to be wonderful.' That changes once you've given him a commitment. It becomes, 'Why didn't you answer the phone on the first ring?' or 'Don't say that in your presentation.' It turns to possessiveness and jealousy and intrusiveness. The difficulty for all women is once we have seen a certain period of consistent behavior, it's difficult to believe that's not the real man. So any woman can fall into it."

Elizabeth Friend's blind date began in the foyer of her Beacon Hill townhouse and ended with a wedding three weeks later on the lawn of her Martha's Vineyard estate. She was in her 30s and recently divorced, a much-honored businesswoman. He was a respected scientist. "It was a marvelous fairy-tale romance," she says. "I had just returned from the South Pacific, and he met me at the airport and said, 'How about a short serenade and a long life together?' It was the most romantic thing I'd ever heard. He is fast and

"In some states, a man who strikes a stranger is committing a felony, but a man who attacks his wife is committing only a misdemeanor."

furious in his romances. He's attractive, intelligent, and to someone from the business world, he seemed noble. It felt like an honor to be a partner to somebody in science. But then he has a dark side, a rage that's totally unpredictable."

It started small. When she became pregnant, he criticized her habits and warned that the baby would be born brain-dead. "I would do things to try and gain his favor," she says. "He would tear down the meals I cooked, and I started keeping menus to prove that I wasn't making things to hurt him. He wanted a nanny who brought a certain station to the house, so I called a friend in Europe and got a French au pair, but he was so nasty that she left within 24 hours. We went through 40 or 50 people working in the house." Then Friend developed a rare blood disease. "He took a can of Lysol, backed me against a wall, and sprayed me because I was filthy," she says. "He got a knife and was going to cut me because I was vile."

> *"The prospect of a becoming a public spectacle is a powerful deterrent to reporting abuse."*

Friend covered her bruises with expensive makeup and actually began a business, all the while trying to "work" on the marriage. "I have a wall full of honors and accomplishments," she says. "There's nothing I've majorly failed at in my life. I'm an enabler. I couldn't believe I couldn't make it better. Successful women may be even more vulnerable to a man who has that sense of smell, a man who's attracted to them and wants to destroy them. And you become a partner in the process. They test you, and you allow them to get away with more."

She managed to convince herself that even such a compromised family life would benefit her child. "I believed I was staying because I did not want my daughter to be without the father that I sometimes saw my husband to be," she says. "But I had a tape of a song that my daughter wrote, about how she was worthless and her mother was scum—things she'd heard her father say. There was a blowup one morning. My husband attacked me, threw me on the ground, and drove off with my daughter in the car. I was bruised and broken and punched in the stomach, and the judge gave me a protective order and removed him from the property. My husband asked the police how to go about getting a permit for a gun."

Low Self-Esteem

A woman of such means and substance shares a flaw with the more prosaic victim of domestic violence: "Something that cuts across all these women is relatively low self-esteem," says Barbara Lewis, Ph.D., a New York City psychologist who counsels battered women. "There's a one-sided loyalty: If a man were truly able to value the woman, he couldn't do this to her. But the woman is made to feel that if she had behaved in a different way, he would have responded differently. A lot of women are into rescuing, and there's a certain grandiosity or hubris about that. She lives in a fantasy world where she's going to change him."

What is even more trenchant for the woman of higher social strata is the disparity between the expectations she and others have about her life and the reality. "We like to look at things simplistically and make assumptions, but in the case of battered women, we often assume wrong," says Sandy Koorejian, executive director of Domestic Violence Services of Greater New Haven, Connecticut. "It's hard to look at someone who's educated, making x number of dollars a year, with x number of people reporting to her, and apparently in charge of her life, and accept that she has allowed someone else to control another significant aspect of her life. We all grew up the same, learning that part of our identity is through a man. We change our names—many women find a lot of solace and security in that—and we give a lot of that stuff away. These women believe that a relationship with a man, even one who hits you, is better than none. And he's saying, 'She has the best clothes. The kids are in the best schools. What does she have to complain about?' We live in a society that values those things, so we tacitly agree."

The prospect of becoming a public spectacle is a powerful deterrent to reporting abuse for any woman living in a neighborhood where the police blotter is routinely reported in the local newspaper. "On the outside, her partner may be considered a fine, upstanding citizen," says Sue Dowling, an advocate at the New Haven service. "That's the mask, the dichotomy, the part that keeps people from knowing what's happening. 'I'm okay, everything is fine.' If they're living in the suburbs, the denial goes along with the manicured lawns and better schools and opportunities for families. The thinking is, 'This is a nice town and I'm a nice person, not a battered wife.' Women with financial stability may have an opportunity to make changes, but the complications come about in other ways: exposure in the community, the loss of the facade."

Abuse Means Failure

Sometimes it's loss of face in the family—or in the mirror. "If I had told my mother what was going on, it would have meant that I had failed," says Janet Dean of Denver, "and I didn't want to hear the I-told-you-so. It was too embarrassing to think I could have been so stupid—that's why I stayed for so long."

Dean became ill after her first year of college, and while recuperating at home, she met a guy, got pregnant, and married him. "There was a lot of chaos before there was any violence," she says. "One night he came home all riled up. He had been fired for smoking pot, and he said, 'We're moving to Texas.' The next morning we packed everything we owned in the back of a Volkswagen bus and moved to Texas

> *"I would lie in bed and think, If he had done to my neighbor what he did to me today, he'd be in jail."*

for a month." The first time she got punched in the face, she was nursing their three-day-old daughter. "I was never so shocked," she recalls. "I thought, What did I do to deserve that?"

Dean's husband would not allow her to go back to college and made it difficult for her to hold a job, preventing her from getting to work on time and moving the family to a remote mountainous region of Colorado. "It was constant survival mode," she says, "always watching out, doing what he wanted. I just got to the point where I thought, if I stay, I'm going to die. I already felt dead emotionally." She moved out with her children, but he continued to harass her—a friend of his had told him, "If you can make them cry, it means they still love you." He showed up one day when Dean's mother was visiting and assaulted both of them, running away before the police arrived. "Three days later he came back and beat me until I almost died," she says. "I was on the floor, crawling down the hallway, trying to call an ambulance. My kids were there—it's still the most awful thing I can imagine—giving me a pillow and blanket. I was in intensive care for two weeks. He was in jail for five months and got two years probation. If he had done it to someone else, he would probably still be in jail for attempted murder."

> *"It's less of an assault crime. I think of it as a hostage situation."*

While Dean was lying on a gurney in the emergency room, she was thinking, "If I live through this, I'm going to do something so this doesn't happen to other women." She went back to college and to medical school, with the support of her second husband, and at 40 is an obstetrician/gynecologist in Denver. She questions every new patient about domestic violence. "It's part of my routine," she says. "I ask about smoking, about drinking, and I ask if there is any history of physical abuse, sexual abuse, or emotional abuse. The ones it's never happened to say, 'No, thank God.' Some of the ones it's happened to say no with a funny look on their faces." Dean offers several levels of assistance: teaching about the cycle of violence, assessing the individual danger, and planning an escape route, with extra car keys and a change of clothes set aside. She's probably saving as many lives as the Pap smear.

A Cycle of Abuse

Anyone without a personal frame of reference for violent behavior might cling to the principle: Hurt me once, shame on you; hurt me twice, shame on me. "But people don't understand the glue that holds these relationships together," says New York City clinical psychologist Karen Greene, Ph.D. "There's a cycle, an escalation of control, and then this incredibly romantic, remorseful period. The romantic part probably marked the beginning of the relationship also—these two against all the calumnies of the world. These people are glued together in an extreme way." The why-doesn't-she-leave issue is a particular conundrum for a middle- or upper-class woman. "Chances are her husband can hire a good lawyer to say she's crazy or popping pills," says Greene. "And she's as likely to be stalked by somebody he hires." Jacquelyn Campbell of Johns Hopkins notes that deciding to leave may not take her out of harm's way. "As the abuse increases, so do his threats, and one of them is 'I'll never let you have the kids.' She may have gone for counseling and gotten a diagnosis of depression—wouldn't you be depressed?—and in the custody hearing he'll say, 'Look at her, she's mentally ill.' For her to leave him is the ultimate slap in the face, and he will continue to harass."

The women whose wealth is dispensed at the discretion of abusive husbands present a poignant picture. "Their situation is actually worse than most of the battered women I deal with," says Richard Gelles of the University of Rhode Island. "The upper-class woman married to the nice Jewish doctor gets zero social services, and the support system in the U.S. is not designed for her. Can you imagine her checking into a shelter, where she's got to share the third mattress from the left? She could go to a motel, but the American Express card is probably in her husband's name, so as soon as the bill comes in he knows where she is."

Margaret Hintz did check into many motels, hotels, and spas. For years she kept a suitcase under the jumper cables in the trunk of her car, and as the seasons changed she'd replace the contents, just as she rotated the clothes in her closet. Once she went to a shelter but felt guilty about taking up the limited bed space. After all, she was married to a millionaire.

Hintz fell in love with a nice young man stationed in the U.S. Air Force in her native Germany, was showered with gifts, and came to the U.S. as a 20-year-old bride. Meeting her in-laws was her first intimation of trouble. "My mother-in-law looked 30 years older than she was," Hintz remembers, "and she cowered. When she put her hand on her husband's shoulder, he roughly pushed her away. Later I asked my husband, 'Why is your mother so afraid of your father?' and he just said, 'What do you mean?'"

The newlyweds lived in Rapid City, SD, where Hintz was alone and homesick while her husband worked long hours at a top-secret military base. "I wanted to surprise him," she says. "When he came home one day, I said, 'Guess what? I got a job!' His whole demeanor changed. He came toward me and hit me so hard that I fell back against the wall and crumbled." The abuse continued for more than 30 years, traversing the country when the Hintzes relocated to Pennsylvania. Hintz raised two children while her husband made a fortune in the electronics business and threatened to kill her. "We had a yacht on the Chesapeake," she says, "and he told me he could knock me over the head and put me in the water, and nobody would ever know. While I was getting hit, he was yelling, 'Why do you make me hit you?' and I was saying, 'I'm sorry.' Women are fixers, and you want to have a happy home or you think somehow you've failed. That's what all the professionals said, all the doctors and clergy. I saw so many. They would say, 'What are you doing wrong? Meet him at the door, fix him a martini, and don't bombard him with your small household annoyances.' When you're told it's your fault, you believe it. But there was always a tiny voice telling me I wasn't wrong. I would lie in bed and think, If he had done to my neighbor what he did to me today, he'd be in jail."

With her son in college and her daughter graduated, Hintz began putting money aside and preparing her escape. When her husband put a piece of broken glass to her throat, she got a protection order and filed for divorce. "The day they served the protection order, the sheriff stayed with me until one in the morning," she says, "until I had the locks changed. They had never seen such hate as they saw in his eyes. Nobody was more shocked than our neighbors. We looked like the perfect family. We went to church on Sundays. I always looked right for PTA meetings. They thought he left me."

Smart and successful men can often be particularly diabolical. A month after Hintz filed for divorce, her husband bought four cemetery plots—but he didn't pay for them. He let the charges stand so that Hintz would be reminded of his implied threat with every monthly statement. She fought like hell for her fair share of the family fortune and now serves on the advisory board of a shelter for battered women as well as working with Pennsylvania Legal Services. She also tried to help one woman with a personal connection: Hintz had an account at a local florist and found out that her former husband had ordered flowers for his new girlfriend on that account. Equipped with a name and address, she sent the woman documentation of the abusive marriage and told her to call if she ever needed help. She never got a response.

Chronic Humiliation and Fear

Despite the dramatic stories, it's a mistake to overemphasize the blackened eyes and broken ribs of battered women, says Evan Stark, Ph.D., director of Connecticut's Domestic Violence Training Project of New Haven. "While injury is a significant piece," he says, "almost always the most salient issue is the chronic humiliation and the fear. Domestic violence may often involve severe injury. But the vast majority of abusive assaults do not result in medically significant injuries. The problem is not only that he's going to knock your teeth out. It's the intimidation, isolation, and control. Once a guy hits you, whenever he says, 'Pass the coffee,' it's something completely different. These women are linked inextricably to feelings of being subordinate, walking on eggshells, having to please him. It's less of an assault crime. I think of it as a hostage situation."

These days there are more efforts to bring the hostages home. In 1994 a mandatory reporting law went into effect in California that requires doctors and other health professionals to report suspected battering, just as they must report suspected child abuse. This is a volatile issue: Many of those who work in the field are opposed to mandatory reporting, arguing that it may actually jeopardize the women it means to help. "I'm sure there was a benevolent motive, but we're concerned about the chilling effect it may have on women," says Debbie Lee, associate director of the Family Violence Prevention Fund in San Francisco. "Given the epidemic proportions of domestic violence, there's a push for screening of the at-risk population, which is all women, just as there is for breast cancer."

There is some concern that mandatory reporting treats women as children. "There is no need for another bureaucracy like the child-welfare services," says Nancy Durborow of the Pennsylvania Coalition Against Domestic Violence. "What we support is some incentive to get doctors and nurses trained on issues of domestic violence for earlier intervention." There are three pilot programs in Pennsylvania: at Mercy Hospital in Pittsburgh, Abington Memorial Hospital in suburban Philadelphia, and Nesbitt Memorial Hospital in Wilkes-Barre. On-site advocates work with the women who come in, and medical personnel are trained in what to look for and how to ask.

The Pennsylvania Coalition also supported a bill in the state senate that would prevent insurance discrimination against victims of domestic violence in issuing policies, such as canceling policies or raising rates. Some companies have denied women health or life insurance because of a medical record of abuse. "The insurance companies have categorized it as 'fair discrimination,'" says Durborow, "like if you decided to be a race-car driver. We're saying that no one chooses to be a battered woman."

In Hollywood's ode to violence, *Natural Born Killers*, an abusive husband and father says pointedly, "If your ass is in my house, it's my ass." Perhaps part of that missive bears repeating to any man who tyrannizes the woman he purports to love: It is your ass . . . that's on the line now.

Rape Is a Serious Problem for Women

by Lynn Hecht Schafran

About the author: *Lynn Hecht Schafran is the director of the National Judicial Education Program, a project of the National Organization for Women Legal Defense and Education Fund.*

The 1995 report on rape from the Justice Department should help to resolve the debate about the figures relied on by Congress and President Clinton in passing the crime bill in 1994.

The findings from the revised national survey of crime victims demonstrate that if researchers asked the right questions, they would find significantly more sexual violence than was previously reported.

In 1994, the then Democratic Congress was criticized for relying on a 1992 study called "Rape in America" when it considered legislation committing money to the Violence Against Women Act, which was part of the crime package.

That study, financed by a grant from the National Institute of Drug Abuse, reported 683,000 rapes a year; Justice Department data at the time had reported 155,000. Congress relied on the "Rape in America" study because many experts testified to flaws in the methodology of the national crime survey.

The Justice Department report, covering 1992–1993 and released after the crime bill was signed, concluded that there were 500,000 incidents of sexual assault a year. These included 310,000 rapes or attempted rapes—twice as many as published in the previous reports—and 186,000 other sexual assaults.

The reason for the doubling of the figure is simple: for the first time, the people surveyed as part of a nationally representative sample of households were asked specifically about rape. (The survey, conducted annually, interviews 100,000 people. It is intended to uncover crimes that are not reported to the police as well as provide more details of reported crimes.)

Unbelievable as it may seem, until this redesign, the National Crime Victimization Survey, as it is called, had asked only general questions about attacks and threats, leaving it to each interviewee to mention rape. The new survey asks whether the person was raped or sexually assaulted in the prior year and whether the assailant was a stranger, a casual acquaintance or someone the victim knew well.

Different Findings

The revised survey produced two distinctly different findings from previous reports. First, the number of rapes and attempted rapes reported for the year 1992–1993 was 310,000 as compared with 155,000 in the 1991 Justice Department report. Second, as opposed to previous findings that more than half of rapists were strangers, the new survey found that 80 percent of rapes were committed by someone known to the victim. This is the same percentage of non-stranger rapes found by the "Rape in America" report.

The statistics in the two studies still differ with respect to total numbers because of methodological differences that are important to understand. Although the redesigned Justice Department survey is a vast improvement, its methodology is not as sophisticated as that used in the "Rape in America" study, which was conducted by the Crime Victims Research Center of the Medical University of South Carolina.

Failing to ask specifically about rape in the earlier crime surveys was absurd. But because the stereotype of rape still involves a stranger jumping from the bushes with a knife, asking about rape directly, as the new Justice Department survey now does, is also inexact.

Many rape victims do not label themselves as such because they mistakenly believe that forced sex can be rape only if the rapist is a stranger. This belief is so powerful that even when the Justice Department survey goes on to ask about sexual assaults by an acquaintance or someone the victim knows well, many do not perceive themselves as having been raped. Given that the vast majority of rapes are committed by someone the victim knows, the potential for error here is high.

Many rape victims also do not label themselves as such because they assume rape means only vaginal penetration. But many states today define rape as any type of sexual assault involving forced penetration. The Justice Department survey has changed its definition of rape accordingly.

> *"The most important point about the new Government findings is that they remind us of how much sexual violence women suffer."*

But that definition is not read to those surveyed unless she or he requests clarification of the terms "rape" and "sexual assault," and then only at the interviewer's discretion. The importance of questions that cover the broader legal definition of rape is demonstrated by the "Rape in America" report where only about half of the the assaults reported involved vaginal rape.

In that study, no one interviewed was asked whether she had been raped. Rather, she was asked four questions about specific threats or acts of force. No one surveyed was asked questions in front of family members.

All of the "Rape in America" interviews were conducted over the telephone, with questions calling for only "yes" or "no" answers. A lack of privacy inhibits candid responses to questions about sex crimes. This is especially so if the victim does not want her family to know about the crime or if the attacker is in the room or believed to be within earshot, both common circumstances.

"Rape in America" found that 10 percent of victims were worried that their families would find out. That is understandable: more than a third of rapes are committed by a relative.

The Effects of Rape

The methodological differences between the new Justice Department survey and the "Rape in America" study are interesting, but they should not be our only focus. The most important point about the new Government findings is that they remind us of how much sexual violence women suffer and of the critical need to reduce it. Whether the actual number of rapes in a year is 300,000 or twice that, each of these assaults means a woman's life is changed forever. We must all work together to bring these numbers down.

Acquaintance Rape Is a Serious Problem for Young Women

by Kathryn Masterson

About the author: *Kathryn Masterson is a contributor to* Style Weekly *magazine.*

Getting smashed and hooking up—they're common expressions in college life. Date rape, as any student who has attended freshmen orientation knows, is part of the campus lexicon, too, since Katie Koestner put a face to the problem in June 1991, when she appeared on the cover of *Time* magazine.

As a freshman at the College of William and Mary in 1990, Koestner was sexually assaulted by a student she had been dating. She reported the assault, and her attacker was banned from any dormitory or fraternity house except his own for four years.

Angry that he was allowed to stay on campus, Koestner went public with her story. The public's response was overwhelming, Koestner says today. "It was one of the first times the words date rape ever appeared in print."

Date Rape Awareness

A wave of date rape awareness followed. Colleges implemented rape awareness programs in freshman orientations. Universities opened women's centers, hired sexual assault counselors and drafted policies covering sexual assault between students.

And nothing, arguably, has changed.

Years after Koestner challenged William and Mary in *Time*, experts on Virginia campuses say that sexual assault—typically between acquaintances—has become the most serious student life issue today.

College administrators face frequent legal challenges from victims, as well as from the accused over the way cases are handled—prompting some to say that

Reprinted from Kathryn Masterson, "Date Rape U.," *Style Weekly*, February 4, 1997.

reporting date rape is a no-win nightmare for everyone.

"I have no doubt that rape is rampant on college campuses," says Amy Spalek, a sexual-assault services specialist at the Richmond YWCA. Of the 20 to 60 calls she gets a month from rape victims, Spalek says most are acquaintance rapes, and a few are always college students.

"Sexual assault—typically between acquaintances—has become the most serious student life issue today."

Tracking the statistics on date rape is difficult because victims rarely report the crime, and few even seek counseling. No one who works with date rape victims thinks the numbers are going down.

When counselor Gay Cutchin conducts sexual-assault awareness programs at Virginia Commonwealth University, she asks how many students in the audience know someone who has been sexually assaulted. The hands go up slowly—until one-half to three-fourths of the people have raised their hands. One in six college women is sexually assaulted during their college years, Cutchin says.

In 1995, a study conducted by the State Council of Higher Education for Virginia found that 15 percent of Virginia's college women said they were sexually assaulted while in college.

College crime statistics, which track the number of rapes reported to the police, are significantly lower than the statistics most counselors give.

In the 2½ years that Virginia Tech has had a women's center, the number of women who came to the center for help after sexual assault has steadily climbed, from 25 in 1994, to 40 in 1995. . . .

According to the American Medical Association, which published the results of psychologist Mary Koss' 1980s survey in its "Facts About Sexual Assault," of 6,159 college students at 32 schools, one in 12 male students admitted to committing acts that met the legal definition of rape. Of the women who said they had been sexually assaulted or raped, 84 percent reported knowing their assailant.

"The Red Zone"

The majority of rapes on campus happen in what's called "the red zone"—the time between the first day of school and the first fall break, counselors say. Most state colleges make some attempt at raising awareness among freshmen of sexual assault, but students say the message is easily ignored or forgotten.

Date rape "shatters women," says attorney Eileen Wagner. "It cuts them off at the knees."

Wagner is best known for representing women who wanted to go to Virginia Military Institute and the female student who accused two football players of raping her at Virginia Tech. In a new and relaxed atmosphere free from parental oversight, young women away from home for the first time quickly trust other students—some of whom may not be so trustworthy, she says. "It's open season for sexual predators."

Wagner says she was raped by an acquaintance while she was in college and repressed the incident for years. More than 10 years later, she says the repressed memory surfaced when she was studying for the bar exam.

Michelle was a victim of acquaintance rape the first semester of her freshman year at the University of Richmond. In the fall of 1994, Michelle (a fictional name to protect her identity) went to an off-campus fraternity party. Inside, a fellow UR student whom she knew from class invited her back to a different room. Expecting to see more people, she found herself in a locked room with nothing more than a mattress on the floor.

She says she resisted his effort to kiss her, but he fought her and pinned her down to the mattress and tried to pull down her tights. "At this point, I thought this guy was completely insane because if I wasn't going to kiss this guy, obviously I wasn't going to have sex with him," she says. "I kept trying to pull the tights up and trying to be nice, but all the time saying no, no, no."

He managed to pull her tights down and penetrated her, she says, but she was able to push him off. When she got home, she threw her tights and underwear into the closet, where they remained until the end of the year. When she finally pulled them out, she saw that they were torn to shreds.

> *"No one who works with date rape victims thinks the numbers are going down."*

Like the vast majority of victims, she never reported her rape at the fraternity party. Instead, she chose to put the attack behind her, she says. When she sees the student who raped her now, she claims it doesn't really bother her the way it once did.

The Frequency

Parents should be alarmed by the frequency of date rape, says Donna Lisker, a sexual-assault educator at Virginia Tech. Although freshmen women must attend programs, "it's like keeping back a river by putting your thumb in a dike."

In September 1996, Virginia Tech student Christie Brzonkala testified before a congressional panel to ask for greater access to rape statistics.

At a press conference, she said, "I thought I was the only person on earth this [rape on campus] had ever happened to. I had no idea that more than 20 rapes had been reported at Virginia Tech during the same time period [1994]. I had never heard of anyone being injured, much less raped in a dorm. I never had a reason to be afraid of a fellow athlete before. I had no way of knowing what happened to me was so common."

The close-knit community of a college campus actually aggravates the number of sexual assaults. Students trust other students whom they meet for the first time, and this trust can be dangerous, Wagner says. Women who are raped are four times more likely to know their attacker than be attacked by a stranger.

Ironically, the closeness of a campus community allows perpetrators to continue attacking people because victims usually will not speak out.

Linda Bips, a counselor at Muhlenberg College in Pennsylvania, says for many women, the rape is too painful, and they choose to deny the problem until much later when it begins to affect their health, their relationships and their work.

Concerned that she would be endangered if she returned to Virginia Tech, Brzonkala dropped out.

Pressing Charges

Victims who choose to press charges have three avenues to prosecute their attackers: campus judicial board hearings, which are held behind closed doors and limit publicity; standard criminal proceedings in a court of law, which can be even more draining than a campus trial, with greater scrutiny of the case; and civil lawsuits, which seek compensation for damages from sexual encounters.

Institutions with centuries of providing higher education find themselves embroiled in administering jurisprudence of the most sensitive, even explosive nature among its students.

The University of Richmond police department is currently investigating a possible date rape that made the front page of *The Collegian*, UR's student newspaper. The campus police report says that a male student assaulted a female student near the campus apartments between 1 a.m. and 2:15 a.m. on Oct. 26, 1996. . . .

The report described the assault as "strong-arm rape," which is defined as a rape where no weapon was used.

The student has told UR administrators that she wants the man prosecuted criminally as well as by the college. At the end of the fall semester, Vice President for Student Affairs Leonard Goldberg said the university was awaiting laboratory test results for any traces of the attacker's semen that could confirm that a sexual encounter occurred.

The publicity surrounding the attack has made students anxious, says Elizabeth Stott, a psychologist at UR's counseling center. "They want to think that it doesn't happen here," Stott says. "The publicity makes them nervous because they see it does."

> *"Date rape 'shatters women. . . . It cuts them off at the knees.'"*

"It didn't make me nervous or scared to walk around campus, but it did make me more aware [of date rape here]," UR senior Melissa Mansfield says.

Still waiting for lab tests and other information, police chief Robert Dillard said, "We don't have any control over it." Dillard says further comment on the case should be forthcoming.

In 1996 at Radford University, an undergraduate female reported to school officials that an acquaintance attempted to have sexual intercourse with her against her will. He was found guilty of "sexual misconduct" by a Radford judicial board and suspended for two semesters.

> *"Parents should be alarmed by the frequency of date rape."*

He then filed suit against three Radford administrators, claiming his right to due process had been violated by the judicial board process. The male student's lawyer argued that Radford had not proven that sexual contact had occurred and that the punishment was "unduly harsh."

A federal judge in Roanoke dismissed the lawsuit, which received ample publicity in the Shenandoah Valley. The victim, whose name was protected, told reporters, "My first inkling was to get [the male student] off campus."

Reaction at Radford among students was that the punishment was too light—comparable to stealing something from another student's room, says student newspaper editor Kevin Porter. . . .

Rape Is Hard to Prove

Unless a woman is battered badly—a rarity in date rape cases—it's difficult to prove that the sex wasn't consensual among acquaintances, says Claire Cardwell, deputy common-wealth's attorney for Richmond. In the courtroom, a date rape trial becomes one person's word against another.

Proving guilt beyond a reasonable doubt is very difficult with only one person's word, Cardwell says.

Sometimes, Cardwell says she isn't sure if the woman should go forward with the case. People have a tendency to be judgmental of a woman's conduct in the situation—what she was wearing, how much she was drinking, and whether she agreed to go back to the man's home or invite him to hers.

Alcohol usually acts as the great uninhibitor.

In 1992, the Center on Addiction and Substance Abuse at Columbia University studied substance abuse on college campuses. Overwhelming evidence suggested that binge drinking was the most common form of substance abuse for college students, reaching "epidemic proportions" in the 1990s.

Forty-two percent of students reported they had engaged in binge drinking—five or more drinks at a time—in the past two weeks, according to the study. One in three college students drinks primarily to get drunk.

CASA also reported that 35 percent of college women reported drinking to get drunk in 1993—more than triple the number reported in 1977.

Combine lowered inhibitions, impaired judgment and reduced motor skills with a party of students who don't know their drinking limits and the mixer or off-campus party is a virtual petri dish for sexual assault.

A UR female student (who asked not to be named) says a night of drinking during a 1995 "beach week" vacation led to her assault.

She drank until she was barely able to stand up straight, went back to her hotel, got sick, and laid down on the bed. One of two male students her friend had brought back to the room from the party was already on the bed.

"He started kissing me and I kissed back. A little later, my clothes were off. I knew he was having sex with me, but I wasn't responding. In my head I was thinking 'What is happening? I don't want to do this.' I fell asleep and woke up with it continuing. I don't even know if he started and stopped. I was blacking in and out, passing in and out. . . ."

The next day, she went home and got tested for pregnancy, sexually transmitted diseases and the HIV. All were negative. When she sees the student on campus now, she says they don't acknowledge each other.

"I don't know if I can call it rape. I was definitely taken advantage of. I never would have done what had happened if I was sober. It's hard to call it rape because I was too drunk to say no."

In a 1995 survey by the State Council of Higher Education for Virginia, 58 percent of women who said they were sexually assaulted said they had been drinking. Sixty-eight percent of the males had been drinking. Sixty-six percent of the women who had been drinking believed they were unable to resist as a result of drinking.

Campus observers warn of a dramatic increase in date rape because of an increase in drinking and the widespread availability of rohypnol, commonly known as the date rape drug. Just $3 a tablet, the drug dissolves quickly in liquid and incapacitates a person for hours.

Peer Educators

At James Madison University in Harrisonburg, students who serve as sexual assault peer educators sit around a table between classes on a January afternoon, talking about the drinking and drug-awareness programs they present to fellow students.

They're stereotypically clean-cut college students—people to whom other students would pay attention in the dormitory or the classroom.

> *"Nobody wants to spoil the fun of the first week of college with too much serious talk of sexual assault."*

Mark (not his real name) is putting the finishing touches on the programs he will present this semester. What makes him different is that he's not a volunteer.

At JMU, he's known as "a sexual assault perpetrator." Speaking to other students is part of his punishment for sexually assaulting another student. Rather than face possible suspension or expulsion, he must complete JMU's sexual assault offender program, a year-long experience designed by Hillary

Wing-Lott, JMU's sexual-assault education coordinator. The program compels perpetrators to make as many as 10 presentations in a semester.

In addition to extensive counseling by Wing-Lott, Mark must tell his story to other students on campus. He's nervous about that. His first presentation will probably be the easiest—he'll be speaking to his fraternity, letting them know that "what happened to me could happen to you."

Mark expects his fellow fraternity members to be understanding when he tells them about the "fine line" he crossed when he took a girl back to his room after a night of drinking. What he—in his alcohol-induced condition—thought was acceptable behavior, he'll explain, was viewed as sexual assault by both the woman and the judicial board.

The rest of the presentations might not be so easy. He'll be speaking to classes and other Greek organizations.

Wing-Lott knows of no other school with a similar program, which is on the cutting edge of campus attempts to deal with the problem of sexual assault. So far, nine students have gone through the program, including two in 1997. Six were referred to Wing-Lott by the criminal justice system. The other three went through the campus judicial system.

Wing-Lott began the program because she felt there was a need for education for students accused of sexual assault. The program achieves two objectives: It educates offenders on what they did wrong, and it takes a proactive approach for the students who listen to the offender tell his story. She hopes those students listen and think, "Well, if I want to hook up, I better not be smashed. I better make sure the girl isn't smashed, either."

When she came to JMU, Wing-Lott says she was the only administrator who was introduced without a title at orientation. She thinks the presenters were afraid parents would ask why JMU needed an office for sexual assault.

Jerry Burgess, a graduate assistant in the sexual-assault education office, says it's a continuous fight to keep sexual assault programs in the freshman orientation every year.

Nobody wants to spoil the fun of the first week of college with too much serious talk of sexual assault.

The Seriousness of Female Violence Against Men Has Been Exaggerated

by Ben Wadham

About the author: *Ben Wadham is a contributor to* XY: Men, Sex, Politics.

With an increasing interest in men and masculinity, a change in the awareness and understanding of gender and power relations is occurring. That awareness is inherently influenced by the way we as individuals within those gender and power relations are socialised. In this western world of overt rationalist logic some of the emerging dialogue is limited and adversarial in nature. One significant example is the recent emergence of literature suggesting that women are as much perpetrators of domestic violence as men, and men are as much victims of domestic violence as women.

Recent research and literature by John Coochey, the People's Equality Network (PEN) and Katherine Dunn claim that contemporary representations of male violence are false. These authors argue that female domestic violence is as prevalent as male domestic violence. They suggest that domestic violence organisations and services, and some prominent women in the domestic violence field, are fudging statistics and actively maintaining a false representation of domestic violence for political and financial purposes.

Coochey is particularly vocal and he focuses on denigrating the recent and current domestic violence research which predominantly considers male violence against women. He does not advance current perspectives and knowledge of domestic violence by offering an alternative which would consider the gendered nature of male and female acts of violence toward their partners. Passages like, "These days people will accept even the wildest claims, as long as they make women out to be victims. Particularly, if they also put men in a poor light," express a conspiratorial and antagonistic stand. Is there a need?

The development of this position demonstrates many men's strong feelings of

Reprinted from Ben Wadham, "The Myth of Male Violence?" *XY: Men, Sex, Politics*, August 1996, by permission. References in the original have been omitted here.

rejection of anything which portrays them in a negative sense. It is important to realise that many streams of feminism and pro-feminist writing do not adopt a simple "all men are rapists" line although they may critique elements of masculinity. Masculinity in most feminist paradigms is seen as constructed, and therefore reflective of an array of power relations and dominant interests, rather than being essentially male. The fact that most research on domestic violence reports predominantly male violence against women is not a personalised attack on men, but a representation of the real safety issues which women and men face from male violence.

Men as Victims

There would be little argument, I suspect, about the incidence of female violence against males. Police and court records in the USA consistently show that 5 percent of men are victims of domestic violence, expressing the need to consider men's experience of violence by a female partner. However, there is a more pressing need to develop a sound, contextual framework for understanding the epidemiology of male and female violence. It is the development of an argument which suggests that men and women perpetrate identical forms and levels of violence as a justification for the re-allocation of services and resources which is problematic. It is especially problematic when it is based upon a selective research model which Coochey, Dunn and PEN continually cite.

The research used by Coochey, Dunn and PEN to support the claim that violence is gender-neutral is an American study titled *Behind Closed Doors*, by Murray Straus, Richard Gelles and Susan Steinmetz. This is an incidence survey, designed to identify how much violence is occurring in households across America, and has been conducted several times. Questionnaires are conducted through a telephone survey with the information collated according to the "Conflict Tactics Scale" or CTS.

The survey involved the interviewer asking a range of questions of either the husband or the wife (not both) from randomly selected households. The questions of the CTS were posed around how the couple settled their disagreements. The interviewee was presented with a list of 18 acts ranging from discussing calmly, cried, threw something at him/her to beat him/her up. These classified acts were intended to measure three things—"reasoning", "verbal aggression" and "physical aggression"—on a scale of either minor violence or severe violence.

"The fact that most research on domestic violence reports predominantly male violence against women is not a personalised attack on men."

The statistics which Coochey, PEN and Dunn cite are mainly reported from studies using the CTS. PEN also base their analysis on another research model used by the VicHealth Injury Surveillance Statistics (VISS). The findings of these research models report equal incidence and prevalence of male and female violence. Steinmetz also used the CTS type of data to proclaim the "battered husband syndrome" in 1978 and there are a range of other studies producing similar findings which use the CTS as the methodological tool.

Coochey endlessly pumps out figures from the Straus et al. study. For example, he states that "one in three households would experience some degree of domestic violence but in half the cases the woman would be the perpetrator" and he uses this finding to substantiate the claim that violence is gender-neutral. Furthermore, PEN suggest that "only studies which are likely to prove useful in the future are those which, like those developed by Straus et al. in the USA, do apply exactly equivalent methodologies to both female and male experience of domestic violence". Dunn paraphrases Straus et al.: "In about half the cases of mutual battering, women were the instigators—the ones who slapped, slugged or swung weapons first. Male violence against passive wives occurred in one quarter of the incidents; in another quarter of the incidents women were the violent partners who attacked non-violent spouses". Straus et al. conclude in their study that "women not only engage in physical violence as often as men, but they also initiate violence as often".

These findings are seriously incongruent with the majority of domestic violence literature. Data from criminal victimisation surveys, hospital admissions, police records, court orders, and spouses seeking shelter and

> *"It isn't too hard to see that a man slapping a woman is a qualitatively different act from a woman slapping a man."*

refuge all show that women are persistently victims of reported assaults. R.P. and E.E. Dobash et al. suggest that police and court records continually indicate that women constitute 90 to 95 percent of such reported assaults. The way authors such as Straus et al. and Coochey can develop such an argument for "sexual symmetry in domestic violence" is by using a very suspect methodology.

Battered Data Syndrome

There are considerable problems with the Straus et al. methodology, as Jack Straton explains. Firstly, the survey questions cannot discriminate between intent and effect. The CTS fails to contextualise the violence; the violent acts are not considered in relation to the events which led up to the act, and there is no consideration of the outcomes, for example the extent of injury or the degree of fear. Moreover, the type of acts of violence are poorly differentiated. For example, having kicked, bit, hit or tried to hit with an object, beat up, choked, or threatened with a knife or fired a gun are all naively grouped as "severe violence". It isn't too hard to see that a man slapping a woman is a qualitatively different act from a woman slapping a man, in terms of the potential for harm, the level of force, the level of fear and the historical context in which such acts are situated.

Another major issue with Straus' studies is they only look at one year so that the possible history of violence which may lead up to a violent response is left out and the violence again is decontextualised. Moreover, there is no means of validating the claims of either spouse as only one spouse is interviewed. Studies by M.V. Szinovacz and E.N. Jouriles and K.D. O'Leary found that spousal accounts of violence differ significantly. This gives grounding to the common knowledge that two people in a violent relationship are going to give different descriptions and accounts of their experience of violence.

Furthermore, Coochey, Dunn and PEN use the *Behind Closed Doors* study selectively. Even Straus et al. point out a number of reasons why abuse against women should remain the focus of intervention. Husbands had the higher rates of the most dangerous behaviours, husbands repeated their violence more often, husbands are more likely to do damage because of their size and strength difference, wives are economically trapped in marriage more often than husbands, and many wives may be using violence to defend themselves. While the "men as victims" argument attempts to substantiate a case for a "battered husband syndrome", it only substantiates a claim for a "battered data syndrome".

> *"Two people in a violent relationship are going to give different descriptions and accounts of their experience of violence."*

The argument of these proponents of "men as victims" is hard-hitting, just like the simplistic media portrayals of violence which have motivated its emergence. It is based upon the idea that similar incidents of violence behaviour mean that the violence, the circumstances leading up to it and the effects and consequences of it are the same also. Coochey in particular fails to elaborate that the *Behind Closed Doors* study also showed that when both partners were violent 44 percent of the husbands used a higher level of violence than their partners compared with 23 percent of the wives who used a higher level of violence. He also failed to say that the study found that the risk of victimisation of women is larger because of significant size differences and relative lack of fighting experience. On average, at the time of the study, men were 45 pounds heavier and 4–5 inches taller than women.

The *Behind Closed Doors* study also showed that if women do use violence it is more likely to be against a violent partner than a non-violent partner. This raises the question about the form and reasons for female violence toward men. The PEN article cites figures from the VISS research which suggest that men suffer more lacerations and puncture wounds than female victims of domestic violence. Women were more likely to suffer bruising, inflammations and pain. The study also states that women used knives more than twice as often as men, as weapons of domestic violence. This data has been used to imply that not only is male/female offending similar but women are more brutal. However, this neglects the reasons and motivations for violence. For example, Straus showed that husbands' threats to use weapons were highly associated with their use and women's threats to use weapons were not as highly associated with their actual use. This suggests that women's use of weapons with little actual violence is a measure of self-defence while men's threats with actual use suggest actual attempts to control.

The Consequences of Violence

Moreover, the consequences of violence need to be considered. A push or punch by a woman may cause rage or laughter in a male while a punch or push by a man can be far more damaging and terrifying. Such a lack of physical power is likely to promote women, if they do "fight back", to use weapons for their own safety or as an equaliser.

Furthermore, if we follow the line of Coochey, Dunn and PEN then we are restricted to considering domestic violence as discrete from other forms of violence. However, violence is not restricted to the domestic sphere and unfortunately, males account for perpetration of 91 percent of homicides, 90 percent of assaults and nearly all sexual assaults and robberies in Australia. Men are also predominantly the victims of violence from other men.

It is counter-intuitive to suggest that women perpetrate the same kinds of violent acts, in the same ways, and for the same reasons as men. It has, historically, predominantly been men who have led armies, gone to war, and commanded expeditionary forces into other countries conquering and colonising. What is more, there are no phrases I can think of which describe the use of force on male partners, like the term "wife-beating" does for men. And there are few historical phrases like "A woman, a dog, a hickory tree, the more you beat them, the better they be," which legitimise female violence against men as this legitimises male violence against women. Moreover, personally as a man it is other men who challenge my feelings of safety, not women.

For me this infers that as men we have an obligation and responsibility to look at male violence, not only for the sake of women, but for our own health and wellbeing.

"While the 'men as victims' argument attempts to substantiate a case for a 'battered husband syndrome', it only substantiates a claim for a 'battered data syndrome'."

Writing an article questioning the emotive methodology of the "men as victims" argument potentially sets up an environment for antagonism. This is, however, what I am attempting to refute. I believe that it is time to consider the real effects of dominant masculine values upon others in the family, the workplace, in politics or in the ways we perceive difference in others. The dominant masculine values of "an unwillingness to talk", to "admit weakness", to "disclose vulnerability". . . or practices of control and "power over" are successful tactics of power but they are also the site of men's undoing.

Men who experience female violence may be unwilling to report their assault because of shame and tensions with their ideas of masculinity, or police may laugh at a man reporting female violence because "no real man would let his wife hit him". Research to date, of issues involving the implications of masculine ideals in men's experience of female violence, has been few and far between. Future research could well illuminate some of these issues. However, this research will take us down the path of considering what

> *"As men we have an obligation and responsibility to look at male violence, not only for the sake of women, but for our own health and wellbeing."*

dominance, control and violence mean for us as men, not leading us into a "battle of the victims".

The research I have criticised is less a cry for the issue of female violence to be addressed and more a representation of dominant interests attempting to perpetuate existing notions of gender and power. A more serious and considered approach would challenge these notions and afford women the attention that male domestic violence (95 percent of domestic violence) requires and those smaller number of men (5 percent) access to services which would provide them with support and safety. A more serious approach would improve both men's and women's lives. Unfortunately, it seems that for some of us the concept of male violence is too bitter a pill to swallow.

The Problem of Violence Against Women Is Exaggerated

by Armin A. Brott

About the author: *Armin A. Brott is a freelance writer in Berkeley, California, and is a frequent contributor to the* Washington Post.

By now, everyone knows about Nicole Brown Simpson and Ronald Goldman, whose brutal murders have kept millions of Americans close to their television sets. But there's a third victim of these killings: the truth about the prevalence of domestic violence and female victimization—a truth maimed almost beyond recognition by the irresponsible use of statistics.

Varying Numbers

Consider the wildly varying number of women who are supposedly beaten by men each year. The National Coalition Against Domestic Violence, for example, estimates that more than half of married women (over 27 million) will experience violence during their marriage, and that more than one-third (more than 18 million) are battered repeatedly every year. Both statistics are widely quoted in the media.

But when I asked Rita Smith, coordinator of the NCADV, where these figures came from, she conceded that they were only "estimates." From where? "Based on what we hear out there." Out where? In battered women's shelters and from other advocacy groups.

Common sense suggests that asking women at a shelter whether they've been hit would be like asking patrons at McDonald's whether they ever eat fast food. Obviously such answers cannot be extrapolated to the country as a whole.

Donna Shalala, secretary of Health and Human Services, offers a lower but still eye-popping estimate. Four million women are battered each year by their male partners—"just about as common as giving birth," she said in a speech in March 1994.

Reprinted from Armin A. Brott, "The Facts Take a Battering," *The Washington Post National Weekly Edition*, August 8–14, 1994, by permission of the author.

But where did Shalala get this figure? From a 1993 Harris poll commissioned by the Commonwealth Fund, in which 2 percent of the 2,500 women interviewed said they had been "kicked, bit, hit with a fist or some other object." Based on about 55 million women married or living with a man, that's a total of 1.1 million. So where did the other 2.9 million come from? They were women who said they had been "pushed, grabbed, shoved or slapped"—not pleasant or condonable, certainly, but also not what most people would call the "terrorism in the home" Shalala referred to in her speech. Shalala—and media reporting the story—also neglected to tell us that fewer than 1 percent of those polled claimed ever to have been beaten up, much less choked or threatened by their partners with a knife or gun.

Shalala's statistics, however, pale in comparison to those issued by various women's advocacy groups. By far the worst distortion of the number of battered women comes from Pat Stevens, a radio talk show host who was interviewed on CNN's *Crossfire* in June 1994. Stevens estimated that, when adjusted for underreporting, the true number of battered women is 60 million. No one bothered to tell *Crossfire* viewers that 60 million is more than 100 percent of all the women in America who are currently in relationships with a man. Instead, Stevens' "estimate" and the other "facts" on the number of battered women serve to fuel the claims that there's an "epidemic of domestic violence" and a "war against women."

The Real Numbers

So how many battered women are there? Murray Straus and Richard Gelles, who have been tracking spousal abuse for more than 20 years, have come up with what are widely believed to be the most accurate estimates available—the National Family Violence Survey (NFVS).

The survey, sponsored by the National Institute of Mental Health, found that there is no violence in about 84 percent of American families. In the 16 percent of families that do experience violence, the vast majority of that violence takes the form of slapping, shoving and grabbing. This is not to minimize the violence that occurs— or the seriousness of some violence against spouses. But the fact is that only 3 to 4 percent of all families (about 1.8 million) have members

"Common sense suggests that asking women at a shelter whether they've been hit would be like asking patrons at McDonald's whether they ever eat fast food."

who engage in "severe" violence—kicking, punching or using a weapon. And a recent study published in the *Archives of Internal Medicine* found that 44 percent of "severe violence" to wives did not cause any injury, and 31 percent caused only slight bruises.

Still, Straus and Gelles estimate that about 188,000 women are injured severely enough to require medical attention. That's a horrifying number, but it's a far cry from the many millions of damaged victims implied by the least cautious users of the statistics.

Another commonly accepted "truth" about domestic violence is that 95 percent of the time women are the victims—and men the perpetrators. But the NFVS—and a variety of other studies—have found that men are just as likely to be the victims of domestic violence as women. Straus and Gelles found that among couples reporting violence, the man struck the first blow in 27 percent of the cases; the woman in 24 percent. The rest of the time, the violence was mutual, with both partners brawling. The results were the same even when the most severe episodes of violence were analyzed. They were also the same when only the woman's version of the events was considered.

Even more interesting are Straus's findings, released in July 1994, that men's violence against women—even as reported by women—has dropped 43 percent between 1985 and 1992. Over the same period, in contrast, assaults by women against men actually increased.

So where did the 95 percent figure come from? From the U.S. Department of Justice, which collects data on the number of reports of domestic violence. But as women's rights groups rightfully claim, reports are not always an accurate measure of the severity of the problem. Certainly, some female victims of domestic violence fail to call the police, fearing retaliation by their abusers. But other

> *"The fact is that only 3 to 4 percent of all families (about 1.8 million) have members who engage in 'severe' violence—kicking, punching or using a weapon."*

Justice Department studies have shown that men—who are socialized to "take it like a man"—report violent victimization much less frequently than women. "They wouldn't dream of reporting the kind of minor abuse—such as slapping or kicking—that women routinely report," says Suzanne Steinmetz, director of the Family Research Institute at Indiana University/Purdue.

Distorted Data

Yet another example of how data on female victimization are distorted is the belief that domestic violence is the most common cause of injury to women. The source for this claim is a 1991 study of extremely poor inner-city women in Philadelphia. In fact, the study did not find that domestic violence was the leading cause of injury even for this group. "And even if it did," says Jeane Ann Grisso, one of the lead researchers of the study, "I'd never apply that conclusion to the total population of American women." Nevertheless, Grisso's study has been widely cited as proof of the epidemic of violence against women.

Several studies done in the 1970s by Evan Stark and Anne Flitcraft also gave rise to another questionable claim: that as many as 50 percent of women's emergency-room admissions are the result of ongoing abuse. They compiled their data by going through medical records in urban hospitals and estimating how many women were battered by using what they called an "index of suspicion." Christina Hoff Sommers, author of *Who Stole Feminism*, has analyzed Stark and Flitcraft's methods and writes: "If a woman was assaulted but the records do not say who hit her, Stark and Flitcraft classify this as a case of 'probable' domestic abuse; if she has injuries to her face and torso that are inadequately explained, they classify it as 'suggestive of

> *"Among couples reporting violence, the man struck the first blow in 27 percent of the cases; the woman in 24 percent."*

abuse.'" That may not seem implausible but it ignores the real possibility that, in the environment studied, women may well have been victimized by drug sellers, pimps and other people they could not identify or would be afraid to identify. Or that the hospital failed to ask or record the information. Moreover, other studies do not support the finding.

Compare Stark and Flitcraft's results to those reached in a 1992 survey of 397 emergency rooms in California. Nurses were asked to estimate the number of patients per month who have been diagnosed with injuries caused by domestic violence. Estimates ranged from two per month for small hospitals to eight per month for large ones. The California study concluded that the number of perceived domestic violence victims was so low because many health professionals are poorly trained in recognizing domestic violence. They may be right, but it's doubtful that that accounts for the entire difference between a handful of domestic violence cases a month and 50 percent of all emergency room admissions.

Distorted statistics notwithstanding, there are clearly women who have been severely battered, and many of them are afraid to leave their batterers—either because they are economically dependent or because they fear further abuse. And in another one of its highly publicized statistics, the National Coalition Against Domestic Violence tells us that women who leave their batterers "increase by 75 percent their chances of getting killed."

When I asked Rita Smith to explain, she conceded that the coalition has no concrete evidence of the effect that leaving a violent partner will have on a woman. I asked Smith whether it bothered her that her organization was responsible for spreading an imaginary statistic. "Not really," she said. "We think the chance of getting killed goes up and we're just trying to make a point here."

Spousal Homicide

In a small number of tragic cases, abusive men do kill their partners—the FBI estimates that about 1,400 women (about 6 percent of all murders) were killed by their spouses or partners in 1992, though not all of the murders were the result of escalating domestic abuse. But the impression one gets is that women are the only ones killed in domestic disputes. Again, this impression is contradicted by the facts. A Justice Department study showed that 41 percent of spousal murder victims were male. Battered-women's advocates claim that those women who kill their husbands do so only out of self-defense. But in an extensive study of women imprisoned for murder, researcher Coramae Richey Mann found that more than 40 percent did not claim they acted in self-defense and 30 percent had previously been arrested for violent crimes. Nor is it the case that female spouse murderers are treated more harshly than their male counterparts. Recent Justice Department statistics show that women convicted of killing their partners receive an average sentence of only six years; men get 17.

Why are these statistics being abused? Obviously some of the data abusers do so with the best of intentions. They are simply trying to get people to sit up and pay attention to the plight of battered women—a truly important goal. But to do so, they've created a false epidemic. If advocates had confined themselves to the truth, domestic violence might have continued to be regarded as a serious, yet curable, problem. But if 19 or 50 or even 100 percent of women are "brutalized," a much more sweeping conclusion is suggested: that all men are dangerous and that all women need to be protected.

This raises age-old ethical dilemmas. Is it okay to lie if your cause is a noble one? After all, distortions about the extent of domestic violence have had some positive effects, opening the public's eyes as well as their wallets. Battered women are now the hottest story in town and Congress passed the $1.8 billion Violence Against Women Act which, among other things, will fund toll-free hotlines, battered women's shelters and education and training programs. It's certainly possible that none of this would be happening if advocacy groups stuck strictly to the facts.

Yet even supposedly harmless "puffing" can have negative consequences. Having fought so hard to be taken seriously and treated as equals, women are again finding themselves portrayed as weak and helpless—the stereotypes that have been traditionally used to justify discriminating against them. As author Katherine Dunn writes, "The denial of female aggression is a destructive myth. It robs an entire gender of a significant spectrum of power, leaving women less than equal with men and effectively keeping them 'in their place' and under control."

But perhaps the worst consequence of the inflation of domestic violence statistics is that a type of ratchet effect develops: The same people who complain that no one listens if they don't exaggerate only find it more difficult to get people's attention the next time around, thus "justifying" yet another inflation. Eventually, the public either stops listening altogether or finds the statistics too absurd to believe. And when we're trying to alleviate the tragedy of domestic violence, the last thing you want anyone to do is laugh.

The Seriousness of Domestic Violence Is Exaggerated for Political Purposes

by Frank S. Zepezauer

About the author: *Frank S. Zepezauer writes and teaches in Sunnyvale, California.*

The U.S. Supreme Court decision *Planned Parenthood v. Casey* has been examined from several perspectives. Now add another. Look once again at these words in the summary of argument: "Mandatory husband notification violates rights of privacy and marital integrity by subjecting intimate marital discussions to state surveillance and control, and *endangering the lives and health of married women compelled to notify abusive husbands of their abortion choice.*"

Abusive Husbands

Abusive husbands? We don't learn their numbers. But we do learn their dangerous potential. If their wives reported an abortion, "they" could respond violently. This possibility generates one of the more tenuous reasons supporting a majority decision which deprived fathers of the right to protect their unborn children, the right even to learn that their children might be in jeopardy.

That is just one of the ways "domestic violence" has been used to leverage significant political gains. There are others, part of a still growing list. Consider, for example, the long battle over joint custody, a post-divorce arrangement which establishes both parents as custodians. When sole custody is awarded, the mother becomes the custodian in the great majority of cases. The father then becomes a "visitor," suffering a severe drop in paternal status. Women's groups generally support sole custody while men's groups campaign for joint custody. And when women's groups lobby legislatures to curtail joint custody,

Reprinted from Frank S. Zepezauer, "The Politics of Domestic Violence," *The Wanderer*, April 25, 1996, by permission of the author.

they almost always warn about the danger of abusive ex-husbands. "Domestic violence" works as their trump card.

It also serves as the definitive rebuttal to critics of feminism. At a Human Life International seminar, a college woman reported intense debates with feminists who, she felt, always managed to get the upper hand. "I can hold my own with them on any subject," she said, "but then they always come up with 'domestic violence' and I'm stumped."

> *"'Domestic violence' has been used to leverage significant political gains."*

"Domestic violence" is, therefore, both a social problem and a political weapon. It is also a big lie. Fashioned by selective data and outright falsehoods, "domestic violence" is in the same league as "international Jewry": propaganda advancing a militant ideology.

The young college woman wanted to know whether anyone knew about domestic violence that had not been filtered by the feminist-friendly media. She is testimony that feminist propaganda has effectively obscured the other side of the domestic violence issue. It exists, mostly in samizdat, challenging the official version. Study it, or go to original sources, and you learn the following:

Spousal Abuse Is a Bi-Gender Problem

Although the term is apparently gender-neutral, "domestic violence" usually refers to wife-battering. O.J. Simpson now symbolizes that perception: the violent, control-obsessed husband who not only beat his wife but ultimately killed her.

The facts reveal a different picture, however. Wives initiate domestic conflicts, both mild and severe, at least as often as husbands. Since 1975, moreover, husbandly violence has decreased while wifely violence has increased.

To be sure, wives are more often the victims in spousal murders—60% against 40%—but the gap is closing, particularly in black families where parity has just about been achieved. Men nevertheless make up 55.5% of all domestic murder victims, those perpetrated by other household members as well as by wives. In any event, a 40% murder rate for wives remains a significant figure when measured against the myth of female nonviolence.

These facts are reported in studies of Western societies going back at least 20 years. The researchers did not rely solely on police records, a misleading source for most of the highly publicized domestic violence data because they report only incidents severe enough to warrant police action. Instead, they investigated what husbands and wives did—and what each said the other did—over a period of time. At least 30 such studies have now been conducted, enough to establish a strong consensus: Wives are as deeply complicit in domestic violence as husbands. They contribute to the heat and tension and rancor which can escalate into physical conflict. They give as well as they take. They are both victimizers and victims.

This politically incorrect assertion finds confirmation in other sources. The belief that females are innately less violent than males was challenged, for example, by Sarah Blaffer Hrdy, who, in *The Woman That Never Evolved,* demonstrated that primates showed few if any sex differences in aggressive behavior. Evidence of aggressiveness parity in humans appeared in *Of Mice and Women.* The book's contributors reported that although men exceed women in physical aggressiveness, women do as well as men in delivering hurtful language and surpass them in using "indirect" methods of violence. These researchers conclude that when it comes to inflicting harm, women do as well—or as badly—as men.

The most significant indication of the female potential for violence comes from studies of lesbians. They show that lesbian relationships are more violent than their heterosexual or male homosexual counterparts.

Ironically, feminists themselves confirm female aggressiveness. They celebrate tough, violent women like Boadicea and the historical Lady Macbeth, as well as a growing list of fictional counterparts such as *Thelma and Louise,* who have become part of a growing cult of "machisma." And feminists insist that when it comes to delivering blows and bullets in police action or military combat, women can hold their own with the toughest men.

Females Are Victimizers, Too

The mythology of "domestic violence" generates an image of widespread husbandly abuse. Yet violence in the home involves all members. Sisters hit brothers, for example, almost as often as brothers hit sisters. And both female and male children hit aging mothers and fathers in the growing scandal of elder abuse. In addition, researchers estimate that an average of 30% of all unmarried individuals, whether dating, engaged, or living together, "have been involved in violence against the opposite sex." One researcher added, "Women are just as likely, if not more likely, to engage in low-level violence."

When it comes to parent against child violence, the sad fact is that mothers inflict more injury than fathers. Roughly 60% of all child abusers are mothers. A Department of Justice report, *Murder in Families,* reveals that if a parent murdered his or her child, the murderer was, in 55% of the cases, the mother. A 1969 report from the *American Journal of Psychiatry* revealed that in murders of infants under the age of one, mothers were responsible in two-thirds of the cases.

Although a powerful faction insists that the victims of abortion are not human, the fact remains that a living being is killed, that roughly 1.5 million are killed every year, and that

> *"Wives initiate domestic conflicts, both mild and severe, at least as often as husbands."*

each of these killings is generated by maternal "choice." It might also be true that male pressure provokes many of these killings. But the mother nevertheless has the final choice in a society where "choice" is now sacred. Thus, in the grim record of filicide, infanticide, and feticide, the mother emerges as the more deadly parent.

Patriarchy Is Not Responsible for "Domestic Violence"

In the radical feminist universe, patriarchy is not simply a kinship system which requires a father. It is also the ultimate evil—what capitalism is to economic Marxism. Seen in this way, "domestic violence" becomes the male class' method of oppressing the female class. The husband supposedly strikes his wife not to express anger or frustration or vindictiveness, but to maintain "male supremacy."

In 1989, for example, a northern California man, Ramon Salcido, killed his wife, children, and mother-in-law in a murderous rampage. A columnist later characterized his crime as "patriarchal violence." She quoted an activist who said that "the violence in this case is not an issue of his sanity, it is an issue of the sanity of a role Salcido was trained to live by—a role the rest of us men have been trained to live by. . . . Rather than pretend that such an act is an aberration, society must recognize the Salcido in all men—or all men in Salcido."

Yet, as with other radical feminist theories, the idea that "domestic violence" serves as an instrument of patriarchal power falls apart before the facts. The surprisingly high level of inter-lesbian violence by itself demolishes the theory. Are all those violent lesbians trying to impose patriarchal values on their battered partners?

> *"Researchers conclude that when it comes to inflicting harm, women do as well—or as badly—as men."*

And are the violent partners necessarily the more dominant? The studies reveal that the *less* powerful partner in lesbian relationships strikes out physically. In such cases—as well as in their heterosexual counterparts—violence becomes a rebellion against dominance rather than a means to maintain it.

Moreover, a comprehensive study has revealed "no direct relationship . . . between patriarchy and wife assault." The author of the report, Donald G. Dutton, reports cross-cultural studies showing that in supposedly highly patriarchal societies, such as Mexico's, assaults on wives run at "about half the rate" found among non-Hispanic whites. After citing the growing evidence on female complicity in domestic violence—in both heterosexual and homosexual relationships—Dutton finds such data "difficult to accommodate from a feminist perspective."

Note also extensive evidence showing that for children the safest place is a household with their biological father. For women, the safest place is a household with their lawful husbands. The intact, marriage-based family—radical feminism's model of patriarchal oppression—is the least violent of all the households now proliferating in our multicultural society.

By the same token, the major source of violent male behavior—both on the streets and in the home—is the single-mother household. The correlation is so strong that social scientists trying to determine a community's potential for violence isolate the percentage of single-mother households as the most reliable predictor.

It is therefore not father-presence in a patriarchal family that breeds violence. It is instead father-absence in the feminist-endorsed single-mother family.

And it is not patriarchal power which is essentially at issue in the "domestic violence" campaign. It is instead the feminist drive for cultural power, part of the radical left's campaign to establish the ultimate egalitarian state. When economic Marxism failed, the left shifted to a gender Marxism in which "women" replaced "workers" as the new proletariat. More than seven years after we celebrated the collapse of Communism, we now see its revised ideology triumphant in our own society.

With the ever-supportive media as a propaganda outlet, radical feminists have therefore used "domestic violence" to win more money and power. They have exploited the O.J. Simpson case, for example, to sell their idea that in household conflicts only men are the problem, and changing them is the only solution.

And they have extracted billions from both private and public sources to finance their campaign. Before the Simpson case, for example, funding for California's battered women's shelters remained at a steady $1.5 million per year. Within weeks after the case broke, female legislators in Sacramento, noting what they called an "unusual window of opportunity," hurried through a measure which increased the funding to $15 million, better than a 1,000% increase in one year. In Congress, a Violence Against Women Act was being considered at a projected cost of $400 million. After the indictment of Simpson—who has done for "domestic violence" what Clarence Thomas did for "sexual harassment"—the funding was placed at $1.8 *billion.*

This money will be controlled *by* women—most of them feminists—and administered *for* women, even though men and boys are as often victimized by household violence. Moreover, this money will further enrich one of the most powerful lobbies in the country.

To say as much is not to minimize the genuine distress that female victims of male-inflicted violence experience. All critics of the feminist "domestic violence" campaign agree that violence against women is serious and needs to be stopped.

"'Domestic violence' is not an epidemic. It is not our major social crisis."

But the same critics insist that it be placed in perspective. Less than 14% of American households experience violence, and less than 3% experience severe violence. "Domestic violence" is not an epidemic. It is not our major social crisis. And it is not, by any means, a male-exclusive pathology.

But, in the hands of ambitious ideologues, it has become a highly successful tool for grabbing power and propagandizing a revolution against the "patriarchal" family.

Feminists Exaggerate the Prevalence of Rape

by Brian Carnell

About the author: *Brian Carnell is a libertarian freelance writer.*

Rape is a heinous crime and our society still does not adequately punish those who commit sexual assaults. For some feminists, though, rape is more than just a horrible crime—it's a political tool to be used to extract every last bit of political influence. This encourages advocacy researchers to exaggerate the number of women who are victims of rape, leading to increasingly inflated numbers based on methodologically suspect studies.

The Official Figures

The United States relies on two primary sources for measuring the level of criminal activity. The FBI's Uniform Crime Reports, started in 1929, collects monthly statistics for law enforcement agencies around the nation. The Bureau of Justice Statistics' National Crime Victimization Survey, started in 1973, relies on U.S. Census Bureau personnel to interview about 101,000 persons in 49,000 households every 6 months over a 3-year period. Sample participants are asked information about criminal activities directed against them.

There are a number of differences between the way the different studies measure crime, the largest being the inclusion of unreported crimes in the NCVS that are obviously excluded for the UCR. In many other areas, however, the two studies use different definitions of crime such that their results are not strictly comparable.

According to the most recent NCVS figures available there were a total of 316,140 attempted and completed rapes in 1994, and 260,310 attempted and completed rapes in 1995. The NCVS estimates 89,620 rapes and attempted rapes were reported to police in 1994 and 67,510 in 1995.

There are two caveats to keep in mind in interpreting this data. First, the 1995 figures are from the BJS preliminary report issued in September 1996. Final figures may end up higher or lower. Second, the statistic for rape and sexual as-

Reprinted from Brian Carnell, "Rape by the Numbers: Why Feminists Can't Do Math," paper published at www.carnell.com/sage/sage_rape_statistics.html (November 1996), by permission of the author.

sault include both men and women.

According to the NCVS, then, in 1994 there were 2 rapes or sexual assaults per 1,000 persons aged 12 or older and in 1995 the rated dropped to 1.6 per 1,000 persons.

For the same period, the UCR reported that women reported 97,464 forcible rapes to law enforcement agencies in 1995 (the lowest level in 6 years). That gives a forcible rape rate of 72 per 100,000 people.

The 1 in 4 Myth

So where does the 1 in 4 figure come in? The 1 in 4 figure is based on the *Ms.* Magazine Campus Project on Sexual Assault, conducted by researcher Mary Koss.

Koss' study asked 6,159 students at 32 colleges a series of questions about their sexual histories. Koss then reported that 15 percent of those surveyed had been victims of rape and 12 percent had been victims of attempted rape an average of two times between [the ages of] 14 and 22.

Koss further calculated that every 12 months 16.6 percent of all college women were victims of rape or attempted rape, giving a 50 percent probability of a female college student being raped over a four-year college career. If Koss' figures are correct, college women who haven't been the victim of rape or attempted rape are in the minority.

"In general, rapes are reported at a far lower level on campuses than in outlying communities."

There are good reasons, however, for thinking her figures are not correct, aside from the fact they deviate from the official figures and most serious scholarly research into rape (many of the scholars who have long been doing research into rape are persona non grata among many feminists because they reach the "wrong" conclusions about the level of rape).

The biggest problem with Koss' study is that 75 percent of the women Koss said were raped did not characterize their sexual encounters that way when asked directly. Eleven percent of those Koss labeled victims said they didn't feel victimized, 49 percent called the experience "miscommunication," 14 percent said it was a crime, but not rape, and 27 percent said they had indeed been raped. Forty-two percent of those Koss identified as rape/attempted rape victims had sex again at least once with the "offender."

Where the Discrepancy Is

Why such a discrepancy? Are college-aged women simply to stupid to realize they've been raped? Although some feminists, such as Susan Faludi, seem to embrace this answer, I believe it's extremely demeaning to women and ignores the flaws in Koss' study.

Koss counted as a victim of rape/attempted rape, for example, anyone who answered yes to either of the following questions:

"Have you had a man attempt sexual intercourse (get on top of you, attempt to insert his penis) when you didn't want to by giving you alcohol or drugs, but intercourse did not occur? Have you had sexual intercourse when you didn't want to because a man gave you alcohol or drugs?"

Forty-four percent of Koss' rape/attempted rape victims were women who answered either of these questions affirmatively. But as sociologist Neil Gilbert points out, the questions are useless since they are so vaguely worded. As Gilbert wrote for a *Society* article on the study, "What does having sex 'because' a man gives you drugs or alcohol signify? A positive response does not indicate whether duress, intoxication, force, or the threat of force were present; whether the woman's judgment or control were substantially impaired; or whether the man purposely got the woman drunk to prevent her from resisting his sexual advances."

The questions could easily have been phrased to include such factors, but instead it was asked in such a way to include both consensual and nonconsensual sexual encounters involving alcohol. Christina Hoff Sommers reports that Koss now concedes this question was overly vague, and those who answered yes should not be counted as rape victims. Apparently this has yet to reach the campus feminists.

Rape Rates on Campus

There is another reason to question the figures—in general, rapes are reported at a far lower level on campuses than in outlying communities. If Koss' figures are correct, the level of reporting for rape is fantastically low.

Gilbert notes, for example, that at the University of California at Berkeley, which is home to 14,000 female students, in 1990 there were 2 rapes reported to police and 40 to 80 students sought help from a campus rape counseling service. If Koss is correct, though, 2,000 women were victims of rape or attempted rape at Berkeley.

That level of reporting is so low, and contradicted by so many other studies with far more rigorous methodological measures than Koss, that it really defies the imagination that people find this study so credible.

The Incidence of Acquaintance Rape Is Inflated

by Christina Hoff Sommers

About the author: *Christina Hoff Sommers is an associate professor of philosophy at Clark University in Worcester, Massachusetts. She is also the author of* Who Stole Feminism? How Women Have Betrayed Women.

Some feminists routinely refer to American society as a "rape culture." Yet estimates on the prevalence of rape vary wildly. According to the FBI *Uniform Crime Report,* there were 102,560 reported rapes or attempted rapes in 1990. The Bureau of Justice Statistics estimates that 130,000 women were victims of rape in 1990. A Harris poll sets the figure at 380,000 rapes or sexual assaults for 1993. According to a study by the National Victims Center, there were 683,000 completed forcible rapes in 1990. The Justice Department says that 8 percent of all American women will be victims of rape or attempted rape in their lifetime. The radical feminist legal scholar Catharine MacKinnon, however, claims that "by conservative definition [rape] happens to almost half of all women at least once in their lives.". . .

The *Ms.* Report

Of the rape studies by nongovernment groups, the two most frequently cited are the 1985 *Ms.* magazine report by Mary Koss and the 1992 National Women's Study by Dr. Dean Kilpatrick of the Crime Victims Research and Treatment Center at the Medical School of South Carolina. In 1982, Mary Koss, then a professor of psychology at Kent State University in Ohio, published an article on rape in which she expressed the orthodox gender feminist view that "rape represents an extreme behavior but *one that is on a continuum with normal male behavior within the culture*" (my emphasis). Some well-placed feminist activists were impressed by her. As Koss tells it, she received a phone call out of the blue inviting her to lunch with Gloria Steinem. For Koss, the lunch was a turning point. *Ms.* magazine had decided to do a national rape survey on college campuses, and Koss was chosen to direct it. Koss's findings would become the most frequently cited research on women's victimization, not so much by established scholars in the field of rape research as by journalists, politicians, and activists.

> "*The majority of women [Koss] classified as having been raped did not believe they had been raped.*"

Koss and her associates interviewed slightly more than three thousand college women, randomly selected nationwide. The young women were asked ten questions about sexual violation. These were followed by several questions about the precise nature of the violation. Had they been drinking? What were their emotions during and after the event? What forms of resistance did they use? How would they label the event? Koss counted anyone who answered affirmatively to any of the last three questions as having been raped:

8. Have you had sexual intercourse when you didn't want to because a man gave you alcohol or drugs?

9. Have you had sexual intercourse when you didn't want to because a man threatened or used some degree of physical force (twisting your arm, holding you down, etc.) to make you?

10. Have you had sexual acts (anal or oral intercourse or penetration by objects other than the penis) when you didn't want to because a man threatened or used some degree of physical force (twisting your arm, holding you down, etc.) to make you?

Koss and her colleagues concluded that 15.4 percent of respondents had been raped, and that 12.1 percent had been victims of attempted rape. Thus, a total of 27.5 percent of the respondents were determined to have been victims of rape or attempted rape because they gave answers that fit Koss's criteria for rape (penetration by penis, finger, or other object under coercive influence such as physical force, alcohol, or threats). However, that is not how the so-called rape victims saw it. Only about a quarter of the women Koss calls rape victims labeled what happened to them as rape. According to Koss, the answers to the follow-up questions revealed that "only 27 percent" of the women she counted as having been raped labeled themselves as rape victims. Of the remainder, 49 percent said it was "miscommunication," 14 percent said it was a "crime but not rape," and 11 percent said they "don't feel victimized."

In line with her view of rape as existing on a continuum of male sexual aggression, Koss also asked: "Have you given in to sex play (fondling, kissing, or petting, but not intercourse) when you didn't want to because you were overwhelmed by a man's continual arguments and pressure?" To this question, 53.7 percent responded affirmatively, and they were counted as having been sexually victimized.

The Koss study, released in 1988, became known as the *Ms.* Report. Here is how the Ms. Foundation characterizes the results: "The *Ms.* project—the largest scientific investigation ever undertaken on the subject—revealed some disquieting statistics, including this astonishing fact: one in four female respondents had an experience that met the legal definition of rape or attempted rape."

The "One in Four" Figure Is Incorrect

"One in four" has since become the official figure on women's rape victimization cited in women's studies departments, rape crisis centers, women's magazines, and on protest buttons and posters. Susan Faludi defended it in a *Newsweek* story on sexual correctness. Naomi Wolf refers to it in *The Beauty Myth*, calculating that acquaintance rape is "more common than lefthandedness, alcoholism, and heart attacks." "One in four" is chanted in "Take Back the Night" processions, and it is the number given in the date rape brochures handed out at freshman orientation at colleges and universities around the country. Politicians, from Senator Joseph Biden of Delaware, a Democrat, to Republican Congressman Jim Ramstad of Minnesota, cite it regularly, and it is the primary reason for the Title IV "Safe Campuses for Women" provision of the Violence Against Women Act of 1993, which provides twenty million dollars to combat rape on college campuses.

> *"Women have sex after initial reluctance for a number of reasons . . . fear of being beaten up by their dates is rarely reported as one of them."*

When Neil Gilbert, a professor at Berkeley's School of Social Welfare, first read the "one in four" figure in the school newspaper, he was convinced it could not be accurate. The results did not tally with the findings of almost all previous research on rape. When he read the study he was able to see where the high figures came from and why Koss's approach was unsound.

He noticed, for example, that Koss and her colleagues counted as victims of rape any respondent who answered "yes" to the question "Have you had sexual intercourse when you didn't want to because a man gave you alcohol or drugs?" That opened the door wide to regarding as a rape victim anyone who regretted her liaison of the previous night. If your date mixes a pitcher of margaritas and encourages you to drink with him and you accept a drink, have you been "administered" an intoxicant, and has your judgment been impaired? Certainly, if you pass out and are molested, one would call it rape. But if you drink and, while intoxicated, engage in sex that you later come to regret, have you been raped? Koss does not address these questions specifically, she merely counts your date as a rapist and you as a rape statistic if you drank with your date and regret having had sex with him. As Gilbert points out, the question, as Koss posed it, is far too ambiguous:

What does having sex "because" a man gives you drugs or alcohol signify? A positive response does not indicate whether duress, intoxication, force, or the threat of force were present; whether the woman's judgment or control were substantially impaired; or whether the man purposefully got the woman drunk in order to prevent her resistance to sexual advances. . . . While the item could have been clearly worded to denote "intentional incapacitation of the victim," as the question stands it would require a mind reader to detect whether any affirmative response corresponds to this legal definition of rape.

Koss, however, insisted that her criteria conformed with the legal definitions of rape used in some states, and she cited in particular the statute on rape of her own state, Ohio: "No person shall engage in sexual conduct with another person . . . when . . . for the purpose of preventing resistance the offender substantially impairs the other person's judgment or control by administering any drug or intoxicant to the other person."

A Close Look

Two reporters from the *Blade*—a small, progressive Toledo, Ohio, newspaper that has won awards for the excellence of its investigative articles—were also not convinced that the "one in four" figure was accurate. They took a close look at Koss's study and at several others that were being cited to support the alarming tidings of widespread sexual abuse on college campuses. In a special three-part series on rape called "The Making of an Epidemic," published in October 1992, the reporters, Nara Shoenberg and Sam Roe, revealed that Koss was quoting the Ohio statute in a very misleading way: she had stopped short of mentioning the qualifying clause of the statute, which specifically *excludes* "the situation where a person plies his intended partner with drink or drugs in hopes that lowered inhibition might lead to a liaison." Koss now concedes that question eight was badly worded. Indeed, she told the *Blade* reporters, "At the time I viewed the question as legal; I now concede that it's ambiguous." As Koss herself told the *Blade,* once you remove the positive responses to the alcohol question, the finding that one in seven college women is a victim of rape drops to one in nine. But, as we shall see, this figure too is unacceptably high.

For Gilbert, the most serious indication that something was basically awry in the *Ms.*/Koss study was that the majority of women she classified as having been raped *did not believe they had been raped.* Of those Koss counts as having been raped, only 27 percent thought they had been; 73 percent did not say that what happened to them was rape. In effect, Koss and her followers present us with a picture of confused young women overwhelmed by threatening males who force their attentions on them during the course of a date but are unable or unwilling to classify their experience as rape. Does that picture fit the average female undergraduate? For that matter, does it plausibly ap-

> *"This is highly convoluted activism rather than social science research."*

ply to the larger community? As the journalist Cathy Young observes, "Women have sex after initial reluctance for a number of reasons . . . fear of being beaten up by their dates is rarely reported as one of them.". . .

Other Researchers Report Low Figures for Rape

There are many researchers who study rape victimization, but their relatively low figures generate no headlines. The reporters from the *Blade* interviewed several scholars whose findings on rape were not sensational but whose research methods were sound and were not based on controversial definitions. Eugene Kanin, a retired professor of sociology from Purdue University and a pioneer in the field of acquaintance rape, is upset by the intrusion of politics into the field of inquiry: "This is highly convoluted activism rather than social science research." Professor Margaret Gordon of the University of Washington did a study in 1981 that came up with relatively low figures for rape (one in fifty). She tells of the negative reaction to her findings: "There was some pressure—at least I felt pressure—to have rape be as prevalent as possible. . . . I'm a pretty strong feminist, but one of the things I was fighting was that the really avid feminists were trying to get me to say that things were worse than they really are." Dr. Linda George of Duke University also found relatively low rates of rape (one in seventeen). She told the *Blade* she is concerned that many of her colleagues treat the high numbers as if they are "cast in stone." Dr. Naomi Breslau, director of research in the psychiatry department at the Henry Ford Health Science Center in Detroit, who also found low numbers, feels that it is important to challenge the popular view that higher numbers are necessarily more accurate. Dr. Breslau sees the need for a new and more objective program of research: "It's really an open question. . . . We really don't know a whole lot about it."

> *"Date rape has swelled into a catastrophic cosmic event, like an asteroid threatening the earth in a fifties science-fiction film."*

An intrepid few in the academy have publicly criticized those who have proclaimed a "rape crisis" for irresponsibly exaggerating the problem and causing needless anxiety. Camille Paglia claims that they have been especially hysterical about date rape: "Date rape has swelled into a catastrophic cosmic event, like an asteroid threatening the earth in a fifties science-fiction film." She bluntly rejects the contention that "'No' always means no. . . .'No' has always been, and always will be, part of the dangerous, alluring courtship ritual of sex and seduction, observable even in the animal kingdom."

Paglia's dismissal of date rape hype infuriates campus feminists, for whom the rape crisis is very real. On most campuses, date-rape groups hold meetings, marches, rallies. Victims are "survivors," and their friends are "co-survivors" who also suffer and need counseling. At some rape awareness meetings, women who have not yet been date raped are referred to as "potential survivors." Their male classmates are "potential rapists."

Has date rape in fact reached critical proportions on the college campus?

> **"If 25 percent of my women friends were really being raped, wouldn't I know it?"**

Having heard about an outbreak of rape at Columbia University, Peter Hellman of *New York* magazine decided to do a story about it. To his surprise, he found that campus police logs showed no evidence of it whatsoever. Only two rapes were reported to the Columbia campus police in 1990, and in both cases, charges were dropped for lack of evidence. Hellman checked the figures at other campuses and found that in 1990 fewer than one thousand rapes were reported to campus security on college campuses in *the entire country*. That works out to fewer than one-half of one rape per campus. Yet despite the existence of a rape crisis center at St. Luke's-Roosevelt Hospital two blocks from Columbia University, campus feminists pressured the administration into installing an expensive rape crisis center inside the university. Peter Hellman describes a typical night at the center in February 1992: "On a recent Saturday night, a shift of three peer counselors sat in the Rape Crisis Center— one a backup to the other two. . . . Nobody called; nobody came. As if in a firehouse, the three women sat alertly and waited for disaster to strike. It was easy to forget these were the fading hours of the eve of Valentine's Day."

In *The Morning After*, Katie Roiphe describes the elaborate measures taken to prevent sexual assaults at Princeton. Blue lights have been installed around the campus, freshman women are issued whistles at orientation. There are marches, rape counseling sessions, emergency telephones. But as Roiphe tells it, Princeton is a very safe town, and whenever she walked across a deserted golf course to get to classes, she was more afraid of the wild geese than of a rapist. Roiphe reports that between 1982 and 1993 only two rapes were reported to the campus police. And, when it comes to violent attacks in general, male students are actually more likely to be the victims. Roiphe sees the campus rape crisis movement as a phenomenon of privilege: these young women have had it all, and when they find out that the world can be dangerous and unpredictable, they are outraged:

> Many of these girls [in rape marches] came to Princeton from Milton and Exeter. Many of their lives have been full of summers in Nantucket and horseback-riding lessons. These are women who have grown up expecting fairness, consideration, and politeness. . . .

The Effects of Inflated Rape Statistics

Much of the unattractive self-preoccupation and victimology that we find on today's campuses has been irresponsibly engendered by the inflated and scarifying "one in four" statistic on campus rape. In some cases the campaign of alarmism arouses exasperation of another kind. In an article in the *New York Times Magazine*, Katie Roiphe questioned Koss's figures: "If 25 percent of my women friends were really being raped, wouldn't I know it?" She also questioned the feminist perspective on male/female relations: "These feminists are endorsing their own utopian vision of sexual relations: sex without struggle, sex without power, sex without persuasion, sex without pursuit. If verbal coercion constitutes rape, then the word rape itself expands to include any kind of sex a woman experiences as negative."

The publication of Ms. Roiphe's piece incensed the campus feminists. "The *New York Times* should be shot," railed Laurie Fink, a professor at Kenyon College. "Don't invite [Katie Roiphe] to your school if you can prevent it," counseled Pauline Bart of the University of Illinois. Gail Dines, a women's studies professor and date rape activist from Wheelock College, called Roiphe a traitor who has sold out to the "white male patriarchy."

Other critics, such as Camille Paglia and Berkeley professor of social welfare Neil Gilbert, have been targeted for demonstrations, boycotts, and denunciations. Gilbert began to publish his critical analyses of the *Ms.*/Koss study in 1990. Many feminist activists did not look kindly on Gilbert's challenge to their "one in four" figure. A date rape clearinghouse in San Francisco devotes itself to "refuting" Gilbert; it sends out masses of literature attacking him. It advertises at feminist conferences with green and orange fliers bearing the headline STOP IT, BITCH! The words are not Gilbert's, but the tactic is an effective way of drawing attention to his work. At one demonstration against Gilbert on the Berkeley campus, students chanted, "Cut it out or cut it off," and carried signs that read, KILL NEIL GILBERT! Sheila Kuehl, the director of the California Women's Law Center, confided to readers of the *Los Angeles Daily Journal,* "I found myself wishing that Gilbert, himself, might be raped and . . . be told, to his face, it had never happened."

The findings being cited in support of an "epidemic" of campus rape are the products of advocacy research. Those promoting the research are bitterly opposed to seeing it exposed as inaccurate. On the other hand, rape is indeed the most underreported of crimes. We need the truth for policy to be fair and effective. If the feminist advocates would stop muddying the waters we could probably get at it.

Is America a "Rape Culture"?

High rape numbers serve the gender feminists by promoting the belief that American culture is sexist and misogynist. But the common assumption that rape is a manifestation of misogyny is open to question. Assume for the sake of argument that Koss is right and that the lower numbers of the FBI, the Justice Department, the Harris poll, of Kilpatrick's earlier study, and the many other studies mentioned earlier are wrong. Would it then follow that we are a "patriarchal rape culture"? Not necessarily. American society is exceptionally violent, and the violence is not specifically patriarchal or misogynist. According to International Crime Rates, a report from the United States Department of Justice, "Crimes of violence (homicide, rape, and robbery) are four to nine times more frequent in the United States than they are in Europe. The U.S. crime rate for rape was . . . roughly seven times higher than the average for Europe." The incidence of rape is many times lower in such countries as Greece, Portugal, or Japan—countries far more overtly patriarchal than ours.

It might be said that places like Greece, Portugal, and Japan do not keep good records on rape. But the fact is that Greece, Portugal, and Japan are significantly less violent than we are. I have walked through the equivalent of Central Park in Kyoto at night. I felt safe, and I was safe, not because Japan is a feminist society (it is the opposite), but because crime is relatively rare. The international studies on violence suggest that patriarchy is not the primary cause of rape but that rape, along with other crimes against the person, is caused by whatever it is that makes our society among the most violent of the so-called advanced nations.

But the suggestion that criminal violence, not patriarchal misogyny, is the primary reason for our relatively high rate of rape is unwelcome to gender feminists like Susan Faludi, who insist, in the face of all evidence to the contrary, that "the highest rate of rapes appears in cultures that have the highest degree of gender inequality, where sexes are segregated at work, that have patriarchal religions, that celebrate all-male sporting and hunting rituals, i.e., a society such as us."

In the spring of 1992, Peter Jennings hosted an ABC special on the subject of rape. Catharine MacKinnon, Susan Faludi, Naomi Wolf, and Mary Koss were among the panelists, along with John Leo of *U.S. News & World Report.* When MacKinnon trotted out the claim that 25 percent of women are victims of rape, Mr. Leo replied, "I don't believe those statistics. . . . That's totally false." MacKinnon countered, "That means you don't believe women. It's not cooked, it's interviews with women by people who believed them when they said it. That's the methodology." The accusation that Leo did not believe "women" silenced him, as it was meant to. But as we have seen, believing what women actually say is precisely *not* the methodology by which some feminist advocates get their incendiary statistics.

Female Violence Against Men Is a Serious Problem

by Philip W. Cook

About the author: *Philip W. Cook is a journalist and lecturer. He is also the author of* Abused Men: The Hidden Side of Domestic Violence.

"Things started out pretty good the first couple of years. Then, she slowly changed. She always had a temper, but then we got into some money problems, and it got worse. She would get mad, and it would escalate all out of proportion. She'd start hitting. She'd slap at my face, and then keep slapping and try to scratch me. I'd put up my arms, or just grab and hold her hands. I never hit her back. I was just taught that you never hit a woman."

Joe S. is one of thirty male victims of domestic violence that I interviewed over a two-year period. Canadian researcher Lesley Gregorash and Dr. Malcolm George in England have interviewed a similar number of such men. Some common patterns of behavior by victims and abusers have emerged; perhaps the most striking is the similarity between female and male victims and their abusers. Of the differences, the biggest is one of public and personal perception. In most cases, male victims are stuck in a time warp; they find themselves in the same position women were in twenty years ago. Their problem is viewed as being of little consequence, or they are somehow seen to be at fault.

Male Abuse

With support from the National Institute of Mental Health, Murray Straus, Ph.D., and Richard Gelles, Ph.D., conducted a nationally representative survey from the Family Research Laboratory at the University of New Hampshire of married and cohabiting couples on domestic violence—the National Family Violence Survey (NFVS). The results were first published in 1977. They followed up the initial survey of more than 2,000 couples with a larger 6,000-couple group in 1985. In minor violence (slap, throw something, push, grab or shove), the rates were equal for men and women. In severe violence (kick, bite, hit with a fist, hit or try to hit with something, beat up, threaten with a knife or gun, use a knife or gun) more men were victimized than women.

Projecting the surveys onto the national population of married and cohabiting couples, the results showed more than eight million couples a year engaging in some form of domestic violence, 1.8 million women victims of severe violence, and two million male victims of severe violence. This means that a woman is severely assaulted every 18 seconds by her mate, and a man is similarly assaulted every 15 seconds. The "every 18 seconds" statistic for abused women is often attributed to the FBI or Justice Department, who have referred to it in publications, but it is not their data. The NFVS figures for abused women are the most often quoted violence in support of funding and attention for domestic violence. Most often, the equal or greater numbers of male victims are simply ignored.

> *"Male victims are stuck in a time warp; they find themselves in the same position women were in twenty years ago."*

To accept the NFVS results for women should mean having to accept the same sources for male victimization. By their own admission in the surveys, women hit first at about the same rate as men do, and women report that self-defense was not the reason for the overwhelming majority of their attacks on their mates. About half of all incidents of violence are one-sided; the rest is mutual combat. The NFVS results have been corroborated by more than thirty other studies in the U.S., Canada and Great Britain. Law enforcement figures are more reliable when used to measure homicide, but near-equality exists in these instances as well: a woman is nearly 25 percent more likely to be killed by her mate than a husband to be killed by his wife, but the rate is virtually equal for black couples.

The overwhelming majority of domestic violence does not result in death; it is expressed in a wide range of actions, both physical and verbal, with control of the other person as an aim. This is a learned pattern of behavior. Most domestic violence would not happen if there were not a history of such violence in the family of origin. Sons of violent parents have a rate of wife-beating 1000 percent greater than those of non-violent parents. Daughters of violent parents have a husband beating rate 600 percent greater. Ignoring violent women and focusing solely on violent men contributes to the cycle of violence for the next generation.

Women Use Weapons

Certainly, a man slapping or shoving a woman is much more likely to inflict injury than a woman slapping or shoving a man. Women, however, are more likely to compensate for their disadvantage in size by using objects and weapons. Studies vary on the ratio of female to male domestic violence injuries. A 1995 report by Barbara Morse of the Institute of Behavioral Science at the University of Colorado shows men seeking medical care for such injuries at about the same rate than did women. Women probably suffer more total injuries ranging from mild to serious, but when it comes to serious injuries where weapons and object use come into play, the gender difference may be smaller than previously thought.

Another argument for ignoring female aggression is to claim that it's much easier for men than for women to leave an abusive relationship. But in fact, if there are children, men may be more likely to feel that they cannot leave, since they know that their chances of getting custody are not very good—and their chances of visitation without interference from a possibly vindictive and abusive spouse are not very good either.

Men also face another factor that abused women today don't face as much—ridicule and isolation.

"The cops show up, and they think it's a big joke," Tim S. explained after his live-in girlfriend hit him in the head with a frying pan, resulting in severe bleeding and a deep cut. "I never did tell anyone [of my friends and family] about all this while it was going on, because they would assume that I had done something to her, or that I deserved it. If there had been a crisis line for men in this situation I would have called it."

Even if a man seeks out a therapist for help, he is unlikely to find one, contends counselor Michael Thomas of Seattle, Washington. "In talking with other therapists, I find that they

> *"In severe violence . . .*
> *more men were*
> *victimized than women."*

rarely even ask questions of their male clients about the possibility of the client being abused. I think a great many clinicians are still resistant to seeing certain types of female behavior as abusive. If the client can't talk about it, it becomes internalized, and it increases the danger of the men exploding in rage themselves, getting depressed or suicidal, withdrawing from relationships, and other effects. I have also heard from female abusers who can't get help. There are very few resources out there, for either victim or abuser."

Recognizing the Problem

Recognition of the problem by therapists, other helping professionals, individuals, government and the news media will come slowly. It should come as no surprise that national surveys show a significant drop in public approval of a man slapping his wife under any circumstances, but no drop at all in approval for a woman slapping her husband.

Of course, the point of any helpful assessment of domestic violence for individuals or for social policy is not to excuse violence. It should not matter who started it, or what the provocation was. The woman who throws things or slaps a man greatly increases her chances of being hit in return. If we excuse violent acts by women by saying that they must have been provoked or were responding to violent acts by men, that would put us in the position of accepting violent acts by men under the same circumstances. Domestic violence is a human problem, not a gender problem.

Sociologists tell us that domestic violence at some level affects a significant minority of British, Canadian, and U.S. couples. It is a tragedy that must be dealt with on an economic, social, legal and spiritual level; but evidence of these problems should not encourage us to declare the family bankrupt. If we can move forward to a better understanding of benevolence and malevolence in both sexes, we will expand the opportunity for constructive rather than destructive relationships.

Chapter 2

What Causes Violence Against Women?

The Causes of Violence Against Women: An Overview

by the National Research Council

About the author: *The National Research Council advises government officials on matters of science, technology, and medicine. In 1995, in response to a request from Congress, the council began to develop a research agenda to increase the understanding and control of violence against women. The following overview is excerpted from the council's report* Understanding Violence Against Women.

A vital part of understanding a social problem, and a precursor to preventing it, is an understanding of what causes it. Research on the causes of violence against women has consisted of two lines of inquiry: examination of the characteristics that influence the behavior of offenders and consideration of whether some women have a heightened vulnerability to victimization. . . . Many theorists and researchers have sought to answer the question, "Why does this particular man batter or sexually assault?" by looking at single classes of influences. . . .

Many of the theories about the causes of perpetrating violence against women are drawn from the literature on aggression and general violence. Both the research on general violence and that on violence against women suggest that violence arises from interactions among individual biological and psychosocial factors and social processes, but it is not known how much overlap there is in the development of violent behavior against women and other violent behavior. Studies of male batterers have found that some batterers confine their violent behavior to their intimates but others are violent in general. The research suggests that, at least in some cases, there may be differences in the factors that cause violence against women and those that cause other violent behavior. Much more work is needed in order to understand in what ways violence against women differs from other violent behavior. Such understanding will be particularly important for developing preventive interventions.

Although current understanding suggests that violent behavior is not caused by any single factor, much of the research has focused on single causes. There-fore, in the following sections several salient findings emerging from each single-factor domain are highlighted to illustrate how each contributes some-thing to the causal nexus of perpetration of violence. . . .

Evolution

From an evolutionary perspective, the goal of sexual behavior is to maximize the likelihood of passing on one's genes. This goal involves maximizing the chances that one will have offspring who themselves will survive to reproduce. In ancestral environments, optimum male and female strategies for successfully passing on one's genes often did not coincide because the amount of parental investment required by males is smaller than that required by females. Males were best served by mating with as many fertile females as possible to increase their chance of impregnating one of them; females, who have the tasks of preg-nancy and nurturing the young, are often better served by pair bonding. Sex dif-ferences in current human mating strategies may be explained as having been shaped by the strategies that created reproductive success among human ances-tors. A number of studies have shown that young adult males are more in-terested in partner variety, less inter-ested in committed long-term rela-tionships, and more willing to engage in impersonal sex than are young adult females. This finding is consis-tent with the optimum evolutionary strategy for males of mating with as many fertile females as possible.

> *"Case histories from battered women often mention the extreme sexual jealousy displayed by their batterers."*

It is theorized that males who have difficulty obtaining partners are more likely to resort to sexual coercion or rape. Extensive evidence of forced mating among animals has been documented. Evolutionary theory also has been used to explain aspects of intimate partner violence. It is theorized that male sexual jealousy developed as a means of assuring the paternity of their offspring. Case histories from battered women often mention the extreme sexual jealousy dis-played by their batterers, and extreme sexual jealousy is a common motive of men who kill their wives.

There is much debate over how much influence evolutionary factors have on modern human beings. Even those who favor evolutionary explanations ac-knowledge that additional factors are necessary to explain sexual assault and in-timate partner violence. . . .

Alcohol

Every category of aggressive act (except throwing objects) has a higher prevalence among people who have been drinking. Alcohol use has been re-ported in between 25 percent and 85 percent of incidents of battering and up to

75 percent of acquaintance rapes. It is far more prevalent for men than their female victims. Considerable research links drinking and alcohol abuse to physical aggression, although adult consumption patterns are likewise associated with other variables related to violence (such as witnessing physical violence in one's home of origin). The relationship of alcohol to intimate partner violence could be spurious, but the relationship of men's drinking to intimate partner violence remains even after statistically controlling for sociodemographic variables, hostility, and marital satisfaction. Men's drinking patterns, especially binge drinking, are associated with marital violence across all ethnic groups and social classes.

The relationship of alcohol to violence is a complex one, involving physiological, psychosocial, and sociocultural factors. The exact effects of alcohol on the central nervous system remain in question, but nonexperimental evidence indicates that alcohol may interact with neurotransmitters, such as serotonin, that have been associated with effects on aggression. Studies have found a genetic basis for alcohol abuse and alcoholism and for antisocial personality traits that are often found among violent offenders. The fact that alcohol abuse and antisocial personality frequently occur together has led to the speculation of common genetic bases, but the evidence remains inconclusive. . . .

> *"Men's drinking patterns, especially binge drinking, are associated with marital violence across all ethnic groups and social classes."*

There are methodological weaknesses in the studies of the links between alcohol and violence, including lack of clear definitions of excessive alcohol use and a reliance on clinical samples with an absence of control samples. Nonetheless, research has consistently found that heavy drinking patterns are related to aggressive behavior, in general, and to intimate partner and sexual violence. However, exactly how alcohol is related to violence remains unclear. Obviously, many battering incidents and sexual assaults occur in the absence of alcohol, and many people drink without engaging in violent behavior. . . .

Sex and Power Motives

Violence against women is widely believed to be motivated by needs to dominate women. This view conjures the image of a powerful man who uses violence against women as a tool to maintain his superiority, but research suggests that the relationship is more complex. Power and control frequently underlie intimate partner violence, but the purpose of the violence may also be in response to a man's feelings of powerlessness and inability to accept rejection. It also has been argued that rape, in particular, represents fulfillment of sexual needs through violence, but research has found that motives of power and anger are more prominent in the rationalizations for sexual aggression than sexual desires. Attempts to resolve the debate about sex versus power have involved laboratory studies of men's sexual arousal to stimuli of depictions of pure violence, pure consensual sex, and nonconsensual sex plus violence. These studies have consistently shown that some "normal" males with no known history of rape may be aroused by rape stimuli involving adult women, especially if the women are portrayed as enjoying the experience. However, sexually aggressive men appear to be more sexually arousable in general, either to consenting or rape stimuli, and rapists respond more than nonsexual offenders to rape cues than to consenting sex cues. Sexually aggressive men openly admit that their sexual fantasies are dominated by aggressive and sadistic material. . . .

Family, Schools, and Religion

Families are where all socialization begins, including socialization for all types of violent behavior. Studies of violent criminals and violent sex offenders have found these men are more likely than other adults to have experienced poor parental childrearing, poor supervision, physical abuse, neglect, and separations from their parents. Increased risk of adult intimate partner violence is associated with exposure to violence between a person's parents while growing up. One-third of children who have been abused or exposed to parental violence become violent adults. Sons of violent parents are more likely to abuse their intimate partners than boys from nonviolent homes. Men raised in patriarchal family structures in which traditional gender roles are encouraged are more likely to become violent adults, to rape women acquaintances, and to batter their intimate partners than men raised in more egalitarian homes. Sexual abuse in childhood has been identified as a risk factor in males for sexual offending as an adult. Experiences of sexual abuse in one's family may lead to inaccurate notions about healthy sexuality, inappropriate justifications for violent behavior, failure to develop personal boundaries, and contribute to communication and coping styles that rely on denial, reinterpretation of experiences, and avoidance.

To the extent that schools reinforce sex role stereotypes and attitudes that condone the use of violence, they may contribute to socialization supportive of violent behavior. Other institutions that have been implicated in contributing to socialization that supports violence against women are organized religion, the workplace, the U.S. military, and the media.

Athletic teams also may socialize children to behavior that is supportive of violence. For example, male athletes may be spurred to greater aggressive efforts by coaches who deride them as "girls." Participation in revenue-producing sports at the collegiate level was found to be a significant

> *"Power and control frequently underlie intimate partner violence."*

predictor of sexual aggression among college students. It is possible that team sports, particularly revenue-producing sports, attract young men who are already aggressive. Whether team sports encourage aggressive behavior or simply

Violence Against Women

reinforce already existing aggressive tendencies remains to be determined. In either case, it appears that participation in team sports is a risk factor for sexual aggression.

Media

Many feminist writers have suggested that pornography encourages the objectification of women and endorses and condones sexual aggression toward women. Both laboratory research and studies of television lend support to this view. Exposure to pornography under laboratory conditions has been found to increase men's aggression toward women, particularly when a male participant has been affronted, insulted, or provoked by a woman. Sexual arousal to depictions of rape is characteristic of sexual offenders. Even exposure to non-explicit sexual scenes with graphic violence has been shown to decrease empathy for rape victims. It appears that it is the depiction of violence against women more than sexual explicitness that results in callousness toward female victims of violence and attitudes that are accepting of such violence.

> "Sons of violent parents are more likely to abuse their intimate partners than boys from nonviolent homes."

It is not only pornography that depicts violence against women. Television and movies are filled with scenes of women being threatened, raped, beaten, tortured, and murdered. A number of studies of television point to the deleterious effects of viewing media portrayals of violence. L.D. Eron found that children who watched many hours of violence on television during elementary school tended to exhibit more aggressive behavior as teenagers and were more likely to be arrested for criminal acts as adults. A meta-analysis of 188 studies found a strong positive association between exposure to television violence and antisocial and aggressive behavior. Those who are exposed to television and cinema violence may also become desensitized to real world violence, less sensitive to the pain and suffering of others, and begin to see the world as a mean and dangerous place. A recently released national study of violence on television found that context of the violence shown was important: television shows virtually no consequences of violent behavior; victims are not harmed and offenders are not punished. It seems that many television depictions of violence send the message that violence works.

None of the studies of television violence has focused specifically on violence against women. The National Television Violence Study found that 75 percent of the targets of violence in television portrayals are males, while only 9 percent are females (the remainder are nonhuman characters). Research has not yet examined the type of violence directed at female victims on television, how it compares with that directed at male victims, and whether there are differential effects on viewers of violence against women and against men.

Societal Influences

For much of recorded Western European and American history, wives had no independent legal status; they were basically their husbands' property. The right of a husband to physically chastise his wife was upheld by the Supreme Court of Mississippi in 1824 and again by a court in North Carolina in 1868. In 1871 a court ruling in Alabama made that state the first to rescind a husband's right to beat his wife. During the 1870s, coinciding with the rise of the child protective movement, there was increased concern that wife beating should be treated as a crime, although few men were ever punished. In the 1890s social casework replaced criminal justice as the preferred system for dealing with family violence and general interest in wife beating waned until the 1960s.

The status of women as property also can be seen in the development of laws concerning rape. Susan Brownmiller (1975) contends that "rape entered the law . . . as a property crime of man against man. Woman, of course, was viewed as the property." She notes that until the end of the thirteenth century, only unmarried virgins were considered blameless in their victimization; married women who were raped were punished along with their rapist. At that time, the Statutes of Westminister put forward by Edward I of England extended the same penalties to men who raped married women as to those who raped virgins. Rape within marriage, however, was, by definition, impossible. Marriage laws traditionally assumed implied consent to sexual relations by wives and allowed husbands to use force to gain compliance. It has only been in recent years that laws have begun to recognize marital rape: today every state in the United States has modified or eliminated the marriage exclusion in its rape laws.

> *"Approximately 25 percent of middle school, high school, and college students state that it is acceptable for a man to force sex on a woman if he spent money on her."*

Sexual Scripts

Expectations about dating and intimate relationships are conveyed by culturally transmitted scripts. Scripts support violence when they encourage men to feel superior, entitled, and licensed as sexual aggressors with women as their prey, while holding women responsible for controlling the extent of sexual involvement. Parents socialize daughters to resist sexual advances and sons to initiate sexual activity. By adolescence, both boys and girls have been found to endorse scripts about sexual interaction that delineate a justifiable rape. For example, approximately 25 percent of middle school, high school, and college students state that it is acceptable for a man to force sex on a woman if he spent money on her.

Since Martha Burt first defined "rape myths" and developed a scale to measure them, a large body of research has examined the role of attitudes and false beliefs about rape on perpetration of sexual assault and on society's response to sexual assault. Typical rape myths include denial of rape's existence (e.g., most rape claims are false, or women generally lie about rape), excusing the rape (e.g., she led him on, he couldn't help himself, rape only happens to "bad" women), and minimizing the seriousness of rape. Despite psychometrically weak measurement instruments, the study of rape myths has provided important understandings about sexual aggression. Not surprisingly, men are more accepting of rape myths than women. A number of studies have found a significant association between acceptance of rape myths and self-reported sexually aggressive behavior.

The early studies of rape myths were performed on college campuses and found that 25 percent to 35 percent of the students accepted a variety of them. Since the mid 1980s, many college campuses have instituted rape awareness and rape education programs. Recent research found fewer than 2 percent of students accepting of sexual aggression or coercion, but up to 36 percent expected that sexual aggression would occur under certain circumstances. S.L. Cook surmises that rape education has made it unacceptable to admit to believing rape myths, but that behavioral expectations are still consistent with acceptance of rape myths. It will be valuable for prevention efforts for research to continue to track any changes in rape myth acceptance and sexual script expectations among students, as well as the general public. . . .

Risk Factors for Victimization

Although most research on the causes of violence focuses on why men use violence and the conditions that support and maintain that violence, some researchers have tried to ask why a particular woman is the target of violence. This line of research has a dismal record of success. A primary problem confronted in trying to identify women's risk factors for violence is the confounding that occurs when traits and behaviors are assessed at some point postvictimization and assumed to represent the previctimization state. An interpretation of current findings is that they represent aftereffects of the violence itself or overly negative self-descriptions triggered by the trauma.

"The only risk marker consistently associated with being the victim of physical abuse was having witnessed parental violence as a child."

Factors that have been at one time or another linked to women's likelihood of being raped or battered are passivity, hostility, low self-esteem, alcohol and drug use, violence in the family of origin, having more education or income than their intimate partners, and the use of violence toward children. However, based on a critical review of all 52 studies conducted in the prior 15 years that included comparison groups, Gerald T. Hotaling and David B. Sugarman found that the only risk marker consistently associated with being the victim of physical abuse was having witnessed parental violence as a child. And this factor characterized not only the victimized women, but also their male assailants. Recent studies also found no specific personality and attitudinal characteristics that make certain women more vulnerable to battering. Although alcoholic women are more likely to report moderate to severe violence in their relationships than more moderate drinkers, the association disappears after controlling for alcohol problems in their partners. On the basis of findings such as these, several writers have concluded that the major risk factor for battering is being a woman.

Pornography Causes Violence Against Women

by Diana E.H. Russell, interviewed by Ann E. Menasche

About the authors: *Diana E.H. Russell is professor emerita of sociology at Mills College in Oakland, California, and the author of* Making Violence Sexy: Feminist Views of Pornography *and* Against Pornography: Evidence of Harm. *Ann E. Menasche is a civil rights attorney in San Francisco, California.*

Ann E. Menasche: Your book, Against Pornography, *attempts to establish a link between pornography and violence against women. How do you define pornography?*

Diana E.H. Russell: I define pornography as material that combines sex and/or the exposure of genitals with abuse or degradation in a manner that appears to endorse, condone or encourage such behavior. I conceptualize pornography as both a form of hate speech and as discrimination against women.

Can you give some examples of what you consider pornographic?

Some examples from *Hustler:* a cartoon showing a jackhammer inserted into a woman's vagina with a caption referring to this as "a cure for frigidity." Or of a woman being ground up in a meat grinder. Photos and descriptions of a woman being gang raped on a pool table, described as an erotic turn-on for the woman.

A cartoon of a husband dumping his wife in a garbage can with her naked buttocks sticking out from the can. A cartoon of a father with a tongue in his daughter's ear and his hands in her pants, again as an erotic turn-on. Or of a boss having sex with his secretary while beckoning his colleagues to come into the room to have sex with her also, with the caption referring to this as her "Christmas bonus."

Pictures of dead, decapitated women with amputated bodies, as well as severed nipples and clitorises. In each of these examples, [*Hustler* publisher] Larry Flynt jokes about rape, battery, sexual harassment, incest, torture, mutilation and death, and presents this violence as sexy.

How do you feel about erotica?

Excerpted from Ann E. Menasche, "An Interview with Diana Russell: Violence, Pornography, and Woman-Hating," *Against the Current*, July/August 1997. Reprinted by permission of the publisher.

I define erotica as sexually suggestive or arousing material that is free of sexism, racism, and homophobia, and respectful of all human beings and animals portrayed.

I find nothing degrading about explicit portrayals of sex per se, though erotica can of course be much broader than that. Even the peeling of an orange can be filmed to make it erotic.

How do you respond to people who point out that it is impossible to obtain a consensus on what is pornography versus what is erotica, that "one person's erotica is another person's pornography?"

> *"[Hustler publisher] Larry Flynt jokes about rape, battery, sexual harassment, incest, torture, mutilation and death, and presents this violence as sexy."*

There is no consensus on the definitions of many phenomena. Rape is one example. Legal definitions of rape vary considerably in different states. Similarly, millions of court cases have revolved around arguments as to whether a killing constitutes murder or manslaughter. Lack of consensus should not automatically mean that pornography cannot be subject to opprobrium or legal restraint, or that we cannot examine its effects.

The Evidence

You state in Against Pornography *that pornography is one of multiple causes of men raping women, other causes being male sex role socialization, sexual abuse in childhood and peer pressure. Could you give a few examples of the research that supports the view that pornography plays a role in causing sexual violence?*

First, there is the experiment by Neil Malamuth in which he shows that being exposed to some typical violent pornography will change those men who weren't force-oriented to begin with into having rape fantasies that they didn't previously have.

Second, there is the research that shows that pornography undermines the inhibitions of those who already have some desire to rape. For example, the work of Dolf Zillmann and Jennings Bryant shows that repeated exposure to pornography for a four-week period increased men's trivialization of rape, increased their callousness towards women, made them more likely to say that rape was the responsibility of the victim and that it was not a serious offense, and increased their estimate of the likelihood that they would rape a woman if they could get away with it.

Perhaps most important of all is James Check's work making comparisons between the effect on men viewing violent pornography, degrading pornography and erotica in an experimental situation.

Check found that the violent material had the most negative effect, the degrading material had the next most negative effects, and the other sexual material had

87

no negative effects at all. The negative effects he documented included an increase in the self-reported likelihood that the men would actually act out a rape.

Katha Pollitt, writing in the February 2, 1997, issue of The Nation *disputed that pornography caused real life harm to women. Pollitt wrote, "any serious discussion of texts that cause real life harm to women would have to begin with the Bible and the Koran: It isn't porn that drives zealots to firebomb abortion clinics or slit the throats of Algerian schoolgirls." How would you respond to that?*

Nonsense! None of us are claiming that pornography is the single cause of violence in the world. Also, Pollitt's not even using sexual violence as examples. If Pollitt had looked at my book, *Against Pornography,* and studied the examples of pornography and the research reviewed there, I don't think she could continue to take such a position.

Pornography as Discrimination

How do you respond to the charge that the Andrea Dworkin–Catharine MacKinnon approach to fighting pornography amounts to censorship that would dangerously restrict free speech?

Dworkin and MacKinnon do not advocate banning or censorship of pornography. What they advocate is that anyone who has been victimized by pornography and can prove it in a court of law should be able to do so. That's not censorship, that's accountability.

It seems that if you make any proposal against pornography, people equate it with censorship. One of MacKinnon and Dworkin's major contributions in this area is to try to recast the debate about pornography—they maintain that this is not primarily a debate about freedom of speech. It's an issue of discrimination against women.

Discrimination based on sex, race, or sexual orientation is not acceptable and, in some instances, it's illegal. Take sexual harassment, for example. There's a law against sexual harassment, that it constitutes discrimination against women and some men.

Catharine MacKinnon is largely responsible for developing this analysis. She conceptualized sexual harassment in this way. Most people don't protest that the laws against sexual harassment constitute an attack on free speech, that men in the workplace should be able to say whatever they like to women, to proposition them and talk about their breasts, and ask them about their genitals and whatever, as an exercise of their freedom of speech.

"Lack of consensus [over the definition of pornography] should not automatically mean that pornography cannot be subject to opprobrium or legal restraint."

It is recognized that such behavior, even though it involves speech, is not acceptable, that it's discrimination and it's abuse of power and it makes a hostile environment against women. Even the display of pornography in the workplace is considered to contribute to a hostile environment and is therefore against the law.

We are making a similar argument, that pornography outside the workplace also makes for a hostile environment, a dangerous environment because it promotes rape and other forms of sexual violence.

> *"Research ... shows that pornography undermines the inhibitions of those who already have some desire to rape."*

Given that this controversy exists, do you think it is helpful to discuss what one thinks about pornography separately from one's position on what should be done about it?

Yes, I think it's imperative! I try to insist that people not start discussing what to do about it before they've discussed if it is damaging or not. If it's not damaging, you don't have to do anything about it.

There are people who take the position that pornography is extremely damaging, but the law isn't the way to handle it. Nikki Craft is one feminist and dedicated activist who takes this stance.

The People vs. Larry Flynt

Could you mention some of the ways that a person can organize against pornography if one is opposed to censorship and disagrees with the Dworkin-MacKinnon approach?

In my book *Making Violence Sexy,* I have a whole section at the end about feminist actions against pornography, none of which constitute censorship or requires the passage of any laws. You can do educational campaigns like the recent campaign against the movie, *The People vs. Larry Flynt.*

We organized press conferences and picket-lines. We were not advocating censorship. We were not even advocating boycotting the movie, although boycotts do not constitute censorship either. Somehow, whenever we express our own First Amendment rights to protest pornography, we're called censors—which is absurd.

I think education is important because half the people who say pornography is fine don't have a clue what they're really talking about. Again and again, we find if you show people what's in pornography, they are shocked, particularly women.

What was the objective of your campaign against the Larry Flynt movie?

Our objective was to educate people about the lies that are told in the movie, to point out the violent and women-hating content of *Hustler* magazine that was completely omitted from the film, and to point out what Larry Flynt is really like, so Milos Foreman and Oliver Stone's efforts to turn him into a hero will be undermined.

Flynt himself has said that the film is a massive free advertising campaign for *Hustler* magazine. Since the movie, the circulation of *Hustler* has gone up, in spite of the fact that the movie has not done so well at the box office. I believe it only made about twenty million whereas it cost about sixty million to make. It was expected to be a great success, but this was before feminists began protesting.

Besides feminists in the Bay Area, who else has spoken against the movie?

Gloria Steinem and Flynt's daughter, Tonya, were major actors in the protests. Feminists in New York and in other U.S. cities as well as in other countries also protested the movie.

In Sweden, feminists took a more militant boycott approach and actually did try and stop men from going to the movie. They were very effective and got a lot of news coverage. Women in England also protested the movie when it opened there on April 11, 1997.

The Need for Activism

How can change come about for women? How can we create a world where women are not kept in our places by violence and the threat of violence?

We need to increase the level of consciousness about male violence against women. We've made some progress in the United States in many areas. For example, sexual harassment is now recognized, it wasn't recognized before. I hope femicide will also become recognized.

The old way of men blaming women for the violence has been challenged by feminists. However, we haven't yet seen a decline in the violence itself.

I often think we would be more effective if women as a gender were more militant in our response. I'm not talking about on an individual level—although I favor that too. But we must join together in organizations to act more militantly, even if those organizations are small four-women ones.

As with pornography, those who are the victims of it, the targets—as Black people are with racist material—really have to be the mobilizers. I think direct action and civil disobedience would be extremely effective for women to use.

We are just a handful of people trying to educate a nation, meanwhile; pornography is a multibillion dollar industry miseducating people. Though many women have been arrested for peace and civil rights work, very few women appear to be willing to get arrested for feminist causes.

> *"Pornography . . . makes for a hostile environment, a dangerous environment because it promotes rape and other forms of sexual violence."*

People talk about a war between the sexes, but it's more like a massacre, because women often don't fight back. And we can't all fight our separate battles in our own homes.

Organizing together is really the secret; organization is the answer to making change. As Andrea Dworkin has said, women have been very good at *endurance* but not at *resistance*. We must change this.

Pornography Does Not Cause Violence Against Women

by Wendy McElroy

About the author: *Wendy McElroy is an author whose books include* XXX: A Woman's Right to Pornography *and* Sexual Correctness: The Gender-Feminist Attack on Women.

"Pornography benefits women, both personally and politically." This sentence opens my book *XXX: A Woman's Right to Pornography*, and it constitutes a more extreme defense of pornography than most feminists are comfortable with. I arrived at this position after years of interviewing hundreds of sex workers. . . .

Anti-porn feminism   Page Mellish of Feminists Fighting Pornography has declared, "There's no feminist issue that isn't rooted in the porn problem." In her book *Only Words*, Catharine MacKinnon denies that pornography consists of words and images, both of which would be protected by the First Amendment. She considers pornography—in and of itself—to be an act of sexual violence. Why is pornography viewed as both the core issue of modern feminism and an inherent act of violence? The answer lies in radical feminist ideology, which Christina Hoff Sommers calls "gender feminism."

Gender feminism looks at history and sees an uninterrupted oppression of women by men that spans cultural barriers. To them, the only feasible explanation is that men and women are separate and antagonistic classes whose interests necessarily conflict. Male interests are expressed through and maintained by a capitalistic structure known as "patriarchy."

The root of the antagonism is so deep that it lies in male biology itself. For example, in the watershed book *Against Our Will*, Susan Brownmiller traces the inevitability of rape back to Neanderthal times when men began to use their penises as weapons. Brownmiller writes: "From prehistoric times to the present, I believe, rape has played a critical function. It is nothing more or less

Excerpted from Wendy McElroy, "A Feminist Defense of Pornography," *Free Inquiry*, Fall 1997. Reprinted by permission of the Council for Democratic and Secular Humanism.

than a conscious process of intimidation by which all men keep all women in a state of fear." How Brownmiller acquired this knowledge of prehistoric sex is not known.

Another tenet of gender oppression is that sex is a social construct. Radical feminists reject what they call "sexual essentialism"—the notion that sex is a natural force based on biology that inclines women toward natural tendencies, such as motherhood. Even deeply felt sexual preferences, such as heterosexuality, are not biological. They spring from ideology.

Men construct women's sexuality through the words and images of society, which the French philosopher Michel Paul Foucault called the "texts" of society. After such construction, men commercialize women's sexuality and market it back in the form of pornography. In other words, through porn man defines woman sexually—a definition that determines every aspect of her role in society. To end the oppression, patriarchy and its texts must be destroyed. . . .

Pro-sex feminism Over the past decade, a growing number of feminists—labeled "pro sex"—have defended a woman's choice to participate in and to consume pornography. Some of these women, such as Nina Hartley, are current or ex–sex workers who know firsthand that posing for pornography is an uncoerced choice that can be enriching. Pro-sex feminists retain a consistent interpretation of the principle "a woman's body, a woman's right" and insist that every peaceful choice a woman makes with her own body must be accorded full legal protection, if not respect. . . .

Dissecting Anti-Porn

Do the specific accusations hurled at pornography stand up under examination?

Pornography is degrading to women. *Degrading* is a subjective term. I find commercials in which women become orgasmic over soapsuds to be tremendously degrading. The bottom line is that every woman has the right to define what is degrading and liberating for herself.

The assumed degradation is often linked to the "objectification" of women: that is, porn converts them into sexual objects. What does this mean? If taken literally, it means nothing because objects don't have sexuality; only beings do. But to say that porn portrays women as "sexual beings" makes for poor rhetoric. Usually, the term *sex objects* means showing women as body parts, reducing them to physical objects. What is wrong with this? Women are as much their bodies as they are their

> *"Every peaceful choice a woman makes with her own body must be accorded full legal protection, if not respect."*

minds or souls. No one gets upset if you present women as "brains" or as spiritual beings. If I concentrated on a woman's sense of humor to the exclusion of her other characteristics, is this degrading? Why is it degrading to focus on her sexuality?

Pornography leads to violence against women. A cause-and-effect relationship is drawn between men viewing pornography and men attacking women, especially in the form of rape. But studies and experts disagree as to whether any relationship exists between pornography and violence, between images and behavior. Even the pro-censorship Meese Commission Report admitted that the data connecting pornography to violence was unreliable.

Other studies, such as the one prepared by feminist Thelma McCormick in 1983 for the Metropolitan Toronto Task Force on Violence Against Women, find no pattern to

> *"Studies and experts disagree as to whether any relationship exists between pornography and violence."*

connect porn and sex crimes. Incredibly, the Task Force suppressed the study and reassigned the project to a pro-censorship male, who returned the "correct" results. His study was published.

What of real-world feedback? In Japan, where pornography depicting graphic and brutal violence is widely available, rape is much lower per capita than in the United States, where violence in porn is severely restricted.

Sex Workers

Pornography is violence because women are coerced into pornography. Not one of the dozens of women depicted in pornographic materials with whom I spoke reported being coerced. Not one knew of a woman who had been. Nevertheless, I do not dismiss reports of violence: every industry has its abuses. And anyone who uses force or threats to make a woman perform should be charged with kidnapping, assault, and/or rape. Any such pictures or films should be confiscated and burned because no one has the right to benefit from the proceeds of a crime.

Pornography is violence because women who pose for porn are so traumatized by patriarchy they cannot give real consent. Although women in pornography appear to be willing, anti-porn feminists know that no psychologically healthy woman would agree to the degradation of pornography. Therefore, if agreement seems to be present, it is because the women have "fallen in love with their own oppression" and must be rescued from themselves. A common characteristic of the porn actresses I have interviewed is a love of exhibitionism. Yet if such a woman declares her enjoyment in flaunting her body, anti-porn feminists claim she is not merely a unique human being who reacts from a different background or personality. She is psychologically damaged and no longer responsible for her actions. In essence, this is a denial of a woman's right to choose anything outside the narrow corridor of choices offered by political/sexual correctness. The right to choose hinges on the right to make a "wrong" choice, just as freedom of religion entails the right to be an atheist. After all, no one will prevent a woman from doing what she thinks she should do.

A Pro-Sex Defense

As a "pro-sex" feminist, I contend: Pornography benefits women, both personally and politically. It provides sexual information on at least three levels:

- It gives a panoramic view of the world's sexual possibilities. This is true even of basic sexual information such as masturbation. It is not uncommon for women to reach adulthood without knowing how to give themselves pleasure.

- It allows women to "safely" experience sexual alternatives and satisfy a healthy sexual curiosity. The world is a dangerous place. By contrast, pornography can be a source of solitary enlightenment.

- It offers the emotional information that comes only from experiencing something either directly or vicariously. It provides us with a sense of how it would "feel" to do something.

Pornography allows women to enjoy scenes and situations that would be anathema to them in real life. Take, for example, one of the most common fantasies reported by women—the fantasy of "being taken." The first thing to understand is that a rape fantasy does not represent a desire for the real thing. Why would a healthy woman daydream about being raped? Perhaps by losing control, she also sheds all sense of responsibility for and guilt over sex. Perhaps it is the exact opposite of the polite, gentle sex she has now. Perhaps it is flattering to imagine a particular man being so overwhelmed by her that he must have her. Perhaps she is curious. Perhaps she has some masochistic feelings that are vented through the fantasy. Is it better to bottle them up?

> *"In Japan, where pornography depicting graphic and brutal violence is widely available, rape is much lower per capita than in the United States."*

Pornography breaks cultural and political stereotypes, so that each woman can interpret sex for herself. Anti-feminists tell women to be ashamed of their appetites and urges. Pornography tells them to accept and enjoy them. Pornography can be good therapy. Pornography provides a sexual outlet for those who—for whatever reason—have no sexual partner. Perhaps they are away from home, recently widowed, isolated because of infirmity. Perhaps they simply choose to be alone. Couples also use pornography to enhance their relationship. Sometimes they do so on their own, watching videos and exploring their reactions together. Sometimes, the couples go to a sex therapist who advises them to use pornography as a way of opening up communication on sex. By sharing pornography, the couples are able to experience variety in their sex lives without having to commit adultery.

Pornography benefits women politically in many ways. Historically, pornography and feminism have been fellow travelers and natural allies. Although it is not possible to draw a cause-and-effect relationship between the rise of pornography and that of feminism, they both demand the same social conditions—namely, sexual freedom.

> *"Viewing pornography may well have a cathartic effect on men who have violent urges toward women."*

Pornography is free speech applied to the sexual realm. Freedom of speech is the ally of those who seek change: it is the enemy of those who seek to maintain control. Pornography, along with all other forms of sexual heresy, such as homosexuality, should have the same legal protection as political heresy. This protection is especially important to women, whose sexuality has been controlled by censorship through the centuries.

Viewing pornography may well have a cathartic effect on men who have violent urges toward women. If this is true, restricting pornography removes a protective barrier between women and abuse.

Legitimizing pornography would protect female sex workers, who are stigmatized by our society. Anti-pornography feminists are actually undermining the safety of sex workers when they treat them as "indoctrinated women." Dr. Leonore Tiefer, a professor of psychology, observed in her essay "On Censorship and Women": "These women have appealed to feminists for support, not rejection. . . . Sex industry workers, like all women, are striving for economic survival and a decent life, and if feminism means anything it means sisterhood and solidarity with these women."

The Purpose of Law

The porn debate is underscored by two fundamentally antagonistic views of the purpose of law in society.

The first view, to which pro-sex feminists subscribe, is that law should protect choice. "A woman's body, a woman's right" applies to every peaceful activity a woman chooses to engage in. The law should come into play only when a woman initiates force or has force initiated against her. The second view, to which both conservatives and anti-porn feminists subscribe, is that law should protect virtue. It should come into play whenever there has been a breach of public morality, or a breach of "women's class interests."

This is old whine in new battles. The issue at stake in the pornography debate is nothing less than the age-old conflict between individual freedom and social control.

Patriarchal Customs Cause Violence Against Women

by Charlotte Bunch

About the author: *Charlotte Bunch is a feminist author and executive director of the Center for Women's Global Leadership at Rutgers University in New Brunswick, New Jersey. She coordinated the Global Campaign for Women's Human Rights at the 1993 World Conference on Human Rights in Vienna and women's human rights activities at the Fourth World Conference on Women in Beijing in 1995.*

Imagine a people routinely subjected to assault, rape, sexual slavery, arbitrary imprisonment, torture, verbal abuse, mutilation, even murder—all because they were born into a particular group. Imagine further that their sufferings were compounded by systematic discrimination and humiliation in the home and workplace, in classrooms and courtrooms, at worship and at play. Few would deny that this group had been singled out for gross violations of human rights.

Such a group exists. Its members comprise half of humanity. Yet it is rarely acknowledged that violence against women and girls, many of whom are brutalized from cradle to grave simply because of their gender, is the most pervasive human rights violation in the world today.

Gender violence is also a major health and development issue, with powerful implications for coming generations as well as society in general. Eliminating this violence is essential to constructing the paradigm of human security—and by that I mean peace, peace at home and peace at large. Without it, the notion of human progress is merely a fantasy.

However, opening the door on the subject of violence against the world's females is like standing at the threshold of an immense dark chamber vibrating with collective anguish, but with the sounds of protest throttled back to a murmur. Where there should be outrage aimed at an intolerable status quo there is instead denial, and the largely passive acceptance of 'the way things are'.

Consider a few facts from this dark chamber—facts that leave no doubt that

Adapted from Charlotte Bunch, "The Intolerable Status Quo: Violence Against Women and Girls," in *The Progress of Nations 1997*, UNICEF, New York, ©1997, pp. 41–45, by permission.

gender violence merits a prominent place on the human rights agenda:

- Roughly 60 million women who should be alive today are 'missing' because of gender discrimination, predominantly in South and West Asia, China and North Africa.

- In the United States, where over-all violent crime against women has been growing for the past two decades, a woman is physically abused by her intimate partner every nine seconds.

> *"It is rarely acknowledged that violence against women and girls . . . is the most pervasive human rights violation in the world."*

- In India, more than 5,000 women are killed each year because their in-laws consider their dowries inadequate. A tiny percentage of the murderers are brought to justice.

- In some countries of the Middle East and Latin America, husbands are often exonerated from killing an unfaithful, disobedient or wilful wife on the grounds of 'honour'.

- Rape as a weapon of war has been documented in seven countries in recent years, though its use has been widespread for centuries.

- Throwing acid to disfigure a woman's face is so common in Bangladesh that it warrants its own section of the penal code.

- About 2 million girls each year (6,000 every day) are genitally mutilated—the female equivalent of what would be amputation of all or part of the male penis.

- More than 1 million children, overwhelmingly female, are forced into prostitution every year, the majority in Asia. In the wake of the AIDS epidemic, younger and younger children are being sought in the belief that they are less likely to be infected.

At first glance, this brutal litany of statistics might seem wildly exaggerated. Yet while it is true that gender violence is a new field of research and studies are often limited in size, it is nonetheless clear that these crimes are, in the main, vastly under-reported. As social scientists are now discovering, the sheer scope and universality of violent acts against women and girls defy even the most educated perceptions.

The Tradition of Male Primacy

Equally shocking is the fact that most gender violence not only goes unpunished but is tolerated in silence—the silence of society as well as that of its victims. Fear of reprisal, censorship of sexual issues, the shame and blame of those violated, unquestioning acceptance of tradition and the stranglehold of male dominion all play their part. In many countries, so does the active or passive complicity of the State and other institutions of moral authority.

In addition, while gender violence is as old as humanity, it is only in the past decade that it has been publicly recognized, systematically studied and legislated against to any significant degree. In the 1990s, such violence finally gained currency on the international level with its recognition as a human rights issue. That is welcome news, and most of the credit goes to women's groups that have struggled against enormous odds to bring the issue to light. But this is no reason for complacency.

As the second millennium draws to a close, there have been reprisals against the progress in the field—rightly regarded as a challenge to male primacy. Some studies even suggest that certain forms of violence against women and girls are on the rise. For gender violence, in all of its varied manifestations, is not random and it is not about sex. It serves a deliberate social function: asserting control over women's lives and keeping them second-class citizens. Constant vigilance is needed to protect the fragile gains made thus far, to continue along the road to equality—and to bring an end to the torrent of daily violence that degrades not only women but humankind in its entirety.

The Intimate Enemy

For tens of millions of women today, home is a locus of terror. It is not the assault of strangers that women need fear the most, but everyday brutality at the hands of relatives, friends and lovers. Battering at home constitutes by far the most universal form of violence against women and is a significant cause of injury for women of reproductive age. Yet it is not the sort of act that commands headlines because it happens behind closed doors and because victims fear speaking out. Even in a comparatively open society like the US, research shows that only 1 in 100 battered women ever reports the abuse she suffers. Crime statistics reveal that most women who are raped know their attackers, as do 40 per cent of female murder victims.

Indeed, domestic violence is tragically commonplace. It occurs across education, class, income and ethnic boundaries. A World Bank analysis of 35 recent studies from industrialized and developing countries shows that one quarter to one half of all women have suffered physical abuse by an intimate partner. And while there are not yet enough data to make accurate country-by-country comparisons, the prevalence and pattern of domestic violence are remarkably consistent from one culture to the next. Statistics on rape from industrialized and developing countries show strikingly similar patterns: Between one in five and one in seven women will be victims of rape in their lifetime.

One might assume that the spreading emancipation of women would

"[Gender violence] serves a deliberate social function: asserting control over women's lives and keeping them second-class citizens."

have diminished the reach of violence. Yet violence in the home has been stubbornly resistant to advances in women's rights. In many Western countries, domestic violence is targeted by law and the media, but it has not summoned the

98

sort of insistent public campaigns as have issues such as driving while intoxicated or smoking.

Further, in most countries today, domestic abuse is officially regarded as a private family matter. While sexual and physical assault are broadly accepted as crimes outside the home, the law in most countries is mute when it comes to attacks within the family nest. Laws that stop at the doorstep of the family are a form of moral hypocrisy. . . .

> *"The issue is changing the perception—so deep-seated it is often unconscious—that women are fundamentally of less value than men."*

In all societies, poverty, discrimination, ignorance and social unrest are common predictors of violence against women. Yet the most enduring enemies of a woman's dignity and security are cultural forces aimed at preserving male dominance and female subjugation—often defended in the name of venerable tradition.

In industrialized societies like the US, where institutions formally frown on gender violence, behaviour belies official pronouncements: rap music insulting women as 'whores'; a popular men's magazine that celebrates gang rape and depicts female bodies being fed into meat grinders; sexual harassment of women trying to integrate into the armed forces; and societal pressures that induce young women to starve themselves or use technology to create 'ideal' bodies, often destroying their health in the process.

In developing countries, violent practices against women are often recognized and defended as strands of the cultural weave. Wife-beating, for example, is considered part of the natural order in many countries—a masculine prerogative celebrated in songs, proverbs and wedding ceremonies.

At their most extreme, expressions of gender violence include 'honour' killings, female genital mutilation and dowry deaths, as well as a deep-seated, even murderous, preference for male children.

In courts of law, the 'honour defence' is institutionalized in some Middle Eastern and Latin American countries, allowing fathers or husbands to walk away from murder. In 12 Latin American countries, a rapist can be exonerated if he offers to marry the victim and she accepts. In one country, Costa Rica, he can be exonerated even if she refuses his offer. The family of the victim frequently pressures her to marry the rapist, which they believe restores the family's honour.

The concept of male honour—and fear of female empowerment—also underlies the practice of female genital mutilation (FGM). This excruciating procedure removes part or all of a girl's external genitalia and causes lifelong health problems for some women. It is aimed at preserving female chastity and marriage prospects and achieves its purpose at the expense of a woman's sexual pleasure and bodily integrity. Up to 130 million women and girls today in at least 28 countries, mostly in Africa, have had their genitals excised to some degree.

Defenders of the rite, who include many women, call FGM a traditional cultural practice of no business to outsiders. This is an old song. Throughout history, 'culture' has been invoked to justify abhorrent practices ranging from slavery to binding women's feet. FGM must be eradicated because it is a grave human rights violation and a public health menace that transcends any and all cultural boundaries. . . .

These are but a few of the ways that society drives home the message that a woman's life and dignity—her human rights—are worth less than a man's. From the day of their birth, girls are devalued and degraded, trapped in what the late United Nations Children's Fund (UNICEF) Executive Director James P. Grant poignantly termed 'the apartheid of gender'. Long after slavery was abolished in most of the world, many societies still treat women like chattel: Their shackles are poor education, economic dependence, limited political power, limited access to fertility control, harsh social conventions and inequality in the eyes of law. Violence is a key instrument used to keep these shackles on.

Changing the Status Quo

There is nothing immutable about the violent oppression of women and girls. It is a construct of power, as was apartheid, and one that can be changed. But because it has been so deeply ingrained, for so long, in virtually every culture remaining on earth, the effort to dismantle the societal structures that tolerate it, or patently refuse even to see it, will require creativity, patience and action on many fronts.

The Convention on the Rights of the Child and the Convention on the Elimination of All Forms of Discrimination against Women protect and promote the fundamental human rights of girls and women. Ratifying and implementing these conventions is the vital first step to lay the groundwork for social and legal reform.

Stopping violence against women and girls is not just a matter of punishing individual acts. The issue is changing the perception—so deep-seated it is often unconscious—that women are fundamentally of less value than men. It is only when women and girls gain their place as strong and equal members of society that violence against them will be viewed as a shocking aberration rather than an invisible norm.

Capitalism Causes Violence Against Women

by Connie Furdeck

About the author: *Connie Furdeck is a contributor to the* New Unionist, *the newsletter of the New Union Party, which, through lawful activities, advocates political and social revolution and the overthrow of the capitalist economic system.*

There is a deepening controversy in our society about the causes and cure for violence, particularly domestic violence.

According to the Senate Judiciary Committee, "As late as 1991 only 17 states kept separate data on domestic violence . . . limited to murder, rape and serious bodily injury." In other words, only incidents with serious consequences were recorded, and then mixed in with other crimes so we had no realization of the widespread extent of the problem.

Since the advent of the women's movement and pressure from grassroots support groups, record keeping and reporting are on the increase—as are the number of incidents of violent behavior itself.

It is estimated that every 15 seconds a woman is battered in the United States by her husband, boyfriend or live-in partner. Over three million children in the U.S. between three and 17 years are at risk of parental violence each year.

The House Committee on Aging estimates there are between 500,000 and one million elderly victims of abuse by their adult children—a vastly unreported domestic crime.

Rape, however, takes the prize as the most unreported domestic crime in America. Most people realize rape is not really about sex, but about dominance. What they don't know is that it is predominantly a domestic issue. According to the National Women's Study, rape by family members and persons with whom the victim is acquainted make up 78% of all cases. Only 22% of occurrences are assaults by complete strangers.

Although very little of the literature on violence deals with the cause of the

Reprinted from Connie Furdeck, "Economic/Emotional Stress Leads to Epidemic of Domestic Violence," *New Unionist,* September 9, 1996, by permission.

problem, the most common reason cited is the need for males to dominate, as if this is somehow a part of their nature.

Psychiatrist James Gilligan presents a thought-provoking contrast. For the past 25 years Gilligan has worked with society's most violent criminals in the Massachusetts prison system. He is also the director of the Study of Violence at Harvard University.

In his book, *Violence: Our Deadly Epidemic and Its Causes,* Gilligan sees violence as rooted in our economic system and points to studies that show that the level of violence in society increases as the gap between rich and poor widens. He writes this is particularly true in the U.S., where less is spent on programs for poor children than in any other industrialized nation. He says the overwhelming majority of violent criminals come from poverty and broken homes, and that their childhoods were filled with physical, sexual and emotional abuse.

In addition to Gilligan's research and other similar studies, anthropology too demonstrates that male domination is learned behavior, rather than part of human nature.

The Rise of the Nuclear Family

Prior to the rise of civilization, humans lived in kinship-based tribal societies. Tribal life reflected a complex network of relationships, duties and obligations. Above all, it was egalitarian and based on cooperation. Women held a respected and mystical status as the producers of children and played a central economic role as the early horticulturists. We need to remind ourselves that humans could not have survived and successfully spread throughout the earth without our ability to cooperate with one another.

All societies since the breakup of tribal life have been class-divided and class-dominated, and men have had the major role as the dominators. Lust for power and organized violence became the norm with our so-called civilization, at the root of which is the private ownership of wealth-producing property.

Nevertheless, violence, particularly domestic violence, was under some modicum of control until the rise of industrial capitalism and its introduction of the nuclear family. Until that time, most people lived in agrarian societies with extended families of grandparents, uncles, aunts and cousins. Divorce, while rare, was not the traumatic event it is today as the extended family system nurtured the children.

This was not by any means an idyllic setting. Certainly there was violence, rape and incest in "the good old days." But men were secure in their roles, and there was not the horrendous, mindless violence that proliferates in today's world.

> *"The level of violence in society increases as the gap between rich and poor widens."*

Today, capitalism is the predominant influence on our lives. Its whole foundation and social structure is based on myths that are contrary to the reality of people's lives. Life is equated to a game, with individuals competing to succeed. Our value is determined by our material possessions, not by our worth as caring, sharing human beings.

The cult of the individual who strives to succeed, whose family rises and falls with the fortunes of the individual, is particularly hard on males. When a man, as provider, loses his job, his identity as a worth-

> *"Violence, particularly domestic violence, was under some modicum of control until the rise of industrial capitalism."*

while person suffers accordingly. For young men brought up in poverty, without the chance at education or "success," the debilitating psychological effects are that much more severe.

When a social system is in decline, and as increasing numbers of its members no longer have a chance at satisfying and worthwhile lives as part of the community, crime and violence increase.

When one reads about the decline of Rome, its orgies and violence, it must be put in the context of the economic changes that had affected people's lives. Great wealth was concentrated in the hands of the few, and the bulk of Roman citizens, who were small farmers, had lost their land and livelihoods. They migrated to the cities looking for work, but couldn't compete with the slave labor of Rome's conquered peoples.

The ruling class tried to divert their justified anger with "bread and circuses." Public spectacles of violence and death were "entertainments" used to release the frustration, boredom and hostility of the unemployed urban masses. The parallels between Rome and our society are striking.

Demanding Change

What can we as a society do to solve this problem of violence in America?

Other industrialized nations have put a great deal of money into their social programs, cushioning the worst effects of poverty. This is not because their business class has a social conscience; it is because their working class is more organized and militant. Witness in France when the politicians threatened to cut social programs [in 1995] and the French workers mobilized more than half the country to fight the cutbacks. The capitalist-controlled government backed down—at least temporarily.

Can we mobilize ourselves to demand appropriate programs to ameliorate the tendency to violence here in the U.S.? Perhaps so, but whatever concessions we win will be a constant struggle to keep, just as has been true of other social gains. In the long run, economics dictates what will be allowed. Given worldwide competition, the prospects look bleak within the existing system.

All previous social systems in human history have gone through periods of birth, maturity, decline and finally death. Ours is no different. It is past reforming. This is why concerned citizens need to look beyond our present system.

We cannot achieve peace and security and an end to violence under capitalism. It poses an ominous threat to our very beings, to our humanity and sense of community. A fundamental economic and political change is needed. We believe the solution lies in building a new society—an economic democracy.

Learned Gender Roles Cause Violence Against Women

by Katherine Hanson and Anne McAuliffe

About the authors: *Katherine Hanson and Anne McAuliffe are director and senior editor, respectively, of the Women's Educational Equity Act Resource Center, a U.S. Department of Education program dedicated to reducing the educational disparity between men and women.*

Violence is not a universal human function; most people go through life without committing violent acts against another person. However, there is a level of historical acceptance and support within any culture for or against violence. Our thinkers and social activists, our spiritual leaders and our teachers are currently searching for alternatives to violence. One answer to reducing violence may lie in a yet relatively unexplored arena—the gender-role socialization of our children within our social systems, including education. While gender-role socialization is not the only cause of violence, it significantly exacerbates the levels of violence when connected to other causes—anger, racism, poverty, learning disabilities, childhood abuse, frustration, attention deficit syndrome—all of which have been linked to violence. Violence takes many forms ranging from one-on-one or gang violence to the abuse, battering, and murder of women. Jackson Katz of Boston's Real Men has noted that "all violence is gendered." This understanding—that the acceptance of violence, particularly among males, is something we inculcate into our children—can have significant implications for the ways in which we view education. By identifying the gendered commonalties of violence we tie the various forms of violence together and can begin to address the underlying issues regarding violence.

Most acts of violence are committed by men, and although this does not imply that all men are violent, violence-prone or accepting of violence as a way of resolving conflicts or attaining power, we have not yet adequately developed

Excerpted from Katherine Hanson and Anne McAuliffe, "Gender and Violence: Implications for Peaceful Schools," *Equity Online*, May 12, 1998, www.edc.org/womensequity/articles/index.html. Reprinted with permission.

societal systems that provide all young men with emotional and intellectual support for nonviolence. As one of the most important systems for acculturating our children to society, we must examine the power and importance of our educational system in changing a paradigm that accepts violence as a male norm to one that assumes male and female norms of empathy and compassion. As society explores new questions and responses to violence, a key intervention point remains the public school system. . . .

Gender as a Social Construct

Gender is a social construction, as are race, class, and ethnicity. Although there are biological differences between males and females, this does not mean that gender-related differences reflect genetic factors. Rather, gender is, in the words of Candace West and Don H. Zimmerman, "the product of social doings of some sort" that results in our framing of what it means to be male or female, a definition that often varies from culture to culture. From birth on, children are taught the norms, values and behaviors of their gender, as perceived by the culture into which they were born. Through this socialization process, children internalize the rules for "masculinity" and "femininity." Because they are learned at a very early age, the meanings attached to gender definitions seem natural, rather than socially constructed. And, because the roots of violence are deeply embedded in our socialization of children, efforts to confront such violence must include a comprehensive examination of the socialization process and the definitions the culture has of appropriate male and female gender roles.

Violence is one of the most disturbing aspects of living in a society that promotes a hierarchy of power in human relationships according to class, race, and gender, among other divisions. Such violence is based in part on cultural assumptions about appropriate roles for males and females. All stem from cultural norms that socialize males to be aggressive, powerful, unemotional, and controlling and that contribute to a social acceptance of men as dominant. Such cultural norms also portray women as dangerous, passive, in need of control and subordinate to men.

These norms serve to create stereotyped gender-role definitions in which males are expected to exercise control and authority aggressively. Males who do not ascribe to such beliefs or behaviors are castigated, harassed,

> *"The acceptance of violence, particularly among males, is something we inculcate into our children."*

and often assaulted. Violence against women and girls becomes a part of the social fabric. Similarly, homophobic violence is supported by a set of norms that unconsciously prescribe our sense of what is appropriately "masculine" and "feminine" in thought, affect, and behavior. These norms define violence against females, nonstereotyped males, gays, and lesbians as reaffirming the natural order of gender appropriate behavior.

106

These stereotyped perceptions of what it means to be appropriately male—to control, to be powerful—have become part of our national mythology, glorified in our media. They are reinforced by a country in which growing numbers of young, urban males are demeaned, tossed aside or corrupted by a society that views them as throw-aways. For many, violence becomes a way to verify that they are, in fact, "men." Violence becomes a way to earn respect, to make an impact, to get what they want. For many young men, violence has evolved into a culture, which anthropologist Glifford Geertz says should be thought of "as the extrinsic genes" because of its deep hold on habits and hearts.

But, as the American Psychological Association's (APA) 1992 conference called "Toward a New Psychology of Men" pointed out, "violent behavior, emotional distance, and higher rates of drug addition among men can't be explained by hormones. The problem is cultural beliefs about masculinity—everything packed into the phrase 'a real man.'" However, even within this culture of violence, we must remember that violence is a choice. As counselors from Emerge, a group for batterers in Greater Boston, and other violence prevention advocates have pointed out, violence is not a constant: individuals make choices about who they will hurt and when. Batterers, for instance, do not beat their bosses or co-workers; they go home and regularly beat their partners. This leads to a need to examine the issues of power, lack of power, and the perception of who is an appropriate target for violence.

> *"Cultural norms . . . portray women as dangerous, passive, in need of control and subordinate to men."*

The nightly news, television entertainment, videos, movies, magazines and video games hold up a mirror to our children of what it means to be adult—male or female—in this society. Countless documents have examined the portrayal of women as helpless victims, ready to be raped, shot, molested, or murdered for entertainment. Thousands of Rambo figures cavort across the screen, spewing mayhem and murder everywhere. Almost all portrayals link violence and sex—for these producers of violent entertainment, violence is sexy. This constant public adulation of violence has its effect in much the same way as did the conscious effort of Nazi propagandists who created films with increasing levels of violence designed to dehumanize their intended victims. Again, according to the APA, "The accumulated research clearly demonstrates a correlation between viewing violence and aggressive behavior." Television and the media contribute to sexual and racial stereotyping. African-Americans are most often portrayed as criminals or victims. Women, especially women of color, are always victims.

Teaching Gender Roles and Violence

However, as much as we would like to lay blame on the media, it must be remembered that the media is us. It is not a faceless industry, but rather groups of individuals who were raised in the same cultural context as the rest of the nation. They, in many ways are acting as mirrors for ourselves, a way to examine what we as a society believe about women, men, and violence.

Recent studies have begun to examine the perception of US society around gender roles. Countless reports talk about boys encouraged to "fight like a man," told that "boys don't cry" or teased for being a "sissy" or "wimp." Girls can be "tomboys"—at least until middle school. But we continue to recount warnings about not straying too far from home, not offending

> *"Stereotyped perceptions of what it means to be appropriately male—to control, to be powerful—have become part of our national mythology."*

men by having strong opinions, not being too physical or athletic. We know about the inherent messages in GI Joe and Barbie, traditional, rigid stereotyped models of masculinity and femininity.

And while some of this social conditioning is changing, [the books] *Failing at Fairness, We've all Got Scars: What Boys and Girls Learn in Elementary School*, and the American Association of University Women (AAUW) study "How Schools Shortchange Girls" point out this persistent problem of equating certain behaviors with maleness or femaleness and again point to the strong role education and schools play in it. For instance, according to Raphaela Best, by the second grade hidden curriculum "taught little girls to be helpful and nurturant. It taught little boys to distance themselves from girls, to look down on them. . . . Through its insistence that boys learn to be boys and girls learn to be girls . . . we make inordinate demands on small boys to become instant men, to live up to macho criteria they are as yet unprepared to meet."

Sports Teach Aggression

This process continues throughout the education cycle. One of the most overlooked arenas of violence training within schools may be the environment that surrounds athletics and sports. Beginning with little league games, where parents and friends sit on the sidelines and encourage aggressive, violent behavior to the college or professional sports arena where brutality is cheered, the message is clear. Violence is sport. For some, sport is a way to act out aggression. As B.J. Gredemeier and D.L. Shields put it, "In sports you can do what you want. In life it's more restricted. . . ."

For too many, however, the model of the athlete or sport figure as aggressive, winning, dominant may be translated into the model for everyday life. Again, the model of athlete as aggressive male is not lost on our children. When New York University professor Martin Hoffman compared the attitudes of men and women, he found women were concerned with fairness, honesty and helping others. Men, he found, were more socialized to egoistic achievement and excess and he found a strong connection with sports to this.

Education as the Carrier of Culture

Our educational system is a primary carrier of the dominant culture's assumptions, norms, and beliefs. For many years gender equity scholarship has documented evidence of the persuasiveness of gender role stereotyping and bias within student-teacher interaction, curriculum materials, classroom behaviors, and course offerings. Schools, then, with their history and role of conveying cultural beliefs and behaviors, play an important role in creating an awareness of the gendered aspects of violence and of countering such behaviors.

School culture can both promote and support violence or it can evolve a culture and socialization process that promotes and sustains healthy violence-free relationships. Through the absence of strong policy and curriculum guidelines, sexuality and gender play a strong role in establishing school organizing principals. Currently, in junior high and high schools, sexuality and gender bias comprise a large part of a hidden curriculum. This hidden curriculum supports the development of violence, and especially gender-based violence, that leads out of school to the street, the workplace and the home. Approaches to dealing with violence among adolescents—as among adults—must have the goal of changing the social structures that create a tolerance for victimization of young women, gays, and lesbians as well as goals that make it possible to prevent and intervene with individual cases of violence.

> *"Currently, in junior high schools, sexuality and gender bias comprise a large part of a hidden curriculum."*

Through education young men and women can unlearn the tolerance of violence and learn how to achieve violence-free, egalitarian relationships. These skills are as critical to students as reading, writing, math, and the use of computers. Since adolescents do not have the knowledge or skills to prevent or react against violence in their own lives or in the lives of friends or family, schools can set standards for healthy violence-free relationships and provide models for students to aim for. The support for nonviolence as a way to be male or female needs to be incorporated into all aspects of the school culture, ranging from policy guidelines to classroom interactions to athletics and sports.

Additionally, for many this work must begin with an examination of the way in which we continue to support or hinder the development of healthy males. And for many, this work must be guided by adult men, with the support of women. Writer, publisher, and educator Haki Madhubuti, talking about violence against women, offered this guidance:

> The liberation of the male psyche from preoccupation with domination, power hunger, control, and absolute rightness requires an honest and fair . . . commitment to deep study, combined with a willingness for painful, uncomfortable and often shocking change. We are not where we should be. That is why rape

exists; why families are so easily formed and just as easily dissolved; why children are confused and abused; why our elderly are discarded, abused, and exploited; and why teenage boys create substitute families (gangs) that terrorize their own communities.

The questions are emerging from all parts of society as are the beginnings of answers. Certainly, as we begin to grapple with what does it mean to be nonviolent, to interact in peaceful ways, to develop a different kind of conversation between individuals, we need to examine honestly and lovingly that part of our cultural identity—what does it mean to be male and female? And just as honestly and lovingly, we must help our young people develop new and more healthful models.

Chapter 3

Are Current Criminal Justice Approaches to Domestic Violence Effective?

Chapter Preface

On August 29, 1996, the California Supreme Court reversed the voluntary manslaughter conviction of Evelyn Humphrey, who had killed her abusive partner, Albert Hampton, four years earlier. The judges ruled that in the earlier trial the jury had not been allowed to consider the expert testimony of psychologists who believed Humphrey suffered from battered women's syndrome.

Battered women's syndrome (BWS) was first described by Lenore Walker in 1977 when she testified to explain the psychological state of mind of women who kill their abusive partners in self-defense. Justifiable self-defense, according to law, requires that one has reacted reasonably to imminent and lethal danger. A battering husband may well provide a "lethal danger," but prosecutors often argue that the "reasonable" response would be for the woman to leave her abusive partner before lethal violence is "imminent."

Walker developed the concept of BWS to explain the constant state of fear that can be induced by continued battering. According to Walker, this fear results in "the victim's inability to predict whether what she does will protect herself from further abuse," a condition often termed "learned helplessness." The victim remains trapped in her situation, but as the abuse escalates, the anxious, hypervigilant victim may finally fight back, perhaps with a weapon, when the violence becomes life-threatening. With BWS testimony, claims the National Organization for Women, "judges and juries are more likely to view the circumstances of battered women defendants realistically and fairly."

BWS remains a controversial defense, however. Cathy Young expresses her doubts: "It's an interesting sort of defense because it assumes the woman is so passive she can't leave a relationship, but she's not too passive to kill." Michael Fumento charges that "battered women syndrome is simply a sign of the times. In a nation of victims, everything can be justified on the basis of claiming some sort of abuse."

Still others reject BWS but maintain that many battered women kill, justifiably, in self-defense. Many feminists, for example, reject the notion that a woman's legal defense should rely on her "helplessness." Author Donald Downs proposes an alternative, arguing that women do not give up their right to self-defense by staying in a dangerous situation: "No one has a legal obligation to leave any kind of relationship."

The controversy surrounding battered women's syndrome is part of a larger argument about whether a traditionally male-dominated legal system should adapt to better serve women. The viewpoints in the following chapter explore other legal debates surrounding violence against women.

Mandatory Arrest Laws Can Reduce Violence Against Women

by Marion Wanless

About the author: *Marion Wanless is a lawyer in Chicago, Illinois.*

"He broke the back door down to get in. . . . He's f—— going nuts. . . . He's going to beat the s—— out of me. Can you get someone over here now?" a terrified Nicole Brown Simpson implored police. Recorded on October 25, 1993, eight months before she was murdered, this 911 call reveals the fear and anxiety of an abused woman.

Nicole Brown Simpson's tragic death has brought domestic violence to the attention of the American public. In the United States, three to four million women are battered each year. This means every nine seconds a woman is beaten by her abuser in this country. Ten of these women die each day. Domestic violence is the leading cause of injury to women, surpassing auto accidents, muggings, and rapes combined. At some point in their lives, one-fifth to one-third of all women will be physically assaulted by a man with whom they have or had an intimate, romantic relationship.

This epidemic cries out for attention and a cure. One possible solution under debate is the mandatory arrest of men accused of abuse. A mandatory arrest law requires police to arrest male suspects if there is probable cause to believe domestic violence has occurred. Mandatory arrest laws always remove the decision to press charges from the victim and usually severely limit or eliminate police discretion. Fifteen states and the District of Columbia have enacted mandatory arrest laws.

A Controversial Solution

Nevertheless, mandatory arrest laws remain controversial: some view them as a simplistic solution to a complex problem, while others fear that mandatory arrest will actually increase domestic abuse. Supporters believe mandatory arrest laws will curtail domestic violence and signify that society finally recognizes that domestic violence is a crime. . . .

[Since the 1960s], society's response to domestic violence has focused almost exclusively on aiding victims. Although necessary and worthwhile, helping victims has not reduced domestic violence. By focusing on the victim, this approach completely ignores the root of the problem. Services for battered women should be collateral to a concentration on the cause of domestic violence—the abusers. Mandatory arrest appropriately shifts the focus away from victims, confirming the fact that domestic abuse is a crime, not just a family dispute. Many believe domestic violence will be eradicated only when society treats it as a crime rather than a family squabble or a lovers' quarrel. Mandatory arrest is a crucial step to criminalizing domestic violence.

Fifteen states and the District of Columbia have enacted mandatory arrest laws for a variety of reasons. First, the states want to shield themselves from potential liability for not providing adequate police protection to battered women. Second, advocates for battered women have campaigned for the laws, exerting pressure on legislators. Third, these governments recognize that joint mediation and counseling, the favored responses to domestic violence in the recent past, do not curtail domestic violence and may even endanger victims. Fourth, despite changes in state laws making it easier for police to arrest in misdemeanor cases, more often than not, police do not make arrests in domestic violence incidents. Finally, domestic violence continues to escalate, and these governments view mandatory arrest laws as an effective weapon in the fight to stop the violence.

> *"Mandatory arrest appropriately shifts the focus away from victims, confirming the fact that domestic abuse is a crime, not just a family dispute."*

In response to the unabated epidemic of domestic violence and other forms of violence against women, Congress passed the Violence Against Women Act. The Act was part of a major federal crime bill signed into law by President Clinton in September 1994. The Act contains a provision authorizing the Attorney General to make grants available to state and local governments to implement mandatory or pro-arrest programs. Grant funds totaling $120 million were made available over three years starting in fiscal year 1996.

The Act provides a significant economic incentive for states to enact mandatory arrest laws. Although several states have already adopted such laws, the question remains: Are mandatory arrest laws truly effective? . . .

Police Role in Domestic Violence

Under existing law in most states, police are not compelled to arrest in domestic violence incidents. In other words, police officers at the scene of a domestic violence incident have complete control over the decision to arrest. Although mandatory arrest statutes restrict police officers' discretion, opponents of these laws overestimate the extent to which police discretion is diminished.

In a poll conducted by the *Cleveland Plain Dealer,* 60% of Ohioans opposed a mandatory arrest law. Survey respondents feared that people would take advantage of mandatory arrest even when violence had not occurred. This fear is unfounded, because even under mandatory arrest laws, police must have probable cause to believe a crime has been committed before making an arrest. The requirement of probable cause prevents the use of mandatory arrest as a means of seeking revenge or retaliation.

> *"Mandatory arrest laws do not prevent police officers from making judgment calls."*

Police argue that mandatory arrest eliminates their control and discretion. They assert that mandatory arrest is too rigid, especially where the facts of a case are in dispute. Mandatory arrest laws do not prevent police officers from making judgment calls. On the contrary, police must still determine if there is probable cause to believe a crime has been committed before making an arrest. If the facts are in dispute, the probable cause determination requires police officers to use their best judgment. Because police constantly respond to situations where facts are in dispute, enforcing mandatory arrest laws should not present any special problems. The only decision mandatory arrest removes from police discretion is whether to arrest if there is probable cause to believe that domestic violence has occurred.

A Dangerous Reluctance to Arrest

Advocates of mandatory arrest cite past police practices and police attitudes toward domestic violence as the foremost reasons for restricting police discretion. They believe the unique situation of the victim in domestic violence cases renders lax police enforcement more dangerous than in other contexts.

Past Performance Historically, arrest rates in domestic violence cases have been very low. Police officers often employ irrelevant criteria such as the "reason" for the abuse or the severity of the victim's injuries in making their decision to arrest. Police officers often discourage victims from pressing charges. Many describe the procedure for obtaining an arrest warrant as arduous and time consuming or counsel victims that their desire to prosecute will probably change. They outline the impact of arrest on abusers—loss of wages, possible job loss, stigma of arrest—and insinuate that the victims do not want to be responsible for inflicting such hardship on their attackers.

Advocates for battered women assert that police are much less likely to make arrests in domestic violence cases than they are in similar incidents between strangers. . . .

Proponents of mandatory arrest reason that if past behavior is indicative of future performance, the decision to arrest should not be left to the discretion of the police. Advocates argue that because police abuse their arrest discretion, the decision to arrest should no longer be theirs.

Police Bias   The arrest decision may be more difficult for police in domestic violence cases than in other contexts. Many male officers may naturally be more sympathetic to male abusers. Numerous officers may labor under the misconception that the victim provoked the attack. Some may feel strongly that police should not interfere in family arguments or lovers' quarrels. Such attitudes make police much more likely to investigate intent and provocation, and consider them as mitigating factors, in responding to domestic violence calls than in other types of cases.

The race or class of the abuser also influences the arrest decision. Minorities are arrested in disproportionate numbers when police have complete discretion. White or upper class abusers are less likely to be arrested.

In short, bias may prevent police officers from making an objective arrest decision, leaving the victim unprotected and the batterer unpunished. Mandatory arrest would prevent police prejudice from affecting the arrest decision.

Unique Danger   Domestic violence is a unique crime in that the dangers of lax criminal enforcement are far greater than in other situations. Incidents of domestic violence are not isolated occurrences. Once battering starts, it will likely recur. . . .

> *"Advocates argue that because police abuse their arrest discretion, the decision to arrest should no longer be theirs."*

One in five women victimized by a spouse or an ex-spouse reports that she has been the victim of a series of three or more assaults in the last six months that were so similar she could not distinguish one from another. In domestic abuse cycles, the violence increases in severity over time. In addition, victim and abuser often live together making domestic violence unlike violence between strangers, where the victim is able to escape to a safe haven and the violence is usually an isolated incident. The battered woman does not have a safe haven, because her home is often where she is abused. The consequence of underenforcement of laws prohibiting domestic violence is that victims are repeatedly abused. . . .

Women's Concerns

Although many advocates for battered women actively support mandatory arrest, others vehemently oppose it. The opponents believe mandatory arrest further erodes victims' self-esteem and contributes to their sense of helplessness by usurping their control. They advocate leaving both the arrest and prosecution decisions to the victim. They assert that mandatory arrest undermines attempts to help victims gain a sense of control over their lives by continuing to foster the pattern of control battered women have experienced with their abusers.

Proponents believe mandatory arrest has the opposite effect—that it empowers victims. They view a victim's act of calling the police as a first step toward ending the abuse. Mandatory arrest lets victims know that the legal system will help them stop the abuse. The realization that they do not have to fight the abuse alone will encourage their efforts to help themselves. Mandatory arrest can get abusers out of the home long enough for victims to make other living arrangements, thereby ensuring their safety. It also provides victims with the opportunity to consider, in peace and safety, their situation and make reasoned decisions about their future.

> *"Mandatory arrest lets victims know that the legal system will help them stop the abuse."*

Some battered women's organizations oppose mandatory arrest because they fear it will lead to increased violence. They worry that an arrest will provoke the abuser to commit greater violence, though badly flawed studies of the effect of mandatory arrest on domestic violence have yielded conflicting findings on this issue. These groups believe each victim is in the best position to judge the potential effect of an arrest. If a battered woman thinks an arrest will result in an even more severe beating, opponents believe mandatory arrest is wrong to expose that woman to such a risk against her will.

Arrest may provoke abusers to commit greater violence. But not arresting batterers is neither an acceptable, nor an effective, way of avoiding this danger. Instead, mandatory arrest should be coupled with provisions such as no-contact and weapon surrender orders which reduce abusers' opportunities to seek revenge. . . .

Sending the Right Message

In the absence of criminal sanctions, the abuser can delude himself about his behavior and avoid taking responsibility. If no one else thinks his behavior is criminal, why should he? The legal system must hold the abuser accountable for his actions and convey a strong message that his behavior is criminal. According to Kathleen Waits, "Arrest thus thwarts denial and evasion of responsibility."

Proponents insist that mandatory arrest is essential to attacking the root cause of domestic violence. According to Waits:

> [The abuser] is violent at home because he has a bully's "sure winner" mentality. He beats his wife because . . . he can get away with it, as long as society does not intervene. In contrast, he doesn't beat his boss or his male acquaintances, not because he is never angry at them, but because the price of such behavior is too great.

As long as an abuser can "get away with it," he has no incentive to change. Only by imposing criminal sanctions, such as arrest, will the abuser be motivated to reform. . . .

Anglo-American society has long condoned domestic violence. Though it has been nearly a century since it was legal in the United States, domestic violence is an epidemic in this country, evidencing an unspoken tolerance for women battering. This unspoken tolerance conveys the message that women are not highly valued, that they are regarded as a man's property to be treated as he sees fit.

The continuing failure to consistently make arrests in domestic violence cases signifies that society still considers domestic abuse a permissible act rather than a crime. Pegi Shriver, who was brutally beaten by her husband, believes the real tragedy of her experience is that the criminal justice system has made him think he did nothing wrong.

Mandatory arrest can change this message. By enacting mandatory arrest laws states send a strong message that domestic abuse will not be tolerated. Mandatory arrest signals that domestic violence is a crime with attendant consequences. . . .

The Overall Criminal Justice Response

In addition to criticizing police for their handling of domestic violence cases, advocates for battered women assert that the entire criminal justice system fails to treat domestic violence as a crime. As Joan Stiles, Public Education Coordinator for the Massachusetts Coalition of Battered Women's Service Groups, points out, "Police response alone will never adequately address the problem of domestic violence; and the police cannot be held accountable for failing to protect battered women if, after an arrest, the rest of the system fails." If batterers are arrested but not prosecuted, or, if prosecuted, merely admonished by judges not to do it again, they will feel licensed by the criminal justice system to continue beating women.

Historically, prosecutors have been as guilty as the police of not taking domestic violence seriously and trying to persuade victims to drop criminal charges. Few men are prosecuted and convicted in domestic abuse cases. Lax prosecution practices undermine the effectiveness of mandatory arrest laws. Since Washington enacted a mandatory arrest law over a decade ago, arrests in domestic violence incidents have soared, increasing six-fold. Prosecution of batterers, however, remains the exception rather than the norm. Seattle police officers are frustrated that they repeatedly arrest the same batterers, but the men are seldom prosecuted and punished.

> *"Without a comprehensive criminal justice system response, an abuser will soon learn that being arrested in a domestic violence incident has no consequences."*

One of the primary ways prosecutors minimize the significance of domestic violence cases is by charging nearly all incidents as misdemeanors rather than felonies, no matter how serious the victims' injuries. Batterers are routinely charged with misdemeanors in spite of the fact that the injuries they inflict are as serious or more serious than injuries inflicted in 90% of the violent crimes that are classified as felonies. Batterers who have slashed, stabbed, shot, clubbed, run over with a car, or doused with gasoline and set fire to their victims are routinely charged with assault rather than attempted murder. Some prosecutors have admitted that the felony charge rate should be higher.

> *"In San Diego, domestic violence cases are treated like homicides, which are obviously prosecuted without the aid of the victim."*

Traditionally, prosecutors do not bring a case to trial unless the victim is willing to testify. Also, prosecutors often acquiesce quickly to a victim's request to have the charges against her batterer dropped. This approach fails to recognize that domestic violence is a crime against society as well as the victim, and gives a batterer too much control over the decision to prosecute. Given the dynamics of an abusive relationship, the batterer is likely to use increased violence and threats to intimidate his victim if he knows it will result in pending charges being dropped. Basing a decision to prosecute solely on a victim's willingness to testify violates the American Bar Association Standards for Prosecutors, which describes the prosecutor's duty as not merely to convict but to seek justice. . . .

Not a Panacea

Mandatory arrest is not a panacea for domestic violence. It is, however, an important step toward ending this epidemic. Given the pervasive tolerance of domestic violence in the United States and traditional police practices, the decision to arrest cannot be entrusted solely to the police. Mandatory arrest ensures a consistent police response on which victims can rely. Police discretion and judgment are not totally eliminated by mandatory arrest statutes; police officers must still ascertain that probable cause exists before making an arrest. Under a mandatory arrest statute, police retain sufficient power to prevent the law from being used for improper purposes such as revenge and retaliation.

Mandatory arrest relieves victims of the burden of making the arrest decision. It provides them with the opportunity to secure safe living arrangements and the chance to peacefully contemplate their situation. Mandatory arrest is an essential step toward ending domestic violence, but without more—including prosecution and penalties commensurate with the nature of the offense—it may not significantly diminish the domestic violence epidemic. Without a comprehensive criminal justice system response, an abuser will soon learn that being arrested in a domestic violence incident has no consequences. Advocates for battered women assert that until the entire criminal justice system, not just the police, takes domestic violence seriously, men will continue beating women with impunity. If the promise of mandatory arrest is to be fulfilled, traditional prosecutorial and judicial responses to domestic violence must be reformed. . . .

Stricter Postarrest Procedures

Statutory postarrest procedures control when and under what conditions arrested batterers may be released from police custody. Without statutory postarrest procedures, arrested batterers may quickly secure release from police custody, minimizing the effect of mandatory arrest on abusers and endangering victims. Certain postarrest procedures are essential to insuring the safety of victims. NIJ studies suggest that postarrest procedures can impact the deterrent effect of mandatory arrest.

After abusers are arrested, they need time for the intense rage of the battering phase of the abuse cycle to subside before they can be safely released from custody. In order to protect victims, arrested batterers should be kept in custody as long as the law will allow. Bail statutes should provide for short-term detention when an abuser's release would endanger his victim. At a bare minimum, victims should be notified prior to their abusers' release so that they can take steps to protect themselves. . . .

Insisting on Prosecution

Only by removing the decision to prosecute from the victims' control will they be protected during the time their abusers' cases are pending. Removing the decision from the victims' control will also eliminate the influence batterers exert over the prosecutorial decision. The National Council of Juvenile and Family Court Judges advises prosecutors: "Victims must not be placed in the position of initiating and managing their own cases. Nor should they make decisions to proceed or withdraw."

Contrary to many prosecutors' beliefs, victim cooperation is not essential to obtaining a conviction. The most effective prosecution strategies employed today are not dependent on victim cooperation. The City Attorney's Office in Duluth, Minnesota, assumes that victims will not cooperate. Rather than relying solely on victims, the office uses police reports to build successful prosecutions. The police reports include detailed statements from the victim and the suspect, descriptions and documentation of injuries, relevant descriptions of the crime scene, statements and identifying information regarding other witnesses, a description of the victim's emotional state, the timing of the victim's statement in relation to when the incident occurred, and information about the suspect's history of abuse or violence. In San Diego, domestic violence cases are treated like homicides, which are obviously prosecuted without the aid of the victim. The law enforcement protocol includes interviewing all children and adult witnesses, recording all statements of the victim, documenting all prior incidents, and taking photographs. Prosecution does not depend on victim cooperation. In fact, San Diego reports a higher conviction rate in cases where the victim does not testify than where she does. . . .

In order for the criminal justice system to effectively curtail domestic violence, penalties commensurate with the offense must be imposed and enforced. By increasing the "cost" of domestic violence through stiffer penalties, more batterers will be deterred from beating women. The U.S. Attorney General's Task Force on Family Violence recommends incarceration of a convicted abuser whenever the victim has suffered a serious injury, there is a history of repeated abuse, or there is a significant threat of continued harm to the victim. The National Council of Juvenile and Family Court Judges recommends that batterers receive more severe sentences for subsequent domestic abuse crimes. . . .

Mandatory Arrest Is the First Step

Mandatory arrest, particularly when part of a comprehensive criminal justice system approach, is an important step toward eradicating the epidemic of domestic violence. Criminal sanctions deter abusers from battering women. In addition, domestic violence legislation, which includes postarrest procedures and tougher sentencing provisions, delivers victims and their children from danger. By adopting mandatory arrest laws, society sends a strong message that violence against women will not be tolerated.

Over the next few years, bills mandating arrest will be introduced in state legislatures across the country in response to funding available through the Violence Against Women Act and growing public outrage over the domestic violence epidemic. Although mandatory arrest is an important weapon in the fight against domestic violence, legislators should not evaluate these bills in a vacuum. A comprehensive response from the criminal justice system is needed. However, change usually occurs incrementally. If mandatory arrest is the first step toward a reformed criminal justice system and the eradication of domestic violence, it is a step that should be taken.

The Violence Against Women Act Is Just

by Joseph R. Biden Jr.

About the author: *Joseph R. Biden Jr. is a U.S. senator from Delaware and the chief sponsor of the Violence Against Women Act.*

The Violence Against Women Act, or VAWA, the major federal law focused on the problem of family violence, provides important safeguards and provisions to protect and help any victim of violence in the home.

On Dec. 1, 1994, Christopher Bailey delivered his unconscious wife to a Kentucky hospital. She had massive and severe kidney and liver dysfunctions. Her face was black and blue and her eyes were swollen shut. She had burn marks on her neck, wrists and ankles, indicating she had been tied up. Police found a puddle of blood in the trunk of the car her husband was driving. They found more blood and evidence of a struggle in two Kentucky motel rooms occupied by Bailey in the preceding days and, finally, a significant amount of blood in the Baileys' West Virginia home, in which the couple last had been seen five days before they arrived at the hospital.

Sonya Bailey, 33, remains in a coma. On May 23, 1995, her husband was convicted of "interstate domestic violence," a federal crime, and was sentenced to life imprisonment.

In May 1996, Rita Gluzman was charged under the same law in connection with the murder of her husband. According to the complaint filed in U.S. District Court, she allegedly traveled from her home in New Jersey to assist in the murder of her husband in New York. Gluzman also faces life imprisonment without parole, if convicted.

A Federal Response to Domestic Violence

What these two cases have in common is that both defendants—a man and a woman—were charged with a federal offense established under VAWA. Until 1994, when this law was enacted, there was no federal crime and there were no federal penalties for crossing state lines for the purpose of committing spousal abuse.

My overriding goal in drafting this legislation and fighting for its passage for almost six years was to end the second-class status of family violence. Consider this: It has long been a federal crime to steal a cow or any livestock and transport it across state lines. Transporting lottery tickets, fireworks, illegally made dentures or illegally cut timber from one state to another also is a federal offense. But a federal crime for transporting a spouse across state lines to assault him or her physically has been on the books for only two years.

Prosecuting such cases in federal court sends a strong message that this country finally will treat family violence as a matter of public justice and no longer dismiss it as a private, personal matter.

VAWA also includes a new federal civil-rights remedy for victims of gender-motivated crime. This means that any victim—man or woman—of a gender-based crime will have the opportunity, in addition to the criminal-justice process, to seek financial redress from their attacker in a federal court.

While VAWA is not biased against men, I make no apologies for the fact that a major accomplishment of the law is to focus attention and resources on the problem of violence against women. Women are by far the most likely victims of family violence. The most recent figures from the Department of Justice show that women were the victims in 92 percent of reported assaults by family members. Millions of American women are battered by their spouses or partners every year. Violence against women has surpassed all other causes of injury to adult women in the United States; according to former Surgeons General C. Everett Koop and Antonia Novello, violence in the home is the No. 1 cause of injury to adult women—affecting more women than breast cancer, heart attacks or strokes.

> *"While VAWA is not biased against men, . . . a major accomplishment of the law is to focus attention and resources on the problem of violence against women."*

Much attention has been diverted lately to a dispute about just how many American women are battered or victims of violence—is it 2 million or 3 million or 4 million a year? More debate occurs about how many women suffer serious physical injury—is it half a million or a million or more a year?

This quibbling about numbers misses the point. No one disputes that the number of battered women is in the millions or that the level of violence in these cases escalates over time. No one disputes the fact that we face a problem of significant magnitude that worsens with no response. The American Medical Association—which, in its 1995 National Report Card on Violence, estimated that "up to four million women a year are battered"—has asked doctors to make recognizing and responding to physical violence in families a medical priority. It is clear that, whatever the precise numbers, this problem cries out for bold action.

But when it comes to family violence, most police officers do not make arrests, most prosecutors do not press charges and most judges do not impose tough sentences and the women and children at risk go unprotected. What was needed was a real solution to this real problem. It took many years of hearings, reports and courageous women who came forward to talk about their abuse to convince Congress that combating family violence and sexual assault should be a national priority. The fight for this legislation took shape as a nationwide educational process, bringing about a slow recognition of the nature and extent of family violence and violence against women and culminating in a national commitment to improve the nation's dismal response.

A Multifaceted Approach

The law passed in 1994 is helping to make this commitment a reality. The years of debate and ultimate passage of VAWA not only provided the resources necessary for action but also created a momentum. Already states have made significant strides in turning the act into action. Police, prosecutors, judges and women across the nation are receiving grants to help them work together to treat family violence as a serious crime. For too long the justice system, like society at large, ignored physical violence between a husband and wife or boyfriend and girlfriend. We cannot change this unless every part of the system begins to work for, and not against, women. The law offers federal grants to state and local coalitions of police, prosecutors, courts and victim services so they can take aggressive action against abusers and offer needed support to women at every step along the way, from arrest to conviction.

To understand why the law calls for this multifaceted approach, consider the unique and complex factors at work in family-violence cases, in contrast to a case of assault between strangers. In an assault case involving strangers, the victim has every incentive to ask the police to arrest the offender. But with spousal abuse, the victim usually lives with the abuser and thus is at risk of retaliation and future abuse. Moreover, when the accused and the victim are strangers, separation of the parties is accomplished easily. But in family-violence cases, the victim and children may be economically dependent on the abuser. Without adequate shelters, victims have no safe place to go with their children and must remain at home with the abuser.

> *"VAWA was passed to help government meet its responsibility to fight family violence."*

Under these circumstances, victims are unlikely to take any steps that might antagonize their abusers, such as seeking arrest or working with prosecutors to press charges. To respond effectively, police must have a policy of mandatory arrest in these cases. Shelters must be available. Prosecutors must resist dropping charges or undercharging family violence cases as misdemeanors. Judges must sentence violent offenders to jail, not just the "slap on the wrist" of probation. And at each step, victims must get the information they need about available support services and about how the justice system can and will work to protect them.

Funding for Police and Shelters

VAWA offers states and localities help in changing the justice system's response to these problems and has allowed the Justice Department to award $26 million in grants since 1994. During the next five years, $120 million will be awarded specifically to help state and local police departments implement mandatory arrest policies in family-violence cases—to ensure arrest whenever there is evidence of physical violence just as in cases of violence between strangers. Another $800 million will be awarded to states to add police, prosecutors, judges and victim services to foster cooperation in making arrests, getting convictions and securing tough sentences in these cases. And another $325 million will be awarded to local battered-women shelters so that women and children will have a safe place to stay when violence forces them from their homes.

This money does not go to federal or state bureaucrats—it must go directly to state and local police, prosecutors, judges and those who run shelters and other support services for battered women.

In passing this law, the Congress made a commitment to the families of America that real help was on its way. And all of the federal dollars provided for fighting family violence come from cutting the federal workforce by 272,000 workers. No new taxes are needed to pay for these programs and not a single dollar will be added to the federal deficit.

Another important development is the opening of the National Domestic Violence Hotline, which is required under VAWA. This toll-free hot line—1-800-799-SAFE—offers 24-hour counseling 365 days a year to all victims of family violence—men and women—throughout the nation. In addition to counseling and immediate assistance, hot-line operators also will be able to connect callers with other community services and shelters.

The Government's Responsibility to Fight Family Violence

Of course, to change our laws, policies and practices we must change the attitudes that have allowed family violence to flourish for so long. And the first step toward changing attitudes is to become informed about the problem and then roll up our sleeves and put the new federal dollars to work fighting family violence whenever it occurs.

Some would say that the government should not get involved in the family— that people must take responsibility for their own lives and live with their choices. But when victims of crime are ignored by the police and the criminal justice system, when they are forced to stay at home because there are no shelters and when there is no safety net to help women who have escaped violence, the government already has become involved. And it has failed to do its job.

VAWA was passed to help government meet its responsibility to fight family violence. We are on the road to changing our dismal record on family violence. I believe there is no turning back.

Laws That Protect Women Should Be Fully Enforced

by George Lardner Jr.

About the author: *George Lardner Jr. is an investigative reporter for the* Washington Post *and chairman of the Fund for Investigative Journalism.*

Kristin Lardner was 21 and studying art in Boston when she got her "abuse prevention orders." She kept them in an envelope in the nightstand by her bed.

She'd gotten the papers to protect her from an exboyfriend, a troubled 22-year-old named Michael Cartier. He'd been charming and affectionate when they first met, and told Kristin tales of an abusive childhood that aroused her compassion. But then his attentions warped into jealousy and violence. On April 15, 1992, ten weeks after they had started dating, Kristin told Cartier she wanted out. He followed her as she walked back to her apartment, knocked her down, and began viciously kicking her. "Get up or I'll kill you!" he shouted before she passed out. When she came to, two passersby were helping her into their car.

Over the following weeks, Cartier called Kristin repeatedly, alternately begging her forgiveness and warning her not to go to the police. She went anyway, and on May 12 got a temporary restraining order telling Cartier to stay at least 200 yards away from her and not to contact her "by telephone, in writing, or otherwise." When he continued harassing her—calling at all hours, trailing her, telling her not to go back to court—she called the police, sure he'd be arrested. She had no reason to think otherwise. Massachusetts had a mandatory arrest law for violators of restraining orders. The words were written in red ink, at the top of her papers: VIOLATION OF THIS ORDER IS A CRIMINAL OFFENSE PUNISHABLE BY IMPRISONMENT OR FINE OR BOTH.

But that didn't happen. Cartier walked out of the courtroom with a smirk on his face and a mere slap on his wrist. The judge made Kristin's temporary order permanent, but simply told Cartier to stay away from Kristin—and incredibly, at Cartier's request, told Kristin to stay away from Cartier too.

Reprinted from George Lardner Jr., "No Place to Hide," *Good Housekeeping*, October 1997, by permission of the author.

On the afternoon of May 30, 11 days after that final court hearing, Cartier confronted Kristin on Boston's Commonwealth Avenue and asked to see her that night. When she refused, he shot her three times in the head, then ran back to his apartment and killed himself.

Kristin Lardner was my daughter. What happened to her was a crime that could have—and should have—been prevented. Her killer ought to have been in jail that awful Saturday—and not only because he was in violation of Kristin's order of protection. Cartier was also on probation for attacking a previous girlfriend: He had been attending a six-week counseling program, and had a six-month suspended sentence hanging over his head, which was supposed to be imposed if he got into trouble again. Kristin knew all this, and told the police, but somehow the paperwork never made it to the judge's courtroom. Had any court official bothered to check Cartier's record, my daughter might still be alive.

> *"Laws are meaningless without vigorous enforcement."*

The Violence Against Women Act

In the five years following Kristin's death, more than 7,000 women across the country were killed by spouses or intimate partners. An estimated two million to four million more are severely and repeatedly beaten by the men they live with, a count that doesn't include women who are dating, divorced, or separated. A recent study determined that one million women are stalked each year, many of them by someone they know, according to Patricia Tjaden, Ph.D., senior researcher at Denver's Center for Policy Research, which just completed the study. "These are conservative estimates," says Tjaden. "Stalking is a much larger problem than previously assumed."

This violence against women has persisted despite an explosion of laws designed to stop it. Starting in 1994, Congress passed a series of laws—collectively known as the Violence Against Women Act (VAWA)—part of which is aimed at addressing the persistent failure of the justice system to deal with domestic violence as a crime rather than as a "private" matter. The legislation includes these provisions:

- It is now a federal crime, punishable by up to five years in prison, for anyone to cross state lines to do bodily injury to a spouse or intimate partner.
- Batterers who cross state lines can be sentenced to prison for up to ten years if they use dangerous weapons, 20 if they cause life-threatening injuries, and life if they kill their victims.
- Stalkers and those subject to protective orders can be prosecuted as felons if they travel from one state to another with the intention of harassing or injuring their victims.
- Those subject to protective orders are also restricted from buying firearms. And, in an even more far-reaching step taken by Congress in 1996, it is now

a federal crime for anyone who has been convicted of even a petty offense involving domestic violence to continue to own or to acquire a firearm.

Some states have also moved to improve their methods for tracking abusers. At the time Kristin got her restraining order, Cartier was not only on probation, he also had been named as the offender in restraining orders filed in two other Massachusetts courts. Knowing that might have forced officials to take Kristin's case more seriously, but at the time there was no mechanism to alert a judge to other cases. Today there is—a computerized, statewide domestic-violence registry that judges are required to consult. It includes a record of all protective orders in the state and violations of those orders. While Massachusetts is still the only state to mandate that judges check the records, almost half of the remaining states now have or are in the process of setting up similar registries. In May 1997, the FBI started a nationwide system that should eventually allow officials to review information from all those states at once.

Apathetic Courts

But laws are meaningless without vigorous enforcement—and there is still very little of that. From 1995 through 1997, U.S. attorneys undertook only 37 prosecutions under VAWA's criminal provisions, according to the Justice Department. That's barely more than one per month for the entire nation. Those provisions are supposed to be applied when state penalties are inadequate, as is very often the case. However, the public remains largely unaware of what the laws say, and as a result, state and federal law enforcement officials—who are supposed to consult with one another in deciding when to use VAWA—haven't paid much attention to it either. This lack of concern is nothing new. "The criminal justice system does not consider a violation of protective orders to be a serious offense," according to a recent study.

Under another provision of VAWA, a woman who receives an order in Connecticut should receive the same protection in Iowa. And, if her stalker follows her there with the intent of harassing her—even if he doesn't actually do her any physical harm—he can be arrested and charged with a felony. "People move easily across state lines," said Attorney General Janet Reno. "A victim . . . must not have to experience [additional] violence in another [state] in order to receive protection there."

However, getting states to cooperate effectively with one another is easy only in theory. Officials in one state often complain that the other

> *"As of October 1997, not a single VAWA prosecution has been brought in Washington, DC."*

state's rules aren't as rigorous. Police say acting under an order issued in another state could subject them to lawsuits for false arrest. Some states even seem to be attempting to undo VAWA by adding conditions that dilute the federal law. Nevada, for instance, will accept another state's orders only as "evi-

129

dence" supporting a temporary or extended Nevada order.

"The states have to realize this isn't some abstract discussion we're having," says Bonnie Campbell, who heads the Justice Department's Office of Violence Against Women. "This is about life and death."

> *"Judges may blame female victims for instigating or causing the violence against them."*

Deborah Fulton knows this all too well. A Washington, DC, mother of five, she has been to court more than 20 times since she first got a protection order in February 1995 against her estranged husband, Jonathan, 41, who lives across state lines in Wheaton, MD. Until recently, he had spent only 36 hours in jail.

Lenient Judges

"They're just not enforcing the order," says Fulton, referring to the DC police. "One time, two officers came. One wanted to arrest him, but the other wanted to know, 'Is he raping you?' He wasn't supposed to be there, but the officers decided to hold off."

Then, on July 8, 1997, Fulton looked out her window and saw her exhusband ransacking her van. She called the police, but Jonathan Fulton was not dissuaded by the female sergeant who responded to the call. "He knocked me down and kicked me right in front of her," says Fulton. Finally, reinforcements arrived, and Jonathan was locked up.

At press time, Jonathan had been charged only with misdemeanors for assault and violating the DC protective order—even though, at the time of his arrest, he was awaiting trial on an earlier charge of violating the same order. Nevertheless, federal officials say it's not yet clear whether they can bump the case up to federal court. As of October 1997, not a single VAWA prosecution has been brought in Washington, DC.

Women seeking protection also face continued resistance by judges unwilling to take these cases seriously. "It's the 'good old boy' thing of giving the benefit of the doubt" to men who beat up their wives and girlfriends, says Senator Orrin Hatch (R-UT), the chairman of the Senate Judiciary Committee and a key sponsor of VAWA. Hatch and others are particularly concerned about judges who exclude evidence of past behaviors. "They don't seem to realize that by the time most batterers come before them, they aren't generally first-time offenders," says Andrew Klein, the chief probation officer for the Quincy, MA, District Court, which has long been a national model for dealing with domestic violence. Case in point: During its first few months in operation, the Massachusetts registry set up after Kristin's murder found that 75 percent of those against whom restraining orders were issued had prior criminal records; 48 percent had histories of violent crime.

A 1993 Justice Department study of selected courthouses across the country confirms Klein's observation: "Judges may blame female victims for instigating or causing the violence against them," it concludes.

The Potential of Protective Orders

Despite these problems, experts agree that in most cases, a protective order is a woman's best defense—when properly crafted and enforced. Travis Fritsch, a leading domestic violence expert based in Lexington, KY, says the orders are frequently and unfairly criticized for not being able to stop a bullet. Beyond that, protection orders do work in many cases. A 1994 study by the National Center for State Courts found that as many as 65 percent of the women who obtain restraining orders report "no problems" six months later. More than 80 percent said they "felt safer."

"It meant that somebody believed me," Jeanne McHann Mahoney says of the order she got in Arlington, VA, after more than 30 years of beatings by her husband. "I was able to say, 'I've had broken bones. He's burned me with cigarettes.' To say all of this to a judge—it opened the door for me. It really did."

But Mahoney continues to live cautiously, two years after her order was issued. She rents a private mailbox so her address can't be traced. She has Caller ID for incoming calls and Call-Blocking. Around her neck, she wears a "panic button" hooked up electronically to the police department. She is still embroiled in divorce proceedings in Mississippi, where her estranged husband lives. He hasn't made court-ordered support payments, but so far he's stayed away.

Another problem is that some thwarted abusers simply direct their wrath elsewhere. In Massachusetts, roughly 15 percent of men who are subjected to orders simply go on to beat up other women.

There are ways that protective orders could be strengthened to deal with men like these. Klein believes violators should get automatic jail time. And treatment programs should last longer, say domestic-violence experts. "Almost half the men named in restraining orders re-abuse their partners physically within two years," says Klein. "A lot of guys can hold anything together for six months, but this is chronic behavior."

"Until the justice system is committed to dealing sternly with violators, protective orders will never be the strong protection for battered women they could be."

In most states, even "permanent" orders expire after a year, and many are granted for far shorter periods of time. The duration can be crucial: Forty percent of those named in protective orders comply with them for as long as the orders last, whether it's 90 days or a year, notes Joan Zorza, a New York City lawyer who has represented some 2,000 battered women, and a board member of the National Coalition Against Domestic Violence in Denver. She thinks truly "permanent" orders—those which are in force until further order of the court—should be more widespread; they are now available in only a few states.

Enforce the Laws Already in Place

Until the justice system is committed to dealing sternly with violators, protective orders will never be the strong protection for battered women they could be. In 1992, the year Kristin was killed, some 6,000 men were arrested in Massachusetts for allegedly violating restraining orders. Eight hundred were put on probation; fewer than 100 went to jail. All of the other cases were dropped.

There's an obvious place to start, says Judge Albert Kramer, the now-retired head of Quincy District Court in Massachusetts. It merely requires that judges and prosecuting attorneys aggressively enforce the criminal laws that are already in place.

Senator Joe Biden (D-DE), the principal author of VAWA, agrees: "The judge got it right," he has said. "If a stay-away order is issued and there is a violation, what we do is lock the sucker up."

I think Kristin would have agreed with that. I know I do.

Strong Laws Are Needed to Fight Violence Against Women

by Robert L. Snow

About the author: *Robert L. Snow is a captain on the Indianapolis police force and the author of* Family Abuse: Tough Solutions to Stop the Violence, *from which the following viewpoint is excerpted.*

After twenty-eight years in law enforcement, after witnessing hundreds and hundreds of family abuse incidents, and after interviewing dozens of people who work in the field of family abuse, I find that there are a large number of changes that must be made in America if we are to stem the tide of family abuse. There are laws that must be enacted, laws that must be changed, and laws that must be enforced if family abuse is to be brought under control. In addition, there are a number of programs working in various parts of the country that need to be transplanted to every part of the country. . . .

Every worker in the criminal justice system, including the police, needs to have yearly training in domestic violence, child abuse, elder abuse, sexual abuse, and financial abuse.

In addition to this training for all members of the criminal justice system, I also believe every major community should have a family abuse advocate system. This is a group of people, often volunteers, who assist family abuse victims. The criminal justice system can be daunting to anyone not familiar with its intricate workings. To help with this problem, in communities that have such a system, an advocate is assigned to a family abuse victim when he or she enters the system, and then assists the victim, up through the trial if necessary, showing the victim how to get done whatever needs to be done.

The first thing done by many victims of family abuse is to gain protection through the use of restraining or protective orders. (Victims of family abuse who fear for their lives or safety should *never* depend on a protective order to really protect them. Particularly when the level of violence has reached the life-threatening stage, these orders can often be of little value, and can even endanger the victims even more.) However, protective orders can be very useful against abusers in a less advanced state of their abuse. According to the National Institute of Justice's research paper *Civil Protection Orders:* "Our research suggests that protection orders can provide a workable option for many victims seeking pro-

> *"Judges . . . should be forced to explain and justify why they are not sentencing a family abuser who violates a protective order."*

tection from further abuse. Furthermore, it appears that when protection orders offer only weak protection, the principal explanation may lie in the functioning of the justice system rather than the nature of protection orders as a remedy." This is so true. I often find that officers don't like enforcing protective orders for the same reason they don't like making arrests in most family abuse situations: because they know that even if they arrest the violator of the protective order the judge will not do anything substantial to him or her.

I'm really not sure why so many of the judges who issue protective orders are so often reluctant to punish abusers who violate them. This is especially difficult to understand because if someone opposed a judge's order in the courtroom, as the abusers who violate protective orders do outside of the courtroom, most judges would not be reluctant at all to throw the person in jail for contempt of court, which is exactly what a violation of a protective order is. I've only seen it happen twice in my career, where a person openly opposed a judge in the courtroom, but both times the judge did not hesitate to use his authority to punish the person. For some reason, however, many judges do not see a violation of a protective order as quite this serious.

Stricter Sentencing Policies

The only answer to this problem, therefore, which will make protective orders actually protective, is near-mandatory sentencing for violators of protective orders. Most judges dislike mandatory sentencing because it does not allow them to make the exception in cases where an exception is applicable. Therefore, judges, like police officers in arresting family abusers, should be forced to explain and justify why they are not sentencing a family abuser who violates a protective order in the cases where they don't. Abusers must know that if they violate a protective order they *will* be sent to jail, and that this is not just a possibility but a near certainty. This will make all but the most desperate abuser stop and think seriously about violating a protective order. The National Institute of Justice research paper cited above states: "In jurisdictions such as Duluth and Philadelphia, where judges have established a formal policy that offenders who violate an order will be apprehended and punished, often with a jail term, both judges and victim advocates report the highest level of satisfaction with the system."

Colorado Springs, Colorado, has a protective order system that I believe should serve as a model for all communities. If a police officer in Colorado Springs responds to a family abuse situation in which he or she believes a protective order is necessary, the officer telephones an on-call judge and explains the situation. If the judge agrees that an order is necessary, the officer then fills out a blank protective order form, and, on authority from the judge, serves it on the abuser, ordering him or her off the property. This order lasts until the end of the next court day, giving the victim time to apply for extended relief.

In addition to the Colorado Springs program, I would also recommend a new program instituted in New York City that adds a bit more protection to protective orders. Working with ADT Security Systems Corporation, the Brooklyn District Attorney has devised a program whereby those abuse victims who are deemed to be in the most danger, even though having a protective order, are given small emergency pendants to wear around their necks. If the victims suddenly find themselves in danger from their abusers, they press a button on the pendant and the police are summoned to the victims' house.

Strengthening Protective Orders

Also needed in every state is a statewide registry of restraining and protective orders. Far too often when a victim crosses a county line the local police have no way of being certain a restraining order presently exists. The state of New Hampshire, however, goes even further than this and makes protective orders issued by courts in other states enforceable in New Hampshire as long as the order is valid in the issuing state. The new Violence Against Women Act has included a similar provision in its expanded protection of women. However, before being enforced nationwide, this provision is being tested in a selected area.

Even the New Hampshire law, though, still isn't enough protection because in many jurisdictions protective orders have a time limit set on them. Protective orders can usually be renewed only once, and then they expire. This does not make sense to me. Protective orders should not expire—period. An abuser doesn't become less dangerous because a year or two has passed. . . . Stalkers have been known to harass their victims for years. For the safety of abuse victims this expiration of protective orders needs to be changed.

A new law passed in New York involving protective orders does give a bit more safety to abuse victims. Under this law, a person violating a pro-

"Needed in every state is a statewide registry of restraining and protective orders."

tective order can be charged with first-degree criminal contempt, a felony, if that person has within the past five years violated a previous order of protection, or if the person injures the victim while violating the order. To make protective orders work, every state should make the first violation of a protective order a misdemeanor with the strong likelihood of jail time as punishment, and the second violation a felony. People served with protective orders must understand exactly what these orders mean: that the served person must leave the victim alone or be willing to suffer the inevitable negative consequences.

In addition to having a law similar to the New York law, I also believe every state should have a law such as the one Indiana has concerning repeat assaults. In Indiana, an assault becomes a felony when it is committed by a person previously convicted of another assault against the same victim. In 1996, this law was amended so that a previous assault now does not have to be against the same victim, but only occur during a family violence incident. As a felony, the assault is then punishable by a term in prison rather than a fine or jail. A March 14, 1996, article in *The New York Times* about two people involved in a violent relationship vividly describes the problem of not having such a law: "Despite evidence that Ms. Komar endured more than a year of repeated beatings that twice sent her to the hospital, her injuries did not, under state law, amount to charges against Mr. Oliver more serious than misdemeanors. Under state law," authors Matthew Purdy and Don Van Natta Jr. wrote, "assaults are treated as felonies only when they cause debilitating injuries, such as broken bones." Mr. Oliver eventually murdered Ms. Komar.

> **"Every community in America should have a family advocacy center."**

Along with the above laws, I also believe an important addition to every state's laws should be one making the neighborhood around battered victims' shelters "no-combat" zones. What this means is that any person who goes to a shelter with the intent to harm or intimidate someone is guilty of a felony. Abusers must be aware that going to a shelter to further terrorize victims will likely end in a prison sentence for them. This is important because citizens must never feel that they are hopelessly trapped in an abusive relationship. There should always be somewhere they can go where they will be safe and can get help.

Community Support and Advocacy

If a state, however, is going to commit itself to making all of this protection available to the victims of family abuse, it must also provide a means for the victims to start a new life without the abusers. Communities must be willing to help victims of family abuse gain economic independence from their abusers through short-term financial assistance, vouchers for day care, subsidized housing, job training, etc. Without this, we are only giving the victims false hope by protecting, but not really helping them. How can all of this be funded? Part of it could come from increased marriage license costs. In 1978, Florida placed a surcharge on marriage licenses that goes to support battered women's shelters. Perhaps getting married should be made a bit more expensive in all states so that couples would have to give it a little more thought. This extra expense could then be put to good use.

Also to assist family abuse victims, I believe every community in America should have a family advocacy center. This idea, which originated in Huntsville, Alabama, brings together in one facility all of the agencies in a community that deal with family abuse problems, such as the police, the prosecutor's office, child protective services, adult protective services, and others. Having all of these agencies working together in the same facility decreases the duplication of effort that often occurs when two or more agencies are investigating the same family or incident. Also, by being physically situated in the same facility, each agency's resources are immediately available to the other agencies. Ideally, a family advocacy center would not be located at the police department or at any other government facility, but in a separate building. In Indianapolis, for example, the family advocacy center is located in a downtown office building. Police departments and other government buildings have the tendency to appear very austere, sterile, and intimidating, which consequently frightens many victims and makes them less than totally cooperative. A family advocacy center, on the other hand, appears much more user-friendly, with bright wallpaper, toys for the kids, and an absence of most police and government paraphernalia.

"Every community needs the coordinated effort that a family advocacy center provides," said John Nolan, head of the Indianapolis Family Advocacy Center. "Cases of family abuse can be handled much more efficiently and effectively in a community with a family advocacy center."

Family Courts

Following on this idea of a combined effort, another necessity in every community is a Family Court. This court would ideally handle cases of child abuse and neglect, divorce, spouse and elderly abuse, child custody issues, and other family-related matters that require a court setting. The advantage of this concept is that it can solve the problem of a single family having several cases that all have the same root cause pending in several different courts. Judge Robert Page, in an article in *Juvenile & Family Court Journal*, stated: "The primary advantage claimed for a family court system is the unification of all complaints, petitions, and case types within one case processing and management system in order to provide a more efficient, less costly and damaging, consistent and longer lasting resolution of the problems presented." This is an excellent family abuse prevention concept needed in every community.

> *"In some jurisdictions in Minnesota, family abuse advocates track family violence cases from the initial call to the police through the prosecution to the sentencing."*

Minnesota has already had a very progressive family abuse program in place for some time, and serves as a model for how the criminal justice system should work. In some jurisdictions in Minnesota, family abuse advocates track family violence cases from the initial call to the police through the prosecution to the sentencing. If something goes wrong with the case, the advocate attempts to find out what part of the system failed in its job. This type of scrutiny makes members of the Minnesota criminal justice system very reluctant to take family abuse cases lightly. . . .

Federal Legislation

In 1994, President Clinton signed the Violence Against Women Act. This law makes it a federal offense to cross a state line to abuse a spouse. Soon afterward, Chris Bailey of St. Albans, West Virginia, severely beat his wife, Sonya Bailey, then stuffed her into the trunk of his compact car and drove for six days through West Virginia and Kentucky before finally taking Sonya to a hospital. She was still in a coma several months later. On 1 September 1995, Chris Bailey, prosecuted under the Violence Against Women Act, received a life sentence in prison.

While the Violence Against Women Act is certainly a welcome addition in the battle against family abuse, another law that I believe needs to be passed and enforced in every jurisdiction is one that prohibits a person under a restraining order, or who has been convicted of family violence, from purchasing or carrying a firearm. Far too often, family abusers stalk their victims while brandishing firearms. We don't allow former mental patients and those convicted of a felony to buy or carry a gun because they have already demonstrated their dangerousness. Well, family abusers are just as dangerous, and in some cases even more so.

> *"Far too often, family abusers stalk their victims while brandishing firearms."*

"The bill would make it clear that if you are not responsible enough to keep from doing harm to your spouse or your children, then society does not deem you responsible enough to own a gun," said Congressman Robert Torricelli, speaking about a law he sponsored that would complement the Brady Bill. [The Domestic Violence Offender Gun Ban became law in the fall of 1996.] California, which already has such a law in effect, recently attempted to amend the law to allow judges to temporarily take away guns already owned by people under restraining or protective orders. . . .

Stalking is a behavior increasingly practiced by perpetrators of family abuse, and another area where reforms can help increase the safety of victims. In 1993, in response to this increasing danger, the Congress of the United States directed the U.S. Department of Justice to develop a model antistalking law that would encourage states to adopt antistalking measures. This model law, recently completed, recognizes that stalking is often characterized by a series of increasingly serious acts, and, because of this, the law recommends that states establish a continuum of charges so that the police can intervene and arrest stalkers in the early stages of the crime. The law also recommends that serious, obsessive stalking be made a felony; that stalkers, once released from custody, be monitored very closely to prevent a resumption of their activities; and that all criminal justice officials receive training about stalkers and their crime. These recommendations should be included in every state's antistalking law. . . .

Much needs to be done if we are to meet and stop the increasing threat of family abuse in America. The problem, however, certainly isn't hopeless. Americans simply need to become much more aware of the problem, and demonstrate a strong commitment to ending it. This, though, can only come about by having citizens and government officials willing to take action.

Mandatory Arrest Laws Do Not Help Women

by Cathy Young

About the author: *Cathy Young is the author of* Ceasefire: Beyond the Gender Wars *and vice president of the Women's Freedom Network, a women's advocacy group.*

In the fall of 1996, Susan Finkelstein's live-in boyfriend was arrested and charged with abusing her. Today, Susan, a 31-year-old free-lance editor in a small Midwestern town, feels that she was abused by the justice system. "I felt so helpless," she says. "I had no rights. Nobody listened to me, nobody wanted to hear my story."

The tale sounds familiar enough—except that what angers Susan is not that her boyfriend was treated too leniently but that he was prosecuted at all.

It all started when Susan and her boyfriend, a 44-year-old college administrator whom I'll call Jim, were having a heated argument on the way home from a party. Both of them, Susan explains, were under a great deal of stress. The quarrel escalated, and Jim decided it would be best to pull over. He wanted to get out of the car and walk, and Susan tried to stop him. "I lost my temper, he lost his temper, and we got into a mutual scuffle," she says. "I may have scratched him, he may have pushed me. It got physical, but there certainly wasn't any beating."

Finally, they cooled down and got back on the road—only to be stopped by a police car. Susan remembers thinking that Jim might have been driving erratically during the fight and might have looked like a drunk driver. But it was something very different. A passing motorist had seen their altercation, written down their license plate number, and called the police.

Despite Susan's assurances that Jim hadn't hurt her and she wasn't afraid of him, he was handcuffed and taken away. Under department policy, an officer told her, they had to make an arrest in a domestic dispute. Says Susan, "I was very upset that they wouldn't listen when I said that I was fine. They said, 'Well, we know that women who are abused often lie out of fear.'"

After spending the night in jail, Jim was arraigned on a misdemeanor charge of domestic violence and prohibited from having any contact with Susan, who had to stay with a friend. Her efforts to convince the judge and the prosecutor that nothing had happened were fruitless.

On a lawyer's advice, Jim pleaded no contest. He had to write a letter of apology to Susan (which he wrote in her presence and mailed to the district attorney's office, which forwarded it to her) and attend 10 weekly counseling sessions for batterers, a three-hour drive away, at a cost of $400. He is acutely aware that his record puts him at risk: "If Susan and I have a loud argument and a neighbor calls the police, I'll be arrested immediately," he says.

The War on Domestic Violence

What happened to Jim and Susan—who are still together as a couple—is not an aberration. It's just another story from the trenches of what might be called the War on Domestic Violence. Born partly in response to an earlier tendency to treat wife-beating as nothing more than a marital sport, this campaign treats all relationship conflict as a crime. The zero-tolerance mentality of current domestic violence policy means that no offense is too trivial, not only for arrest but for prosecution. Consider these recent examples:

In 1996, Seattle City Councilman John Manning, who came home one day and was shocked to find his wife loading her things into a truck, was charged with assault for grabbing her shoulders and sitting her down on the tailgate (causing no injuries). He pleaded guilty to misdemeanor domestic violence, received a deferred prison sentence, and agreed to complete a treatment program for batterers. (The *Seattle Times* editorialized that the case gave "a public face" to the tragedy of domestic violence.)

The same year, Michigan Judge Joel Gehrke made headlines when he gave convicted spouse abuser Stewart Marshall a literal slap on the wrist, citing the wife's adultery with her husband's brother as a mitigating factor. This episode, which provoked cries about judges who go easy on wife beaters, should have raised questions instead about frivolous prosecutions. Aside from the fact that many of the jurors believed Chris Marshall had set up the incident as a leverage-gaining divorce tactic, Stewart's assault consisted of grabbing her by the sweatshirt and pushing her; she did not suffer a single scrape. A woman juror who backed Judge Gehrke's decision explained that the jury "had to say guilty" because "if you touch, it's battery."

> *"The War on Domestic Violence is a mix of good intentions . . . , bad information, and worse theories."*

In those cases, at least, the alleged victims wanted a prosecution. But increasingly, women who don't—like Susan Finkelstein—find their wishes ignored. This issue was brought into the spotlight by the 1996 Texas trial of football star Warren Moon, whose wife Felicia was forced to take the stand against him. In a less famous case in St. Paul, Minnesota, two years earlier, Jeanne Chacon, an attorney, tried not only to drop battery charges against her fiancé, Peter Erlinder, but to serve as his lawyer. Though Chacon herself had called the police and accused Erlinder of "slamming" her to the ground, she quickly changed her story: Abused as a child, she explained that she was prone to violent outbursts, and that Erlinder had merely restrained her with a "basket-hold" technique recommended by her own therapists. Her therapists corroborated her story, and Chacon had several violent episodes while the case was pending. Still, prosecutors insisted on going to trial—which, like the Moon case, ended in acquittal.

> **"Mandatory arrest rules often force cops to act against their better judgment."**

Like many crusades to stamp out social evils, the War on Domestic Violence is a mix of good intentions (who could be against stopping spousal abuse?), bad information, and worse theories. The result has been a host of unintended consequences that do little to empower victims while sanctioning state interference in personal relationships.

Feminist Ideology

The battered women's advocacy movement, which has led the campaign against domestic abuse, is heavily influenced by radical feminist politics and tends to frame the issue in terms of a male "war against women." The mission statement of the National Coalition Against Domestic Violence links "violence against women and children" to "sexism, racism, classism, anti-semitism, able-bodyism, ageism and other oppressions." Booklets funded by government and by charities such as United Way assert that "battering is the extreme expression of the belief in male dominance over women."

Such thinking is responsible for such widely circulated factoids as "domestic violence is the leading cause of injury to American women," "battering causes more injuries to women than car accidents, rapes, and muggings combined," or "25 to 35 percent of women in emergency rooms are there for injuries from domestic violence." These patently false numbers (data from the Justice Department and the Centers for Disease Control and Prevention suggest that less than 1 percent of women's emergency-room visits are due to assaults by male partners, and that about 10 times as many women are injured in auto accidents) are complemented by increasingly expansive definitions of abuse.

Thus, in her landmark book, *The Battered Woman* (1979), psychologist Lenore Walker writes that "a battered woman is a woman who is repeatedly subjected to any forceful physical *or psychological* behavior by a man in order to coerce her to do something" (emphasis added). While Walker focuses primarily on women who have been physically assaulted, she also talks about men "battering" their wives by, for example, being inattentive. Pamphlets distributed by family violence programs stress that one doesn't have to be hit to be abused and list such forms of abuse as "calling you names," "criticizing you for small things," or "making you feel bad about yourself." A booklet published by the state of New Jersey, *Domestic Violence: The Law and You*, informs the reader that she is a victim of domestic violence if she has experienced "embarrassment or alarm because of lewd or shocking behavior" or "repeated verbal humiliation and attacks."

The Move Toward Pro-Arrest Policies

These ideas have consequences. By 1982, largely due to lobbying by advocacy groups, a majority of states expanded police authority to make arrests in misdemeanor assaults which the officers had not actually witnessed—a move applauded by most law enforcement personnel and family violence researchers. But as the rate of arrest remained low, many states and jurisdictions began to go further and *mandate* arrests, a policy viewed with far more ambivalence. This trend has been boosted by the post–O.J. Simpson-trial attention to domestic abuse and by incentives for pro-arrest policies in the federal Violence Against Women Act of 1994.

Such policies have undeniably increased the number of arrests. It is far less clear, however, that they have had a significant impact on spousal abuse. Christopher Pagan, who was until recently a prosecutor in Hamilton County, Ohio, estimates that due to a 1994 state law requiring police on a domestic call either to make an arrest or to file a report explaining why no arrest was made, "domestics" went from 10 percent to 40 percent of his docket. But, he suggests, that doesn't mean actual abusers were coming to his attention more often. "We started getting a lot of push-and-shoves," says Pagan, "or even yelling matches. In the past, police officers would intervene and separate the parties to let them cool off. Now those cases end up in criminal courts. It's exacerbating tensions between the parties, and it's turning law-abiding middle-class citizens into criminals."

Many police officers agree—though all of those who were willing to discuss their misgivings asked that their names not be used, given the charged nature of the subject and their criticism of official policy. "We need domestic violence law but we need common sense, too," says a veteran small-town policeman in New Jersey. The officer stresses that he doesn't miss the days when a woman could be bruised or bloodied and you couldn't arrest the man unless she was willing to risk enraging him further by signing a complaint.

> *"The effects of mandatory arrest are compounded by no-drop prosecutions."*

But today, he says, the law has gone to the other extreme: "Sometimes the wife's begging, 'Don't arrest him, the kids are here,' and you *have to* arrest."

It's not just male officers who chafe at having their hands tied. A woman I'll call Sally Gilmore, a sergeant on the nearly all-male police force of a working-class New Jersey town, feels that mandatory arrest rules often force cops to act against their better judgment. She recalls responding to a quarrel between a woman and her ex-boyfriend, who had come over to pick up his things. After being told that he couldn't be arrested for shouting at her, the woman suddenly "remembered" that he had also hit her and pointed to a bruise on her leg. "I asked, 'When did this happen?' and she said, 'Just now,'" says Gilmore. "Well, this bruise was days old. He said he didn't hit her. I basically knew she was lying, but I had no choice."

No-Drop Prosecutions

The effects of mandatory arrest are compounded by no-drop prosecutions. The assumption behind no-drop policies is that when women recant or refuse to press charges, it is out of fear or dependence. But reality is far more complex. The woman may feel, rightly or not, that she is not in danger and can handle the situation better without the complications of a legal case; or the lines between aggressor and victim may be blurred; or the charge may have been false, made in anger, and later regretted.

"Some crusaders openly argue that domestic violence should be taken more seriously than other crimes."

A counselor with a family violence intervention program in Florida who generally favors no-drop prosecutions saw this happen with her own daughter Angela—a troubled young woman with a severe drinking problem—and her live-in boyfriend. One evening, says the counselor, who also requested anonymity, an intoxicated Angela wanted to go out to buy more liquor: "Her boyfriend won't give her the money. So she goes out to the corner and calls the police saying he has locked her out—which he probably had because he didn't want trouble—and fills out a report saying he threatened her, she's afraid of him, and so on." The police took her home and arrested the young man. The next day, a now-sober Angela was appalled by what she had done and tried to back out—to no avail. With her mother's help, she hired a lawyer, and her boyfriend was eventually allowed to plead no contest. . . .

Singling Out Domestic Violence

Curiously, battered women's advocates (and journalists who take their cue from the activists) continue to claim that police and the courts treat domestic abuse less seriously than non-family assaults. In fact, this may not have been true even prior to feminist-initiated reforms. In the 1992 book *Policing Domestic Violence*, University of Maryland criminologist Lawrence Sherman concludes that underenforcement of assault and battery laws was hardly unique to domestic violence. He cites data from the 1970s showing that police were reluctant to intervene in *any* violent personal dispute, be it a marital squabble, a neighborhood quarrel, or a bar brawl. All else (such as injury) being equal, the rates of arrest were similar for domestic and non-domestic cases. Certainly, more recent studies show no evidence of discrimination against battered women. Analyzing the handling of violent offenses in 1987–88 in Arizona, feminist criminologist Kathleen Ferraro found—to her own surprise—that while most attacks of any kind were either not prosecuted or were charged as misdemeanors,

> *"It seems so ironic that in trying to give women a voice, [prosecutors] are taking away their voices."*

felony assaults were *less* likely to be dismissed if they involved spouses or partners (even though the victims in domestic cases were much more likely to request a dismissal). Nor did the victim-offender relationship affect the severity of the sentence.

Nowadays, however, some crusaders openly argue that domestic violence should be taken *more* seriously than other crimes. In 1996, the sponsor of a New York bill toughening penalties for misdemeanor assault on a family member (including ex-spouses and unwed partners) vowed to oppose a version extending the measure to *all* assaults: "The whole purpose of my bill is to single out domestic violence," Assemblyman Joseph Lentol said. "I don't want the world to think we're treating stranger assaults the same way as domestic assaults."

These arguments, however, are rooted in the paradigm of domestic violence promoted by the battered women's movement: the woman, powerless and trapped by economic or psychological dependency, is victimized by the brutal, domineering man who uses force to impose control. Certainly, some cases fit this model; but many others do not. . . .

Overzealousness

Undoubtedly, there are cases in which victims of intimate violence are badly let down by the system, sometimes with fatal results. But apathy and excessive zeal can coexist—just as horror stories of children yanked from parental homes on flimsy suspicions of abuse coexist with ones of abused children handed back to their tormentors. Indeed, when apathy and excessive zeal do coexist, the policy implications are often disastrous. Douglas Besharov, a child welfare expert at the American Enterprise Institute, compellingly argues that overzealous probes of frivolous claims of child abuse lead to underenforcement where action is needed most because the system is too bogged down in trivial pursuit to single out the serious cases.

It's probably the same with domestic violence. The system, says sociologist Richard Gelles, fails to differentiate between minor charges of abuse and cases rife with danger signs—such as the events leading to the death of Kristin Lardner, the daughter of *Washington Post* reporter George Lardner. (The former boyfriend who fatally shot her in May 1992 before killing himself had a long history of criminal behavior; yet after assaulting Kristin, he was not jailed, despite violating his probation.) Indeed, manipulators may be more likely to get the system to work to their advantage than real victims, too scared or too unsophisticated to navigate its channels.

Even if the dangerous cases are caught early, some people are going to be badly hurt or even killed by their mates. Such things are not always predictable. And we might ask, without creating a new "abuse excuse," whether being denied access to his children might not push a nonviolent person over the edge. "People with nothing to lose are dangerous people," says James Fagan, a Massachusetts attorney and state legislator.

The most obvious casualties of the War on Domestic Violence have been men, particularly men involved in contentious divorces. But it has also hurt many of the women who are its intended beneficiaries. Part of the problem is the one-size-fits-all approach to domestic violence. For many couples in violent relationships, particularly those involved in mutual violence, joint counseling offers the best solution. But if they have come to the attention of the authorities, it's one form of counseling to which they are unlikely to be referred. Couples therapy is vehemently opposed by battered women's advocates—ostensibly out of concern for women's safety, but also because of the implication that both partners must change their behavior.

Paternalism

A few years ago, James Dolan, first justice of Dorchester District Court in Massachusetts, warned that the system may be engaging in "benign abuse" by "denying women the right to continue a relationship without submitting to the authority of the court." Dolan may have been stretching the term *abuse*, but quite a few women might agree with his assessment.

And then there are the women who, often on the basis of a misunderstanding or a single, trivial incident blown out of proportion, are labeled as victims against their will. "It was very paternalistic, even if women were involved in the system," says Susan Finkelstein, reflecting on her experience. "At one point, I told a prosecutor that I didn't appreciate being told what was best for me by someone who didn't even know me. She said, 'It strikes me as odd that you don't appreciate the fact that we're trying to protect you.' What I said didn't matter. It seems so ironic that in trying to give women a voice, they are taking away their voices."

The Violence Against Women Act Is Unjust

by Jeremy Rabkin

About the author: *Jeremy Rabkin is a professor of government at Cornell University in Ithaca, New York.*

Remember the four Los Angeles policemen charged in the beating of Rodney King? After their acquittal of state criminal charges by an all-white jury, they were retried on federal charges—before a more racially balanced jury—and sent to prison. On the other side of the continent, Lemrick Nelson was charged in the fatal stabbing of Yankel Rosenbaum, a young Hassidic scholar, in the midst of anti-Semitic rioting in the Crown Heights neighborhood of Brooklyn, New York. Acquitted by a predominantly black and Latino jury, Nelson was also retried on federal charges before a different jury and also convicted on the second go-round and given a severe prison sentence.

Federal Retrials as Double Jeopardy

Cases like this, where federal prosecutors get to retry a failed state prosecution, are still relatively rare. But they are becoming common enough for some legal scholars to express concern that we are gradually abandoning the Fifth Amendment guarantee against "double jeopardy"—that is, allowing the same defendant to be "twice put in jeopardy" of criminal penalties for "the same offence." Technically, the federal trials are not for the state offense of assault or murder but for the separate federal offense of "deprivation of rights." In the most celebrated cases, however, federal prosecutors essentially have presented the same evidence regarding the same actions of the accused—but before a different and more carefully selected jury. If we do this for some cases, why was this not considered, say, in the O.J. Simpson case? Why were the families of Simpson's victims left to pursue civil claims on their own, where they could win punitive financial damages but not have any chance to see Simpson sent to prison?

Does this have something to do with the fact that, in the case of the four L.A. policemen, the acquittal on state charges provoked several days of ferocious ri-

Reprinted from Jeremy Rabkin, "More Equal Than Others," *The American Spectator*, May 1997, by permission of the author.

oting by angry blacks in Los Angeles? Does it have something to do with the fact that a sizable part of New York's Jewish community mobilized to demand justice in the aftermath of the Crown Heights riot, triggering a political upheaval that ultimately helped to drive incumbents Mayor David Dinkins and Governor Mario Cuomo from office? In contrast, no organized political constituencies rallied to demand justice for the killing of Nicole Simpson and Ron Goldman.

> *"These days it takes much less scandal for Congress to unleash federal prosecutors against the sorts of crimes usually handled by the states."*

It is true that, in the case of O.J. Simpson, there was no relevant federal statute on which to launch a new prosecution. The federal statute under which the L.A. cops were tried descends from a "civil rights" measure enacted after the Civil War, and covers only "deprivation of rights" on "account of race" and "under color of state law" (meaning, by state or local government officials, like policemen). The Lemrick Nelson case was tried under a more expansive 1968 "civil rights" statute, which makes it a federal crime for private individuals to interfere, "by force or threat of force," with any other person's attendance at public schools or use of any other state facility "because of [that person's] race, color, religion or national origin." (Nelson was charged with interfering with Rosenbaum's right to use the public streets, where the murder took place.)

The O.J. Simpson case could not be pigeon-holed into either of these federal statutes. But the absence of other applicable statutes deserves notice in itself: Congress has never enacted a generalized authorization for federal retrial of cases that don't come out right at the state level. Until quite recently, moreover, both of these exceptional federal statutes were almost always invoked to provide an initial, not a second, prosecution—invoked, that is, to remedy the delinquency of Southern sheriffs and prosecutors, not Southern juries. Whether or not it is now a threat to American ideals of justice to deploy these statutes for prosecutorial appeals, everyone must acknowledge that these statutes were initially devised to deal with criminal-justice systems in the old South that were massively and blatantly racist, and a terrible stain on American justice.

Expanding Federal Authority via Civil Rights for Women

But these days it takes much less scandal for Congress to unleash federal prosecutors against the sorts of crimes usually handled by the states. That is the lesson of the Violence Against Women Act, one of the strangest elements in President Clinton's pork-laden 1994 anti-crime package. The name is a giveaway to the histrionic nature of this measure. No previous Congress would have dared to name a "civil rights" measure as an "act for the special protection of blacks from racist violence." VAWA has a whole subsection called "Civil Rights for Women."

In fact, Congress did not quite have the courage of its own bombastic rhetoric. The substantive prohibitions prohibit "gender bias," affirming a general "federal right to be free from crimes of violence motivated by gender"—rather than specifically targeting bias crimes against women in particular. But the Clinton Justice Department has taken the cue. It now has a special "Office of Violence Against Women"—headed, of course, by a woman, who boasts on her résumé that she was an official delegate to the Beijing Conference on Women's Rights.

VAWA provides a general civil remedy for victims of "crimes of violence motivated by gender" (so that victims can sue their gender-biased perpetrators in federal court). A federal appeals court is now weighing claims that this sweeping provision exceeds constitutional limits on federal authority. Perhaps anticipating such objections, VAWA contains much more restricted criminal provisions, covering only "interstate domestic violence"—a phrase that perfectly encapsulates the statute's weird combination of overreaching rhetoric and oddly legalistic restraint. Federal prosecutors are not empowered to try (or retry) any person's "crime of violence" against "that person's spouse or intimate partner"; they may prosecute only such crimes that also involve the crossing of a state line.

Yet all sorts of criminals cross state lines. Most of them still get prosecuted by authorities in the state in which they committed the crime. Perpetrators of domestic violence are less likely than others to cross state lines in the course of their crimes, since

> *"The most evident bias in the jury system is anti-male."*

their victims, by definition, are quite close to home. So why do we need this special federal back-stop for "domestic violence"? VAWA's champions insisted that it was necessary because state officials do not take domestic violence seriously—because they do not take seriously the concerns of women.

Gender Bias in the Courts

But it is rather unclear who really suffers more from official "gender bias" in this area. It is true, as VAWA advocates proclaim (and as President Clinton emphasized in a 1995 proclamation on "National Domestic Violence Awareness Month"), that women are relatively more likely to be killed by family members or "intimates" than are men. But the notion that family life is a special danger to women is a twisted feminist fantasy. According to a 1993 study by the Bureau of Justice Statistics, women who are unmarried or separated are actually twenty-five times more likely to suffer violent attack than married women who live with their husbands.

In absolute numbers, moreover, far more men than women are killed each year by family members or "romantic partners." "Domestic violence" takes less of a death toll among men only in percentage terms, because men are, overall, three times as likely as women to be fatalities of violence. If anyone needs protection from "violence," it is men. True, most of the violence that is killing men is not the result of "gender bias." But so what? Are we more shocked by "gender bias" than by murder? What young black men—by far the largest single category of murder victims—got from the 1994 Omnibus Crime package was midnight basketball.

If we are going to obsess about "gender bias," the most evident bias in the jury system is anti-male. According to another recent study by the Bureau of Justice Statistics, men who kill their spouses are far more likely to be convicted than are female spouse-killers (only 6 percent of wife-killers are acquitted, compared with 27 percent of husband-killers). Men also tend to get much longer prison sentences for such crimes (the spouse-killing average is sixteen years for men, six years for women). The likely reason for such disparities is that juries are more inclined to see a female killer as having acted in self-defense or in response to provocation, while they are more inclined to view a male perpetrator as a dangerous killer who will kill again if not punished. Such assumptions are certainly understandable. Men are, in general, more violent than women. But that is stereotypical thinking. In other contexts, that sort of stereotypical thinking could, in itself, be denounced as "gender bias."

Unjust Changes to Criminal Procedure

More remarkable and more telling than VAWA's selective targeting of new federal jurisdiction are the very selective changes, enacted at the same time, to the federal rules of criminal procedure. The rules now allow evidence of past practice by the defendant to be presented to the jury in order to demonstrate "propensity" to commit the crime. Rules of evidence in criminal cases usually forbid prosecutors from telling juries about the past misdeeds of the defendant. (The theory is that such information would prejudice jurors, encouraging them to think the defendant was the sort of person who would do the crime or the sort of person who deserved to be punished anyway, no matter what the evidence in the case at hand.) VAWA leaves these restrictive rules in place for every crime—except sexual assault and child molestation.

The Justice Department's Office of Violence Against Women does not even try to minimize the altered perspective implied by this change in the rules. A recent Justice press release

> *"If it is good for juries to hear allegations of past misconduct by an accused rapist, why not also let juries hear about the past practices of accused muggers [or] terrorists?"*

boasts that these changes will "provide the basis for informed decisions by juries regarding questions of propensity to commit future crimes in light of the defendant's past conduct." So what if the defendant didn't commit the actual crime with which he is charged? The "past conduct," by the way, can be established by testimony of witnesses who never pursued their charges to police or prosecutors.

Now it may be that most juries will discipline themselves to focus on the precise evidence in the case at hand. It may also be that the existing rules are too restrictive. But if it is good for juries to hear allegations of past misconduct by an accused rapist, why not also let juries hear about the past practices of accused muggers, terrorists—or politicians accused of bribery? Why is it that we only get criminal procedure reform, like federal retrial of failed state prosecutions, when organized political constituencies demand it? And why is it that we then deliver these fixes only to the groups with the political muscle to claim them?

The entrance to the Supreme Court building bears the inscription, "Equal Justice Under Law." Is it just a slogan?

Domestic Violence Laws Are Anti-Male

by Sally L. Satel

About the author: *Sally L. Satel is a psychologist and lecturer at the Yale School of Medicine and a member of the National Advisory Board of the Independent Women's Forum, a conservative women's advocacy group.*

Let's call him "Joe Six Pack." Every Saturday night, he drinks way too much, cranks up the rock 'n roll way too loud, and smacks his girlfriend for acting just a bit too lippy. Or let's call him "Mr. Pillar of the Community." He's got the perfect wife, the perfect kids. But he's also got one little problem: every time he argues with his wife, he loses control. In the past year, she's been sent to the emergency ward twice. Or let's say they're the Tenants from Hell. They're always yelling at each other. Finally a neighbor calls the police.

Here is the question. Are the men in these scenarios: a) in need of help; b) in need of being locked up; or c) upholders of the patriarchy?

Most people would likely say a) or b) or perhaps both. In fact, however, c) is the answer that more and more of the agencies that deal with domestic violence—including the courts, social workers, and therapists—now give. Increasingly, public officials are buying into Gloria Steinem's assertion that "the patriarchy requires violence or the subliminal threat of violence in order to maintain itself." They are deciding that the perpetrators of domestic violence don't so much need to be punished, or even really counseled, but instead indoctrinated in what are called "profeminist" treatment programs. And they are spending tax dollars to pay for these programs.

A portion of the money for the re-education of batterers comes from Washington, courtesy of the 1994 Violence Against Women Act (VAWA). To obtain passage of VAWA, feminist organizations like the National Organization for Women and even secretary of Health and Human Services Donna Shalala, pelted legislators with facts and figures: "The leading cause of birth defects is battery during pregnancy." "In emergency rooms, twenty to thirty percent of

Excerpted from Sally L. Satel, "It's Always His Fault," *Women's Quarterly*, Summer 1997. Reprinted by permission of the Independent Women's Forum.

women arrive because of physical abuse by their partner." "Family violence has killed more women in the last five years than Americans killed in the Viet Nam War." Happily, these alarming factoids aren't true. But the feminist advocacy groups were able to create new bogus statistics faster than the experts were able to shoot the old ones down. And some of the untruths—like the fiction that wife-beating soars on Super Bowl Sunday—have become American myths as durable as the story of young George Washington chopping down the cherry tree.

> *"[VAWA] money is being used to further an ideological war against men—one that puts many women at even greater risk."*

Still, the problem of domestic violence, even if grossly exaggerated, is horrific enough. So Congress generously authorized $1.6 billion to fund VAWA. Few taxpayers would begrudge this outlay if it actually resulted in the protection of women. But instead there is increasing evidence that the money is being used to further an ideological war against men—one that puts many women at even greater risk.

The Feminist Theory of Domestic Abuse

The feminist theory of domestic abuse, like the feminist theory of rape, holds that all men have the same innate propensity to violence against women: your brother and my boyfriend are deep down every bit as bad as [convicted batterer and child abuser] Joel Steinberg. Men who abuse their mates, the theory goes, act violently not because they as individuals can't control their impulses, and not because they are thugs or drunks or particularly troubled people. Domestic abuse, in feminist eyes, is an essential element of the vast male conspiracy to suppress and subordinate women. In other words, the real culprit in a case of domestic violence is not a violent individual man, it is the patriarchy. To stop a man from abusing women, he must be taught to see the errors of the patriarchy and to renounce them.

Thus, a position paper by the Chicago Metropolitan Battered Women's Network explains: "Battering is a fulfillment of a cultural expectation, not a deviant or sick behavior." Thus, too, the Seattle-based psychologist Laura Brown, a prominent feminist practitioner, argues that feminist psychotherapy is an "opportunity to help patients see the relationship between their behavior and the patriarchal society in which we are all embedded."

As well, feminists have stretched the definition of abuse to include acts of lying, humiliation, withholding information, and refusing help with child care or housework, under the term "psychological battery." A checklist from a brochure of the Westchester Coalition of Family Violence agencies tells women if their partner behaves in one or more of the following ways, including "an overprotective manner," "turns minor incidents into major arguments," or "insults you," then "you might be abused."

153

With money provided by VAWA, this view has come to pervade the bureaucracies created to combat domestic violence. In at least a dozen states, including Massachusetts, Colorado, Florida, Washington, and Texas, state guidelines effectively preclude any treatment other than feminist therapy for domestic batterers. Another dozen states, among them Maine and Illinois, are now drafting similar guidelines. These guidelines explicitly prohibit social workers and clinicians from offering therapies that attempt to deal with domestic abuse as a problem between a couple unless the man has undergone profeminist treatment first. Profeminists emphatically reject joint counseling, the traditional approach to marital conflict. Joint counseling and other couples-based treatments violate the feminist certainty that it is men who are always and solely responsible for domestic violence: any attempt to involve the batterer's mate in treatment amounts to "blaming the victim."

Aggressive Law Enforcement

The dogma that women never provoke, incite, or aggravate domestic conflict, further, has led to some startling departures in domestic law. Hundreds of jurisdictions have adopted what are called "must-arrest" policies: that is, when local police are called to a scene of reported domestic abuse, they must arrest one partner (almost always the man) even if, by the time the authorities arrive, the incident has cooled off and there is no sign of violence, and even if (as is often the case) the woman doesn't want the man arrested. Many of these

> *"We treat women as brainless individuals who are unable to make choices."*

same jurisdictions have also enacted "no-drop" policies—meaning that if a woman does press charges, she will not be permitted to change her mind and drop them later. Under VAWA, $33 million was spent in 1997 on the "Grants to Encourage Arrest" program, which uses federal money to induce localities to adopt must-arrest policies. In 1998, the budget of the "Grants to Encourage Arrest" program jumped to $59 million.

Of course, it's hard to feel sorry for men charged with abuse. And there is a satisfying, frontier-justice aspect to the feminist treatment programs: what better punishment for a loutish man than to make him endure hours of feminist lecturing? The trouble is, domestic violence—as these same feminists constantly remind us—is no joke. And there are virtually no convincing data that this feminist approach to male violence is effective.

Policies That Backfire

Indeed the paternalistic intrusiveness that characterizes so much of feminist domestic violence policy frequency has the unintended consequence of harming the very women it was meant to protect. Judge William S. Cannon, who has handled thousands of domestic violence cases through South Bay (San Diego)

Family Court, finds that "about eighty percent of the couples we see in court end up staying together." Nonetheless, the California legislature has made it mandatory for judges to issue a restraining order separating the parties in all domestic violence cases. "It's ridiculous," the judge says of this mandatory separation, "each situation is different." Sometimes a woman doesn't want the separation, particularly if the threat from her husband is mild. "If the woman feels relatively safe, she might well rather have her kids' father home with the family," Judge Cannon says. In California, however, this option is no longer open to women. As Judge Cannon says, "We treat women as brainless individuals who are unable to make choices. If a woman wants a restraining order, she can ask us for it."

> **"Many victims of domestic abuse do want to hold their families together."**

Persuading victims of domestic violence that they need no psychological help or are never to blame can also backfire, because it pushes many women away from seeking counseling that they plainly need. A prosecutor from Southern California, who preferred not to be identified, told me that many of the women he refers to treatment reject his advice. "They're influenced by the prevailing view in the advocate community that tells them they don't need help. Meanwhile, I'm accused of blaming the victim," the prosecutor says. Some of these women return to husbands who injure or even kill them, when a therapist might have helped them find the strength to stay away. Others end up doing the killing themselves, a tragedy that has happened "more than once on my watch," the prosecutor said. The defense attorneys then claim that the wife is "a victim of battered woman syndrome. They'll say the system failed her because she was never referred for professional help."

It is likewise far from clear that must-arrest policies help victims of domestic abuse. Several studies—including one by Lawrence W. Sherman of the University of Maryland, whose early study on mandatory arrest in a single midwestern city actually gave rise to the program's popularity—suggest that mandatory arrest can escalate spousal violence in some men by further enraging them, and causing them to seek revenge on their lovers once they are released from jail.

Viewing Batterers as Untreatable

But the implicit goal of feminist treatment and legal responses is to separate women from their abusive partners—no matter what the circumstances, and no matter how fervently the women wish otherwise. Many shelter counselors interviewed by Kimberle Crenshaw of the UCLA School of Law believe that a batterer is incapable of breaking the cycle of abuse and the woman's only hope of safety is to leave the relationship. In a *New York Times Magazine* story about spousal abuse, writer Jan Hoffman summed up the advice of Ellen Pence, founder of the much-replicated Duluth Abuse Intervention Program and a staunch believer that all batterers are gripped by a hatred of women: "Ellen Pence's advice to women in battering relationships is simply this: Leave. Leave because even the best of programs, even Duluth's, cannot ensure that a violent man will change his ways."

Not very encouraging words from a nationally regarded expert. Perhaps if feminist treatment of domestic violence recognized some cold truths about women and intimate violence, success rates might improve.

For example, contrary to the prevailing view of battered women as weak, helpless, and confused, professor Jacquelyn Campbell reported in 1994 in the *Journal of Family Violence,* that the majority of battered women do take steps to end the abuse in their relationships. In truth, the average abused woman is not Hedda Nussbaum (the obsessed lover of psychopath Joel Steinberg). The sad facts, as discussed by Christine Littleton in the 1993 book *Family Matters: Readings on Family Lives and the Law,* are that many "women who stay in battering relationships accurately perceive the risks of remaining, accurately perceive the risks of leaving, and choose to stay either because the risks of leaving outweigh those of staying or because they are trying to rescue something beyond themselves"—such as their family.

And here is the cruelest failure of profeminist therapy. Since many victims of domestic abuse do want to hold their families together, and since they are trying to weigh the risks of staying with an abusive mate, it does them an enormous disservice to put a dangerous man through a program that cannot fulfill its promise to cure him. "The woman thinks to herself, 'Well, now he's changed,' so she goes back to him and drops her guard. Sometimes with devastating effects," says Dr. Richard J. Gelles, of the University of Rhode Island's Family Violence Research Program, a pioneer researcher in domestic violence. Professor Richard M. McFall, an expert on marital violence with Indiana University, observes that "typically, the man comes out of a useless mandated treatment program no less violent than when he went in, but now he's got a clean bill of psychological health.". . .

> "States are basing rigid treatment policy on rhetoric and ideology, not data."

A One-Size-Fits-All Approach

Many advocates are also apparently so blinded by ideology that they are unable to draw distinctions between types of abusers. Some men, for example, are first-time offenders, others are brutal recidivists, others attack rarely but harshly, others frequently but less severely, and many are alcoholics. Such a heterogeneous population cannot be treated with a one-size-fits-all approach. Amy Holtzworth-Munroe, an associate professor of psychology at Indiana University, says, "states are basing rigid treatment policy on rhetoric and ideology, not data."

Take the case of "Don," a senior administrator at a southern university. Arrested once for slapping his wife (they are still together), Don was required to attend a Duluth-model program. About fifteen men sat for three hours on ten consecutive Wednesday nights in a classroom headed by two counselors. "The message was clear," Don told me, "whatever she does to you is your fault, whatever you do to her is your fault. It would have been a lot more helpful if they taught us to recognize when we felt ourselves being driven into positions where we lash out.

> *"Women must share responsibility for their behavior and contributions to domestic violence."*

The message should have been 'recognize it, deal with it, and quit hitting.' But all they gave us to work with was guilt." According to Don, "bathroom and cigarette breaks were filled with comments about the whole thing being stupid. In the sessions, group discussions among participants were not allowed to develop—maybe the leaders were afraid we'd unite and challenge their propaganda." Rather than improve their relationships, Don felt the therapy only helped to increase polarization between men and women. "Wives went to support groups and we went to our groups."

Complementing these biases was an equally great omission: the role of alcohol in domestic violence. Though studies show a persistent correlation between intoxication and aggression in families, Don's group leaders were adamant that alcohol was never a cause of violence. Don claimed, however, that "every man in the room had been drinking when he was arrested." Booze, of course, is never an acceptable excuse for bad behavior, but there's no question that alcohol pushes some people into violence. Feminist theory downplays the relevance of alcohol abuse, and as a particularly foolish result in Don's program, failed to make sobriety a condition of the treatment for domestic batterers.

Glenna Auxiera, a divorce resolution counselor in Gainesville, Florida, attended a training course on male batterers sponsored by the Duluth Abuse Intervention Program. She reports being "stunned" by what she heard. "The course leaders were fixated on male-bashing," Auxiera says. "I was a battered woman, too, and I see the part I played in the drama of my relationship. Hitting is wrong. Period. But a relationship is a dynamic interaction and if both want to change, counselors should work with them."

Couples Can Overcome Their Problems

But this, of course, is precisely what state guidelines in nearly half the country now or will soon prohibit as the first course of treatment. They would outlaw, for instance, the kind of help that saved the decade-long marriage of a midwestern couple we'll call "Steve and Lois M." Mr. and Mrs. M. were regarded by their community as a model couple. Mr. M. was in fact a high-profile businessman. But two or three times a year, he turned violent. After their last fight, in which he gave Mrs. M. a fractured arm, she gave him an ultimatum: unless he went with her to marriage therapy, she would take their nine-year-old son and leave. He agreed, and the couple saw Eve Lipchik, a Milwaukee, Wisconsin expert in family therapy. "One can still deplore the aggression and be an advocate for the relationship when two people want to stay together and are motivated to make changes in the relationship," says Lipchik. "It's too easy to stuff people into boxes labeled villains and victims."

Mrs. M. did not feel "blamed" when she and her husband saw Lipchik together for four months with follow-up sessions at six and eighteen months. She got what she most wanted: her marriage saved and the violence ended. Of course, the happy ending of the story of Mr. and Mrs. M. does not necessarily await every combative couple: spousal assault is a difficult behavior to change. But with a good therapist, difficult change is not impossible. Richard Heyman, of the State University of New York at Stony Brook, found that group conjoint therapy (several couples treated together) produced a significant reduction in both psychological and physical aggression immediately following treatment and one year later. This applied when the couple was intact, the degree of violence not severe, and the couple acknowledged that aggression was a problem, and often a mutual one.

Of course, joint-therapy is not for everyone. It may even be outright dangerous when the man causes frequent injury or when the woman is afraid of him. Not only will the

> **"The battered women's movement has outlived its useful beginnings."**

woman be hesitant to tell the truth in counseling sessions, but her husband might well retaliate for disclosures she makes to the counselor. A woman in such a situation is at real risk and must protect herself though she may find it hard—psychologically and physically—to pull away. For her, writes Dr. Virginia Goldner, "the ideological purity and righteous indignation of the battered woman's movement is all that protects her from being pulled back into the swamp of abuse." Maybe so, but more often the violence is less intense and, as psychologist Judith Shervin writes, "men and women are bound in their dance of mutual destructiveness. . . . Women must share responsibility for their behavior and contributions to domestic violence."

Violence by Women

These contributions are far bigger than feminists are willing to admit. According to the landmark 1980 book, *Behind Closed Doors: Violence in the American Family* by Murray A. Straus, Richard J. Gelles, and Suzanne K. Steinmetz, about twelve percent of couples engage in physical aggression. Severe violence such as punching, biting, kicking, or using a weapon is as likely to be committed by wives as husbands—at a rate of about one in twenty for both sexes. Rates of less severe assault such as pushing and grabbing are also comparable, about one in thirteen for both men and women. . . .

After reviewing the available research, Straus concludes that twenty-five to thirty percent of violent married and cohabiting couples are violent solely because of attacks by the wife. About twenty-five percent of violence between couples is initiated by men. The remaining half is classified as mutual. This is true whether the analysis is based on all assaults or only potentially injurious and life-threatening ones. (These findings are corroborated by other studies, including the 1991 Los Angeles Epidemiology Catchment Area study, and the 1990 National Survey of Households and Families.) . . .

Anyone still inclined to blame domestic violence on the patriarchy and male aggression ought to take a look at the statistics on violence against children. A just-released report from the Department of Health and Human Services, "Child Maltreatment in the United States," finds that women aged twenty to forty-nine are almost twice as likely as males to be "perpetrators of child maltreatment." According to a 1994 Department of Justice report, mothers are responsible in fifty-five percent of cases in which children are killed by their parents. The National Center on Child Abuse Prevention attributes fifty percent of the child abuse fatalities that occurred between 1986 and 1993 to the natural mother, twenty-three percent to the natural father, and twenty-seven percent to boyfriends and others.

Finally, consider domestic aggression within lesbian couples. If feminists are right, shouldn't these matches be exempt from the sex-driven power struggles that plague heterosexual couples?

Instead, according to Jeanie Morrow, director of the Lesbian Domestic Violence Program at W.O.M.A.N., Inc. in San Francisco, physical abuse between lesbian partners is at least as serious a problem as it is among heterosexuals. The Battered Women's Justice Project in Minneapolis, a clearinghouse for statistics, confirms this. "Most evidence suggests that lesbians and heterosexuals are comparably aggressive in their relationships," said spokeswoman Susan Gibel.

Some survey studies have actually suggested a higher incidence of violence among lesbian partners, but it's impossible to know for certain since there's no reliable baseline count of lesbian couples in the population at large. According to Morrow, the lesbian community has been reluctant to acknowledge intimate violence within its ranks—after all, this would endanger the all-purpose, battering-as-a-consequence-of-male-privilege explanation. Morrow's program treats about three hundred women a year but she wonders how many more need help. Because they are "doubly closeted," as Morrow puts it, women who are both gay and abused may be especially reluctant to use services or report assaults to the police.

More Problems than Progress

Like so many projects of the feminist agenda, the battered women's movement has outlived its useful beginnings, which was to help women leave violent relationships and persuade the legal system to take domestic abuse more seriously. Now they have brought us to a point at which a single complaint touches off an irreversible cascade of useless and often destructive legal and therapeutic events. This could well have a chilling effect upon victims of real violence, who may be reluctant to file police reports or to seek help if it subjects them to further battery from the authorities. And it certainly won't help violent men if they emerge from so-called treatment programs no more enlightened but certainly more angry, more resentful, and as dangerous as ever.

Aggression is a deeply personal and complex behavior, not a social defect expressed through the actions of men. Yet to feminists, it can only be the sound of one hand slapping: the man's. So long as this view prevails, we won't be helping the real victims; indeed, we will only be exposing them to more danger.

Chapter 4

How Can Violence Against Women Be Reduced?

Chapter Preface

For fifteen years the Domestic Violence Project/SAFE House women's shelter of Ann Arbor, Michigan, was located in a hidden, rural location, following the conventional wisdom that the best way to protect women from their batterers is to keep them hidden. The period immediately after a woman leaves her abuser is usually the most dangerous—enraged batterers will often increase the severity, frequency, and methods of abuse in an attempt to re-establish power and control. According to Richard Gelles of the Family Violence Research Program at the University of Rhode Island, the risk that an abuser will kill his victim increases by 75 percent when she tries to leave. Shelters play a crucial role in intervening against this escalation of violence, and many communities take keeping the location of these havens secret very seriously. In Georgia, for example, it is a misdemeanor to knowingly reveal the location of a shelter.

However, across the nation a growing number of shelters are bucking tradition (and, say critics, taking an unnecessary risk) by publicizing their locations. In 1995 the Ann Arbor Domestic Violence Project/SAFE House embraced this out-in-the-open approach, moving into a highly visible downtown building. Susan McGee, the program's executive director, explains the decision: "By insisting the battered woman hide away, we were reinforcing the idea that they had done something shameful, that they had done something wrong, and the community wasn't responsible." Responding to charges that this rationale is naive, advocates of public shelters say they still consider safety the top priority, but rely on tightened security or proximity to a police station rather than secrecy. The debate continues, but most national women's organizations have not yet taken a position on whether shelters should publicize their locations.

Whatever approach they take to security, shelters aid thousands of women each year simply by providing a supportive, protective community for women while they try to break free of an abusive relationship. The viewpoints in the following chapter explore a variety of approaches to reducing violence against women, from therapy for individuals and couples to educating society as a whole. But as the National Coalition Against Domestic Violence explains, the most important concern for many women is more immediate: "The primary service needed by a battered woman is the provision of safety. She must have a place of refuge from the batterer."

The Criminal Justice System Can Reduce Violence Against Women

by Albert R. Roberts

About the author: *Albert R. Roberts is a professor of social work and criminal justice at Rutgers University in New Brunswick, New Jersey, and is the author of over fifteen books, including* Sheltering Battered Women *and* Helping Battered Women: New Perspectives and Solutions, *from which the following viewpoint is excerpted.*

We have come a long way during the past two decades as responsive prosecutors, judges and legislators have begun to recognize family violence as a serious crime. All fifty states have passed civil and/or criminal statutes to protect battered women, and prosecutors' offices are beginning to implement efficient systems of screening and prosecuting cases. Police and courts in a small yet growing number of jurisdictions have set up a round-the-clock method of issuing temporary restraining orders and providing advocacy as the cases move through court. Although court-mandated, probation-operated batterers' counseling programs have been developed on a limited basis, more are needed.

The court system is still plagued, however, with many problems in its handling of family violence cases, including

- Judges, trial court administrators, case managers, and intake officers who tend to minimize the dangers that abused women encounter and who discourage them from following through with criminal or civil complaints.
- Overloaded dockets and overworked judges in large cities that result in the court's inability to schedule a hearing and a trial date in a timely manner.
- A lack of specialized training on family violence for court personnel.
- Abused women who fail to call the police or go to court because they believe that the criminal justice system will not be able to protect them.

- A lack of counseling programs to which the court can refer both the batterer and the victim.

From time to time, the court system does all it can to issue and enforce a restraining order, but still the batterer flies into a rage as a result of the court's involvement and murders the woman who had sought the court's protection. Occasionally the court itself has been the site of violence, when an enraged batterer has brought a concealed weapon into the courthouse and shot his partner while she was seeking protection from the court.

> *"It was not until 1988 that all fifty states took family violence laws seriously and passed acts that created civil and criminal remedies for victims of family violence."*

What are the statutory provisions for the effective handling of domestic violence by prosecutors, judges, and the courts? What changes were made at the end of the 1970s and the decade of the 1980s in state laws, family law remedies, and criminal assault statutes to benefit battered women? Under what circumstances, in most states, can a woman obtain a restraining or protective court order against her abusive partner? This [viewpoint] attempts to answer these questions related to changes in the legislative and judicial responses to the crime of domestic violence.

The Response of the Courts and Judges

Family courts and criminal courts are unique American institutions. Their primary function is to provide a public forum for resolving legal disputes of a criminal or family nature. The courts' powers and organizational structures vary from state to state, but for the most part, many of the states' statutes are uniform with regard to the responsibilities of judges, prosecutors, and attorneys. The overwhelming majority of criminal and family law cases are settled without a trial. A family court judge often has courtroom administrative responsibilities; that is, he or she may also preside over bail hearings, probation revocation hearings, and child custody hearings and also may issue search warrants, restraining orders, and/or protective orders.

The availability and commitment of judges to protect the legal rights of battered women differ from state to state and within the states. For example, during the mid-1980s, Cook County (Chicago), Illinois, followed by Marion County (Indianapolis), Indiana, established a special court with a specially trained magistrate to hear all domestic violence cases.

Court Orders

Judicial intervention on behalf of battered wives is a recent phenomenon. In 1976, Pennsylvania took the lead as the first state to pass legislation recognizing wife battering as a crime. By 1980, forty-four states had enacted legislation that dealt with family violence, but it was not until 1988 that all fifty states took family violence laws seriously and passed acts that created civil and criminal remedies for victims of family violence.

Temporary restraining orders (TROs) became one of the most frequently used legal options for battered women during the 1980s. Although the protection order is known by different names across the country, it is most commonly referred to as an *order of protection*, a *restraining order*, or a *temporary injunction*. An order of protection can stay in effect for up to one year. The purpose of these court orders has been to prevent violence by one family member against another. The court orders usually forbid the alleged abuser from making contact with the victim, and in some cases, the order specifies the distance that the abuser must maintain from the person who requested the order. Depending on the state law, the court order may mandate that the abusive spouse move out of the house, refrain from terroristic threats of abuse or further physical abuse, pay support for the victim and minor children, and/or participate in a counseling program aimed at ending the violence or chemical dependency (both the batterer and the victim may be required to enter counseling).

In the past in most jurisdictions, a battered woman needed a lawyer to prepare documents for a civil (family or domestic relations) court order. But now, in most states, an abused woman may file a petition in the appropriate court and represent herself in the hearing. The batterer is given reasonable notice of the hearing and is asked to be present. He can hire an attorney to represent him, but legal representation is not required. The hearing for the temporary and permanent order of protection is before a judge; there is no jury.

> *"In most states, an abused woman may file a petition in the appropriate court and represent herself in the hearing."*

The fearful and endangered victim must convince the judge that she was physically or sexually abused. Although some judges have been very compassionate and sensitive to the needs of battered women, others tend to blame the women for provoking the assaults. The judge usually has complete discretion over whether to grant a temporary restraining order and, seven to fourteen days later, a permanent restraining order. If the judge does not believe that the woman is in danger of further abuse, the case may be dismissed.

The most serious drawback of orders of protection is that they are extremely difficult to enforce. Because the police cannot be available twenty-four hours a day, seven days a week, the courts and police rely on the victim to call them if the batterer violates the court order. If the batterer violates any of the conditions of the protection order (e.g., tries to get into the victim's apartment), he will be in contempt of court or guilty of either a misdemeanor or criminal offense (depending on the state code).

There is wide variation, from one state code to another, in the penalties for violating a restraining order. Abusers can receive from fifteen days to six months in jail, probation and mandated counseling, or up to a $500 fine. An additional disadvantage of the court order is that instead of restraining the abuser, it may provoke him into retaliating against the victim with even more violence.

Judges need specialized training on the myths, dynamics, and effects of domestic violence, as well as on the court-mandated treatment needs of abusers. In the early 1990s, several statewide judicial conferences focused on family violence issues and policies. In addition, the National Council of Family and Juvenile Court Judges initiated two demonstration projects in 1990. The first project, funded by the Department of Justice, concentrates on improving family court practices with abused women through technical assistance. The second nationwide project, funded by the Conrad Hilton Foundation, is developing training materials for the court personnel, judges, district attorneys, and probation officers.

Probation

County and city probation departments can play an important role in optimizing the delivery of services to batterers and their victims. Unfortunately only a very few probation departments offer any assistance to abusers, battered women, or their children. Probation officers can provide early identification of serious cases and presentence reports on batterers (including a detailed psychosocial history, criminal history, and relationship problems), monitor batterers' restitution orders, and either conduct or refer batterers to six-month court-mandated group-counseling programs. These types of programs are provided by the San Francisco Probation Department and the Ocean County Probation Department in New Jersey. . . .

Prosecution of Family Violence Cases

In the past, it was very rare for batterers to be held accountable and to be punished for abusing their spouse or girlfriend. As discussed in the previous section, judges in different parts of the country are beginning to receive training on the enforcement of protection orders and the necessity of sentencing violent batterers to jail and/or court-mandated counseling. Because judges are viewed as the supreme authorities of their courtroom, they wield significant power. Thus when a batterer who violates probation or a restraining order is given a stern lecture or a short-term jail sentence, it gives the perpetrator as well as the community an important message—that domestic violence will not be tolerated by the criminal justice system.

> *"Most victim advocates believe that more domestic violence cases should be actively prosecuted."*

Prosecutors also have the potential to break the cycle of violence. Most victim advocates believe that more domestic violence cases should be actively prosecuted, particularly those acts involving alleged abusers with prior criminal histories. Although other advocates believe that most abusive men are generally law-abiding citizens and, at the same time, that the first- or second-time abuser has the potential to change, the victim still needs to be protected. Therefore, deferred prosecution pending the outcome of a six-week, twelve-week, or six-month batterers' counseling program is the preferred prosecutorial alternative. The least useful approach is to encourage plea agreements (plea bargains), with the sole intent of reducing the prosecutor's caseload and clearing the court's calendar, rather than protecting the victim.

> *"When prosecutors take official responsibility by . . . filing charges themselves, they are sending the important message that domestic violence is a serious crime against the state."*

Responsive prosecutors have been instituting promising strategies and policies in regard to family violence, which have improved the different stages of the prosecution process. The first innovative stage has been the early identification of abuse cases and the filing of criminal charges by the prosecutor's office. The victim/witness assistance unit in the prosecutor's office conducts a phone interview with each violently battered woman within a few hours after her abuser's arrest. If it determines that the alleged abuser has caused serious bodily harm to the victim or that the abuser has been convicted of any assaultive crime, then the advocate will help prepare the victim to testify and collect eyewitness testimony from neighbors or photographs and x-rays of the victim's injuries. The other model, the Domestic Abuse Intervention (DAI) Programs, was developed in Duluth and Minneapolis, in which staff interview and council victims after an arrest is made. A staff member then meets with prosecutors before the arraignment hearing to make sure that the prosecutors have all the necessary information and background evidence to prosecute the case.

In order to prevent batterers from intimidating and pressuring victims to drop charges or restraining orders, a growing number of prosecutors sign the criminal complaints themselves or file charges based on the arresting officer's signed complaint. When prosecutors take official responsibility by signing and filing charges themselves, they are sending the important message that domestic violence is a serious crime against the state, not a personal matter. Several prosecutors (e.g., Madison, Wisconsin, and South Bend, Indiana) do not allow the battered women to drop charges except in the case of extraordinary circumstances. In the majority of domestic violence arrests, however, neither the prosecutor nor the police will sign a criminal complaint. And in those cases in which the victim signs the complaint, most change their mind after their spouse apologizes and swears never to hit them again.

Sentencing options include traditional probation, pretrial diversion, probation, and intensive supervision in a biweekly counseling program, a stipulated order of continuance pending completion of a diversion program, and a presumptive sentence of thirty to sixty days in jail with the sentence suspended for one year pending compliance with an agreement that the batterer have no contact with the victim and complete a counseling program. The main problem with these innovative sentencing options is that most courts and prosecutors have limited staff resources and refuse to assign enough staff to screen applicants and monitor the abusers' attendance at and cooperation with the diversion program. Even when three to five full-time staff are assigned to these projects, they often fail because the community does not have enough alcohol rehabilitation, drug treatment, and/or group-counseling programs for the hundreds of batterers in need of treatment. Nevertheless, some jurisdictions have assigned adequate staff to operate a comprehensive domestic violence treatment program. The Minneapolis project employs thirteen full-time staff members augmented by nearly fifty trained volunteers. In both Minneapolis and Duluth, when the civil courts determine that abuse has taken place, the batterer is required to participate in educational and counseling groups. The court can also order a chemical dependency and psychological evaluation, and the abuser is required to sign a contract stipulating his responsibility to participate in the court-ordered treatment program. The staff regularly monitors his compliance with all aspects of the court order, including limited or no contact between the defendant and the victim. Then, in the few cases in which the abuser violates the court order, the prosecutor has the documentation to obtain a conviction.

More Supportive Courts Are Needed

Navigating the court system is generally a time-consuming and overwhelming ordeal for victims of violent crime. But for a woman who has been a victim of repeated physical abuse, degradation, and terroristic threats by a spouse or boyfriend, the thought of going to court may be so intimidating that no effort is made to get legal protection.

"Every . . . judge in state and county courts throughout the United States needs specialized training in handling battered women and abusive partners."

Protection or restraining orders are now available in every state as well as the District of Columbia. Thirty-two states have passed child custody statutes, which mandate courts to consider domestic violence when making custody awards and granting visitation rights. As of January 1993, fourteen states and the District of Columbia had enacted statutes mandating arrest for perpetrators of domestic violence. Thirty-three states also now have preferred or proarrest policies at the discretion of the police officer.

In order to ensure that the legal rights of battered women are fully protected, however, more needs to be done. Every court clerk, case manager, legal advocate, and judge in state and county courts throughout the United States needs specialized training in handling battered women and their abusive partners. All courts need systematic guidelines, simplified mandatory forms, and step-by-step instructions for processing court orders. Police officers and court clerks should have a brochure available to disseminate to all victims of domestic violence. This brochure should provide information on the battered woman's legal rights and options, instructions on how to obtain a court order or restraining order, and a list of local community resources.

Programs That Empower Women Can Reduce Violence Against Women

by Neil Websdale and Byron Johnson

About the authors: *Neil Websdale is a professor at Northern Arizona University's department of criminal justice in Flagstaff. Byron Johnson is a professor at Lamar University's Justice Center in Beaumont, Texas.*

Intrafamilial violence directed against women is part of a set of structural relations and social practices that, as Sylvia Walby puts it, allow men to "dominate, oppress, and exploit women." We agree with Kathleen Ferraro who observes that treating woman battering as a "crime problem" diminishes the social and political significance of interpersonal violence against women. According to Ferraro, "it is vital that battering not be viewed only as a crime, but also as a manifestation of structured gender inequality."

This view is supported by a large number of empirical studies that reveal that it is mostly men who control women through violence and women who bear the brunt of serious injuries. Women who attack their husbands usually do so out of desperation and self-defense.

Criminal justice policies will always be of limited utility in reducing the revictimization of battered women by their abusive partners because those policies do not systematically address women's social and political disadvantage. Traditionally, violence against women in families has been seen as a misdemeanor offense, even though the injuries sustained by many women would attract felonious charges if perpetrated by a man she did not live with or know well. After a decade of federally funded studies on the impact of arresting batterers at domestics, researchers and policymakers still debate whether mandatory arrest is an effective intervention tool that reduces the revictimization of women. . . .

Psychological explanations have tended to identify battered women as accomplices to their own victimization. They become emotionally paralyzed and un-

Excerpted from Neil Websdale and Byron Johnson, "Reducing Woman Battering: The Role of Structural Approaches," *Social Justice*, Spring 1997, by permission of *Social Justice*.

able to work their way out of abusive situations because they suffer from learned helplessness. Consequently, much therapy with battered women ends up reinforcing women's subordination rather than challenging their social and political disadvantage and incorporating that disadvantage into emotionally supportive strategies. Unlike psychological approaches, we contend that a more effective way to reduce woman battering is to empower battered women (by providing independent

> *"It is vital that battering not be viewed only as a crime, but also as a manifestation of structured gender inequality."*

housing and job opportunities) to break away from violent relationships, if they so choose. In suggesting such an approach, we do not mean to set up a false dichotomy between housing/work related issues and all the personal/emotional contradictions and ambiguities of ending an intimate relationship.

The Kentucky Job Readiness Program

In this viewpoint we report case study findings from a unique federally funded project in Kentucky that was designed to reduce the revictimization of battered women by providing battered women with job training, employment, independent living skills, independent housing, assistance with negotiating the welfare system, education, legal support, childcare, and a multitude of other services. This preventive "structural" intervention is known as the Kentucky Job Readiness Program (JRP). The JRP has been in operation in Kentucky for four years (1990 to 1994) and has been funded by a U.S. Department of Labor demonstration grant. By the fall of 1994, the JRPs operated in seven of the 16 spouse abuse shelter sites in Kentucky. No other state has implemented JRPs exclusively in their spouse abuse shelter system. The uniqueness of the Kentucky JRPs makes it all the more important to report the case study findings on the revictimization rates of battered women receiving JRP interventions. . . .

Since the late 1970s, 16 spouse shelters have formed to provide women with refuge from violent men. Spouse abuse centers in Kentucky provide a range of services for their clients, including some or all of the following: safe shelter, nonresidential counseling, support services, clothing, legal advice, economic assistance, counseling, childcare, access to medical services, transportation, assistance in finding housing, and a range of other informal supports. The majority of women using the services of spouse abuse shelters are poor. . . .

The innovative JRPs were designed not only to extend the baseline of shelter services, but also to provide a comprehensive range of preventive interventions, including economic self-sufficiency, emotional empowerment, autonomous living skills, and practical support. This self-sufficiency was not designed to translate only into the acquisition of minimum-wage jobs, but also to provide women with a substrate of skills and confidence, which, if their circumstances and individual leanings permitted, would enable them to climb the career ladder. In a nutshell, the JRPs were a structural attempt to confront the problem of battered women having no other choice but to return to violent households. The philosophy behind these structural interventions is that battered women, contrary to the astructural approach of theorists such as Lenore Walker, do not suffer from learned helplessness and are not emotionally paralyzed to the point that they cannot effectively problem-solve. Rather, if given real opportunities to confront their victimization and poverty through job training, learning independent living skills, and independent housing, battered women will seize upon them and demonstrate tremendous resourcefulness under very trying conditions.

The Nature of JRPs

The JRPs are multifaceted preventive programs that very pragmatically confront the structural disadvantages of battered women. Each component is designed to confront a particular structural impediment, which, if overcome, gives battered women a chance to redirect their considerable resistive powers away from mere physical and emotional survival and toward the construction of a more peaceful lifestyle, usually with their children.

JRP employment counselors usually meet with interested potential enrollees early on during their first week in shelter. Counselors may have read clients' files before making initial contact. Screening refers to the way in which JRP staff assess the appropriateness of a potential client for enrollment. Across all sites, very few interested clients are screened out by JRP personnel. JRP staff know from

> "A more effective way to reduce woman battering is to empower battered women (by providing independent housing and job opportunities) to break away from violent relationships."

experience that employment skills are an essential component to the pursuit of economic independence. These skills provide not only a means of financial support, but also a much needed confidence boost for entry into a world often denied them by their violent and controlling partners.

JRPs offer a wide range of skills training and services to battered women. Programs include the provision of training services, support services, housing services, and job placement services.

The unpaid, marginalized, and trivialized nature of the household labor performed by many clients diminishes their self-esteem concerning their work capabilities. The JRP, through the notion of transferable skills, attempts to invert women's self-deprecating observations about their potential employability. As Ann Oakley and Christine Delphy argue, the work of housewives is unpaid and unrecognized because they are housewives and not because of the nature of the work they do. The same work in the socialized labor market would be paid. JRPs invert this structural disadvantage by identifying the numerous skills battered women possess from their housework and present the possibility that JRP clients could be paid to use these skills. Alternatively, this baseline of skills could be refined and reoriented to the more social world of the labor market, as opposed to the isolated and personalized private sphere of housework.

Empowering Women

Training services consist of various interventions designed to prepare battered women for the world of work and independent living. These include, but are not limited to, the following: job counseling, job training/job search, and remedial education and literacy. Job counseling is the process of assisting participants to realistically assess their abilities, needs, and potential, and providing guidance in the development of participants' vocational goals and the means to achieve those goals. Job training/job search is the process of helping participants to develop or enhance their job-seeking skills. In most cases, a job search may include a structured activity focusing on building practical skills and knowledge in order to identify and initiate employer contacts and interviews. This knowledge includes labor market information, job application/resume writing, interviewing techniques, and finding job openings. Remedial education and literacy entails instruction in reading comprehension, math computation, language arts (writing and verbal communication), and reasoning skills that enable an individual to function in the labor market. JRP support services greatly extend the baseline of spouse abuse shelter services and better prepare clients for the difficult task of economic self-sufficiency. These support services offer assistance with transportation, food/meals, personal needs, clothing, work equipment, money management, self-esteem/motivation, independent living/life skills, daycare, and advocacy.

Battering relationships are often characterized by abusive men controlling the movements of "their" women. Solving the problem of getting around the power plays of an abusive relationship is another way in which the JRPs confront the structural disadvantage of battered women. Transportation is provided to participants so they can travel to training, shelters, job interviews, and jobs. At times, participant placement funds have been used to buy clients secondhand cars. Such provision is particularly valuable in rural areas where public transportation is very limited. JRPs also provide food for clients and their children. Other personal needs are also provided, including goods and services such as toothbrushes, shampoo, other personal hygiene supplies, pen and paper, false teeth, eyeglasses, and shower and laundry services. Cloth-

> *"If given real opportunities . . . , battered women will seize upon them and demonstrate tremendous resourcefulness under very trying conditions."*

ing for women who are entering the job market is important, particularly when certain jobs require special clothing. For example, overalls may be purchased for women entering nontraditional jobs and suits may be provided for those entering clerical work.

Structural Subversion

Interventions around clothing are not just pragmatic. They symbolize a subversiveness in terms of the presentation of the self in everyday life, since many battered women either did not "dress up" or were likened to whores by their abusers for doing so. Similarly, some employers require employees to own certain kinds of equipment (e.g., tools for construction or carpentry work) and the JRPs were sometimes able to provide these. Money management and budgeting workshops teach some clients how to handle money. Financial training is essential, especially since many women have never been allowed by their abusers to own and control their own money. Women are given the opportunity to attend individual or group meetings to enhance their self-esteem and increase their motivation for life and work. Independent living/life skills are offered to assist the individual to learn how to cope with everyday problems. JRPs also offer assistance with locating appropriate daycare services. Such services are essential if women are to enter the world of paid employment. Finally, legal advocacy may involve hooking the client up with the appropriate legal services or making clients aware of some of their legal rights *vis-à-vis* issues such as emergency protective orders, child custody, and child support.

> *"Housing offers physical and emotional space away from the abuser, who was used to managing his 'castle' in certain ways."*

Structural subversion is also seen through providing independent housing. This housing offers physical and emotional space away from the abuser, who was used to managing his "castle" in certain ways. JRP housing services (mostly public housing) for battered women include emergency housing assistance, transitional housing placement, permanent housing placement, deposit and rent assistance, assistance with furnishings and moving, and housing assistance counseling. . . .

Having identified, celebrated, refined, and extended many of the unrecognized skills possessed by battered women, these JRP clients are often ready to consider entering the world of paid employment. JRP job placement services include job development, direct placement, post-placement follow-up, self-help support groups, and mentoring. Job development is the process of marketing a JRP participant to employers, including informing employers about what the participant can do and soliciting and securing a job interview for that individual. In cases where the JRP staff have developed linkages with local private employers, a job may be "developed" or created for a particular participant. Direct placement is a job placement after intake, enrollment, and receipt of case management, support services, and/or housing services, but without the benefit of job training services. Post-placement follow-up services are designed to support program participants once employment is secured. Self-help support groups are meetings of JRP participants who provide positive reinforcement for each other and improve their personal comfort in learning new things, searching for jobs and housing, and attaining long-term success in the workplace. Mentoring is accomplished as an experienced person, teacher, or counselor intervenes on a battered woman's behalf. The mentor becomes a champion of the client and over a long period of time can be counted on for emotional support and career guidance. . . .

The Study

As part of the official evaluation of the U.S. Department of Labor Demonstration Grant, the Kentucky Domestic Violence Association (KDVA) gathered 153 case studies on JRP clients who passed through the program between 1991 and 1994. These case studies were written by JRP staff and counselors at participating shelters and detailed the program participation and post-shelter residence living situations of JRP graduates. Case studies were completed on women who had been out of shelters for at least three months and sometimes up to one year. To learn more about the workings of the JRPs and to improve the program, JRP staff constructed case studies on clients who had a variety of experiences in the program. They were specifically asked not just to write about the "success" stories where battered women overcame tremendous obstacles and found and retained high-paying jobs. Indeed, most of the JRP women did not dramatically change their economic situation by obtaining well-paying jobs. . . .

> *"Women who live separately from their abusers are significantly less likely to be revictimized than women who remain with their abusers."*

Findings

Demographic Profile of the JRP Clients. We provide summary demographics of all 684 cases to provide readers with a broad appreciation of the demographic features of all the women who passed through the JRP from 1991 to 1994. JRP clients had the following characteristics:
- Average age was 31.85 years;
- 78.1% were Caucasian, 18% African American, 0.8% Asian or Pacific Islanders, 1.4% Hispanic, 1.1% American Indian or Alaskan Natives, 0.6 "other";
- 28.4% were married, 32.2% separated from their husbands, 19% single, and 19.7% divorced;
- 63.3% had children aged six and over;
- 40.4% had high school diplomas, 21.6% GEDs, 16% vocational certificates, and 2.4% college degrees;
- 16.3% were employed, 77% unemployed, and 6.7% not in the wage-earning

labor force. Nearly all of the women had worked for wages at some time in their lives (96.7%); and

- 42.9% were service workers, 13% laborers, 12% marketing/sales, and 9.9% technical or support staff.

Statistical Analysis of JRP Service Delivery and Revictimization. Our analysis of the 153 cases indicates that all battered women who participated in the JRP took advantage of job training and services, 67.32% of participants secured employment, and 85.62% of clients secured housing and lived independently of their abusers. Perhaps most significantly, 82% of battered women experienced no revictimization.

An analysis of the 125 clients out of 153 who experienced no revictimization revealed the following:

- Ninety-eight of these clients had independent housing and jobs and were not living with family or friends.
- Twenty-four clients acquired housing, but were not employed.
- Two had jobs and were living independently of their abusers either with family or friends.
- One had completed the JRP and had no housing independent of the abuser and no job.

Women who live separately from their abusers are significantly less likely to be revictimized than women who remain with their abusers. Of those women who secure independent housing, 97.6% report no further

> *"JRPs cut to the heart of both class and gender power relations for this group of batterers and their victims."*

victimization. Conversely, of those women who return to their abuser, 86.36% report further victimization. These findings strongly suggest that providing independent housing arrangements to formerly battered women has a profound effect on their revictimization.

Women who secure employment are significantly less likely to experience further battering from their abuser. Seventy-six percent of the women who were employed as a result of the JRP report no further victimization. On the other hand, among the women not able to secure employment, 40% were revictimized. Although not as significant as independent housing, employment is still an important factor in whether women are victims of further violence.

Additional analysis reveals patterns related to employment, housing, and further victimization:

- Of the 98 women who were able to acquire housing independent of their abuser (i.e., not with friends or family) and found employment, 93 (95%) experienced no further victimization.
- Of the 33 women who secured independent housing but no job, 29 (88%) experienced no further victimization.
- Only five women who indicated they were living with their abuser were

able to secure and retain jobs. Three of these five were revictimized.

- Seventeen women returned to live with their abuser and could not find employment. All but one (94%) experienced further victimization. . . .

Making Sense of the Effects of JRPs on Revictimization

The battered women who form the subject of this study are working class and poor. The gendered capitalist workplace offers them, and most other women, low-paying jobs. Their ongoing brutalization is often accompanied by extreme isolation from friends and family. Many of them earn little money and often do not work for wages. They are usually heavily dependent upon their batterers for economic support. In rural areas of the state, this dependence is compounded by geographical isolation, a sociocultural milieu that dictates highly stereotypical roles for women, and a dislocation from the potentially supportive institutions of the state. We have argued that the plight of battered women in Kentucky's shelters is deeply rooted in the social disadvantage of women. . . .

As noted, the JRPs cut to the heart of both class and gender power relations for this group of batterers and their victims. If battered women are provided with both outside economic and emotional support, roughly 70% express a keen interest in living apart from their abuser and less than 30% see couples, individual, or family counseling as viable alternatives. This finding is supported by the JRPs, which show women to be keen to change their situation. These findings tell us that the long-term solution to battering must include major structural interventions that remain cognizant of the way in which both poverty and patriarchy intersect to keep women in violent relationships. . . .

Failed Criminal Justice Solutions

Much of the debate about solutions to the problem of woman battering has narrowly focused on criminal justice strategies such as mandatory arrest. Woman battering is not solely, or even primarily, a problem that is amenable to criminal justice solutions. Criminal justice solutions sometimes temporarily remove batterers from the family. In most cases he returns to that unchanged family environment and often engages in further acts of violence. Strategies such as mandatory arrest alone will not stem the tide of violence against women within families.

Our data show that the Kentucky JRPs, and especially the provision of independent housing and the acquisi-

> *"Criminal justice 'solutions' ignore or downplay the social generation of crime."*

tion of employment (with the latter contributing to a lesser, but still highly significant, degree), reduce the revictimization of battered women residing in the JRP shelters. We contend that this structural intervention is potentially more powerful than the approach of criminal justice systems, which are limited to astructural interventions such as arrest, conviction, incarceration, and/or counseling. As noted, all of these criminal justice "solutions" ignore or downplay the social generation of crime. Theoretically, we have explained the preventive impact of the JRPs largely in terms of empowering women to move beyond their violent relationships. Battered women in Kentucky often find themselves trapped in these abusive relationships, not because they suffer from learned helplessness or battered woman syndrome, but because of structural forces such as poverty, low educational qualifications, no childcare options, no safe affordable alternative housing, and little enthusiasm on the part of most judges or police to incapacitate batterers long enough to provide women with time to think through their options. . . .

Moving Toward Multifaceted Preventive Approaches

The documented evidence from the JRP case studies strongly suggests that a multifaceted community response is potentially a much more effective way of reducing or preventing the revictimization of battered women. Woman battering is a wide-ranging social problem that has at its heart the intersecting power relations of gender and class. We contend that such a problem must be comprehensively addressed by interagency cooperative efforts that strike at the disadvantageous position of women in abusive relationships. Woman battering must not be seen astructurally as a criminal justice problem, but rather structurally as an economic, public health, labor, housing, human rights, and educational issue.

Our findings suggest that much more funding should be made available for preventive programs that change the structural conditions affecting battered women's options concerning leaving violent familial relationships. The implications of our research go well beyond developing structural interventions to reduce the revictimization of battered women. If the power imbalance between men and women in abusive relationships can be effectively altered and revictimization subsequently reduced, then is it not reasonable to suggest that by moving toward equality for women in their relationships with men that we might lower the outbreak of woman battering in the first place? Put simply, if structural interventions can reduce revictimization, why shouldn't they lower initial victimization?

Churches Can Reduce Violence Against Women

by Paul A. Cedar

About the author: *Paul A. Cedar was president of the Evangelical Free Church of America until 1996, when he left to become president of Mission America, a national networking and evangelism ministry.*

The statistics are staggering. Estimates of the number of women beaten every year in the United States range from 2 million to 4 million. That means that somewhere in this nation, a woman is beaten on the average of every 16 seconds.

If that were not enough, thousands of women are killed each year by their husbands, ex-husbands, or boyfriends.

The situation is so serious that in 1992 the Surgeon General reported that the abuse of women by husbands or boyfriends was the leading cause of injuries to women aged 15 to 44.

The human tendency is to pass the blame for abuse on to someone else. Many blame "the system." In other words, the police should do more to solve the problem, or the government needs to enact better legislation, or, for some feminists, men need to be understood as "bad" while women must be recognized as "good."

Others would assign the blame to the "victim." They would assert that no one needs to be abused. They contend that the solution is for the abused person simply to leave the marriage or relationship, or to press charges against the abuser, or to return the abuse. In other words, the victim needs to "get tough" with the person who is abusing her. Unfortunately, research shows that the most violent abuse takes place after the abused woman tries to leave.

The Church's Role

For Christians, at least two questions emerge. First, does the problem of the abuse of women exist among Christians involved in evangelical churches? And, if so, what can and should we be doing about it?

Although it is difficult to identify specific statistics, it is obvious that the problem of spousal abuse is much involved in the lives of many professing

Reprinted from Paul A. Cedar, "Abused Women: How Can the Church Help?" *Moody*, September 1995, by permission of the author.

Christians. In my years of counseling as a pastor, I became increasingly appalled by the abuse of spouses by those claiming to be committed followers of Jesus Christ.

Abuse is initiated and practiced by both husbands and wives. However, the majority of cases in the church are situations where women are abused by a husband, ex-husband, or boyfriend.

What steps can we take to help these battered and abused women? And what kind of help and redemptive ministry can we provide for the Christian who has become abusive?

Practicing Prevention

The first thing we can do is take the initiative in every possible way to prevent abuse before it ever begins. Studies show that few men are abusive early in their relationships or during the first months of marriage. In addition, the abuse of a wife or a girlfriend usually begins with verbal abuse and/or threats. Those should be clear warning signs to every thoughtful Christian woman.

The church can provide strategic preventative ministries including the following:

• *Ministry to children and parents.* Because much abusive behavior is developed during childhood, it is important for Christian parents to be equipped to be effective in the spiritual discipline and training of their children. Violence and abuse are sinful. Paul warned the Galatian Christians that the "acts of the sinful nature" include hatred, discord, jealousy, fits of rage, selfish ambition, dissension, and factions. All of those sins are related to sin of abuse. Paul concluded that "those who live like this will not inherit the kingdom of God" (Gal. 5:19-21). Children need to learn what attitudes and behavior are sinful and what the consequences of sin will be. They also need to be invited to be forgiven of their sins and to be delivered from patterns of sinful behavior through denying themselves, taking up their crosses daily, and following Jesus.

• *Premarital counseling.* Every local church should provide effective counseling sessions for young people preparing for marriage. Abuse should be addressed in some detail. Because most abusive persons have grown up in an environment of abuse, it is important to discover whether either partner has grown up in such an environment. If so, special counseling should be provided for the person

> *"Every local church should provide effective counseling sessions for young people preparing for marriage. Abuse should be addressed in some detail."*

who has experienced or witnessed abuse. The future partner also should be equipped to recognize the early signs of abuse in order to seek help before the abuse is acted out.

• *Preaching and teaching the Word of God.* The pastor needs to give spiritual leadership to the balanced teaching of the Word of God in the local church:

from the pulpit, in Sunday school classes, in small groups, and in family devotions. This should include the role of men as husbands and fathers. One of the special challenges many men seem to face in the evangelical church is an exaggerated view of the dominance of men and the submissiveness of women.

Evangelical Chauvinism

The misquoting and misinterpretation of Scripture is often used to defend a deadly and demeaning kind of male dominance I would call evangelical chauvinism. I realize this kind of abuse is usually not deliberate. Many Christian men have come to believe sincerely that they should dominate and even control their wives.

In my opinion, they misunderstand tragically the biblical role of the husband and father. There is no teaching in the Scriptures that gives husbands the right to abuse or control their wives or any other woman.

Instead, the Bible teaches graphically that men should "love their wives" and that they should do so in the same way "Christ loved the church and gave himself up for her to make her holy. . . . In this same way, husbands ought to love their wives as their own bodies" (Eph. 5:25-28). That kind of husband will not abuse his wife, his children, or any other person.

Our model for Christian husbands and fathers is that of our Heavenly Father. We should love as He loves, nurture as He nurtures, and encourage as He encourages.

In the creation account, the Bible

> *"The misquoting and misinterpretation of Scripture is often used to defend a deadly and demeaning kind of male dominance."*

tells us it was not good for man to live alone. So God declared, "I will make a helper [helpmate] suitable for him" (Gen. 2:18). In the Hebrew text, the same word translated "helper" or "helpmate" is used to describe one of God's ministries to us as our "help" or "helper" (see Psalm 33:20; 70:5; 121:2). We do not try to dominate or abuse our Lord who is our helper. And neither should Christian men ever abuse women.

At the same time, there is a legitimate role for a Christian father and husband to give spiritual leadership to his wife and children. But it is not the role of a tyrant, dictator, or abuser. It is the same role the loving Christ has with His church. Christian men are to love their wives and to lovingly give themselves to help their wives grow in the grace and nurture of our Lord so that together, both husband and wife will become authentically holy—like Jesus Christ!

• *Marriage seminars and retreats.* In helping prevent abuse in Christian families, pastors should not merely preach about marriage. They should see that the church provides regular seminars, retreats, or other ministry resources to strengthen marriages and equip both husbands and wives to be more loving, gentle, encouraging, and supportive of one another. The apostle Peter instructed husbands specifically when he wrote, "Husbands, in the same way be considerate as you live with your wives, and treat them with respect as the weaker partner and as heirs with you of the gracious gift of life, so that nothing will hinder your prayers" (1 Peter 3:7).

• *Promise Keepers.* Although none of us can be certain that this movement will be long-lived, we can do all we can to encourage men of local churches to take advantage of this

> *"Abuse is not merely a social ill or an act of criminal behavior. It is sin."*

strategic ministry. I am convinced that as men are strengthened in their walk with God, they will become better husbands and fathers.

A Supportive Church Environment

In addition to being preventive, we need to be proactive in dealing with abusive behavior. There are several important ingredients that can be provided by every local church of every size and every sociological setting:

• *An open and loving spiritual environment.* Most abused women are afraid to discuss their needs with any other person until the abuse has become violent and destructive. They hesitate because they believe they will be judged or that others will not believe them.

In the context of a church family, any believer should be able to discuss concerns with the pastor or another Christian friend with full confidence. The apostle Paul encouraged us to "carry each other's burdens, and in this way you will fulfill the law of Christ" (Gal. 6:2). No Christian woman should ever have to carry the burden of abuse alone. There should be such a loving, trusting, and respectful spirit in the congregation that any Christian can receive loving and sensitive counsel and encouragement immediately for any problem—including abuse.

• *Practical help.* Every Christian woman who is being abused should receive not only the concern and sympathy of other Christians, but also the practical help she needs. The apostle John addressed that basic principle when he asked, "If anyone . . . sees his brother [or sister] in need but has no pity on him, how can the love of God be in him?" (1 John 3:17). He then concluded, "My children, love must not be a matter of words or talk; it must be genuine, and show itself in action" (1 John 3:18 NEB).

The very essence of participation in the church is that we share our resources with one another. In the early church, "all the believers were one in heart and mind. No one claimed that any of his possessions was his own, but they shared everything they had. . . . Much grace was upon them all. There were no needy persons among them" (Acts 4:32-34). The church family needs to be ready to provide a safe place for abused women, appropriate counseling, or crisis intervention.

• *Prayer support.* Whenever we encounter a crisis in our lives, we do well to begin by falling on our face before God to ask for His wisdom and guidance. The rate of success in resolving or overcoming the abuse of women in the secular world is not at all encouraging. Some would say it is almost non-existent.

In contrast, Christians have all the resources of God at their disposal. Abuse is not merely a social ill or an act of criminal behavior. It is sin. As we have seen, it is what Paul calls an act of the sinful nature. It involves our spiritual enemy—the devil. The first step we should take against such behavior is spiritual assault. It is prayer that unleashes the ministry of the Holy Spirit to convict a person of sin.

Paul put it in these terms: "For though we live in the world, we do not wage war as the world does. The weapons we fight with are not the weapons of the world. On the contrary, they have divine power to demolish strongholds" (2 Cor. 10:3,4). When one of the members of a church family is being abused, we would do well to mobilize all the members to join in prayer for our Lord's protection and provision for the woman who is being abused. The Lord can go where we cannot go and do what we cannot do. Whenever abuse comes to any woman, it is time for members of her church family to weep, to humble themselves, and to gather for united prayer.

Ministering to the Abuser

The church needs to reach out with the love of Jesus Christ to minister not only to the abused woman, but also to the man who has been abusing her. I realize this is a remarkably radical idea in our secular world. Unfortunately, it seems to be just about as radical in Christian circles.

In the scores of articles and books I have read on the subject of abuse, virtually no one seems to be addressing the problem of the person who is inflicting the abuse. While some acknowledge that he often has been raised in an abusive environment or is under unusual stress, the idea that he can be helped or that his conduct can be changed is usually ignored.

That is where the church can offer hope in what seems an impossible situation. I believe there are several specific steps that we can take to help the person who is guilty of abusing another—especially when that abuser professes to be a Christian or is a member of the church family:

> *"The idea that [the abuser] can be helped or that his conduct can be changed is usually ignored. That is where the church can offer hope in what seems an impossible situation."*

• *Pray for him.* Once again, I believe we should begin with prayer for both the abused and the abuser. Without the intervention of our Lord, there is little hope for any abusive situation.

• *Initiate crisis intervention when it is appropriate.* One of the special challenges is that the abuser is usually someone the victim loves deeply. That's why it's difficult for an abused woman to report the abuse or to leave her abusive situation.

The key is to offer the abused woman both authentic hope and a means where love can be extended to the man she loves so deeply. The purpose of crisis intervention is not to *punish* the abuser, but to attempt to *rescue* him from sin and death.

I will never forget the first time I was involved in such a rescue attempt. I was on the staff of a large evangelical church. A woman had come to one of my pastoral colleagues to reveal that she had been abused for years by her husband and that he was now beginning to abuse their children. Although she had tolerated abuse for a long time, she simply could not allow her children to be abused.

> *"The purpose of crisis intervention is not to* **punish** *the abuser, but to attempt to* **rescue** *him from sin and death."*

I was asked to be a member of the crisis intervention team. After a great deal of prayerful preparation, we went with the abused wife to the office of her husband, who was a respected executive in a large business. We went to lovingly confront him and his sin. We gave him the alternative to leave his office immediately with us to enter a Christian counseling facility where he would receive appropriate help, or his family would have to leave him to be safe from his abuse. He was assured that his employer was fully aware of the situation and supported his getting help immediately.

In turn, we expressed our deep love and concern for him and his family; it was our desire not to punish him but to help him and to do all we could to restore his family.

He made the right choice that day. The good news is that he was wonderfully restored to an intimate and loving relationship with Christ and then with his wife and family. Today, he is an outstanding Christian leader in his home, his church, and his community.

I am convinced that God sometimes uses this confrontive approach to bring abusive men to their senses. It is important, however, that the pastor or a qualified Christian counselor give prayerful and careful leadership to the "interventive" ministry.

False Promises vs. True Repentance

• *Call the abuser to repentance.* Addictive abusers are frequently remorseful immediately after abusing the women in their lives. They often cry openly, ask for forgiveness, and promise to never abuse again. Unfortunately, the remorse is usually short-lived and the cycle repeats itself.

In contrast, authentic repentance includes not only initial feelings of regret or remorse, but also a dramatic change in behavior. Christian repentance means "to turn from a given sin" and follow Christ unreservedly. This requires a radical change in direction and behavior. It is a spiritual experience that begins with confession and concludes with a deep commitment to follow Jesus as Lord.

I am convinced that only the Holy Spirit can set abusers free from the pattern of violent and destructive behavior. Only the Holy Spirit can replace the "acts of the sinful nature" with love, joy, peace, patience, kindness, goodness, faithfulness, gentleness, and self-control (Gal. 6:18-23).

In writing to the Christians in Colosse, Paul instructed them to "put off" whatever belonged to their earthly nature. In turn, he encouraged them (and us) to "put on" the "new self" and to clothe ourselves "with compassion, kindness, humility, gentleness, patience . . . and love which binds them all together in perfect unity" (Col. 3:5-14).

That is what every abuser needs—to be transformed by the power of the resurrected Christ—to be made into a new creation (2 Cor. 5:17). Only Christ can bring about that radical change of direction and behavior. Only He can bring authentic and ultimate hope to an abusive situation.

Physicians Can Reduce Violence Against Women

by Sarah M. Buel

About the author: *Sarah M. Buel is an assistant district attorney in Norfolk County, Massachusetts, a member of the Department of Justice's Advisory Council on Violence Against Women, and a frequent lecturer on the topic at law and medical schools.*

Many were outraged by the 1988 murder of 6-year-old Lisa Steinberg by Joel Steinberg, her adoptive father. Mr. Steinberg also brutalized Lisa's adoptive mother, Hedda Nussbaum. On February 12, 1988, Mrs. Nussbaum was referred to the Bellevue Hospital Emergency Room from a battered women's shelter, due to the severity of her injuries. Mrs. Nussbaum presented with multiple fractures, explaining that she had fallen down a flight of stairs. Fortunately, the physicians determined that the injuries had been sustained in a beating. She was treated and admitted to the Bellevue Psychiatric Unit for 5 days. At that time she disclosed the truth of her own abuse and that of her children. Yet on February 17, 1988, Mrs. Nussbaum was released to her battering husband's custody. The hospital's report was referred to the New York City Department of Human Resources, but its investigation found no evidence of child abuse, apparently deeming the serious injuries to Hedda Nussbaum to be of no consequence.

Progress Has Been Made

Since Hedda Nussbaum's hospital visit many physicians, nurses, and medical professionals have made great strides in developing more effective interventions with family violence victims. These efforts are due, at least in part, to the leadership roles taken by the American Nurses Association, the American College of Obstetricians and Gynecologists (ACOG), and the American Medical Association (AMA). Each has produced comprehensive guidelines, standards of practice, and informational materials to assist medical professionals in improving their practices. These publications have contributed significantly to the available domestic violence literature and have served as a catalyst to galvanize

Excerpted from Sarah M. Buel, "Family Violence: Practical Recommendations for Physicians and the Medical Community," *Women's Health Issues*, vol. 5, no. 4, Winter 1995, pp. 158–69. References in the original have been omitted here. Reprinted by permission of the Jacobs Institute of Women's Health.

other professional organizations to action. For example, there now exists a nationwide program to provide free reconstructive surgery to indigent battered women. Advocates herald the program, as a victim's recovery can be impeded by constantly being forced to see the scars of abuse.

Additionally, many state medical organizations and specific commissions have taken up the difficult challenge of producing practical materials for the professionals and the battered patients. The Massachusetts

> *"Medical professionals [are often] the front line: the first to see a victim or the first person in whom the victim will confide."*

Medical Society produced an outstanding packet, *Campaign Against Domestic Violence,* then mailed it to every physician in the state. They have followed up with articles, seminars, press releases, and the formation of the Physicians Domestic Violence Roundtable to provide the opportunity for information-sharing, collaboration, and training. . . .

Increasingly, hospitals are inviting domestic violence experts to present on domestic violence issues at grand rounds, medical schools are inviting guest lecturers on the topic, and medical organizations are highlighting this area at their educational training programs. Dr. Richard Jones, as president of ACOG, probably began the trend when he made domestic violence the cornerstone of his presidency, speaking world-wide on the issue and instituting major changes in his own practice and hospital. Dr. Jones was the catalyst for tremendous efforts, including providing domestic violence materials to every ACOG member and arranging a panel of colleagues to present on domestic violence as the presidential program at the ACOG Annual Clinical Meeting in 1993.

Why the Medical Community Must Work Against Abuse

Initial questions might include the following: Why should health professionals get more involved in family violence issues? Isn't this best left to the criminal justice system? First, the community desperately needs the involvement of medical professionals because so often they are the front line: the first to see a victim or the first person in whom the victim will confide about the abuse. This affords the physician the opportunity to intervene with safety planning and a myriad of resources that can prevent further harm and possible homicide. As achieving and maintaining good health for patients are medical goals, safety must surely be seen as part of that paradigm.

Second, courts have been more willing to hold hospitals liable for the acts or omissions of their staff, with clear responsibility on the shoulders of physicians, nurses, and other hospital employees. A string of recent cases has not so much suggested that the hospitals caused the negligence, rather that they did not act responsibly to prevent it. A 1991 Pennsylvania Supreme Court opinion stated that not only must physicians follow the standards of care, but that nurses and other hospital staff are obligated to "question a physician's order which is not in accord with standard medical practice." Given that routinely asking patients about abuse (i.e., on every visit asking, "Have you been hit or threatened since the last time I saw you?") is now considered the standard of care, it is clearly the medical professional's failure to ask that will subject him or her to potential liability.

Third, family violence cannot simply be left at the doorstep of the police, courts, shelters, emergency medical providers, or any one community entity. It is only in those communities with a multidisciplinary, integrated response that a reduction in family violence is achieved. The city of San Diego, by forging a close police, prosecutor, medical, mental health, and educator partnership, reduced its domestic violence homicide rate by 59% between 1993 and 1995. Phoenix has achieved a 30% reduction in its domestic homicide rate by instituting a similar protocol. The Nashville Metropolitan Police Department boasts a 71% drop in its domestic homicide rate for 1994 and the first quarter of 1995, as a result of the establishment of a similar coordinated community response. The recommendations contained herein do not represent an effort to "medicalize" the problem of family violence, but rather to identify the most productive roles for medical professionals, given the need for cross-disciplinary involvement. For each profession (e.g., law, education, mental health, business, religion, and social work) similar corresponding guidelines have been developed. . . .

Educate Yourself and Colleagues

Know and Use Community Resources. Find out about visiting shelters (if permitted) and determine what services you and/or other medical professionals and students might provide in such settings. For example, in some communities, physicians and nurses are going into shelters to provide health services to victims and their children. Other physicians, such as Dr. Elaine Alpert in Boston, have offered free medical care to victims and arrange with colleagues to assist with other needs. By speaking with victims, offenders, and children who have lived with the abuse, medical professionals can learn more about what interventions are most helpful.

However, only trained batterer's therapists should take on the task of confronting the batterer and determining what intervention program is most appropriate. Well-intentioned, but misguided advice at a recent medical conference suggested that the physician could align himself or herself as an ally of the batterer, working together to stop the violence. Noted batterers' expert Dr. David Adams cautions that not only can the batterer dupe the doctor into believing that the abuse has stopped when in fact it may be escalating, but such intervention can be quite dangerous for the victim, physician,

> *"It is only in those communities with a multidisciplinary, integrated response that a reduction in family violence is achieved."*

and staff. The role of the physician with the victim is to 1) routinize inquiry about abuse, 2) discuss safety planning, 3) state clearly, "You do not deserve to be abused," and 4) refer to appropriate shelter and advocacy programs. In working with the abuser, the provider's role is to refer the batterer to a certified batterer's intervention program, where a danger/lethality assessment and treatment plan can be completed.

> *"In working with the abuser, the [medical] provider's role is to refer the batterer to a certified batterer's intervention program."*

In Boston, several nurses and doctors participated in police ride-alongs to gain a better understanding of what their crisis response involved. Some have found it helpful to attend a batterer's intervention program meeting, to learn more about the ways that a sense of entitlement to power and control impact the batterer's behavior over time. Many medical professionals have also learned a good deal by asking experienced advocates about areas of concern and how they can help. . . .

Abuse Prevention Tactics

Routinize Inquiry About Abuse. The standard of care requires that each patient is asked on every visit, "Have you been hit or threatened since the last time I saw you?" If the patient is being seen for the first time, an explanation can be offered: "Due to the high incidence of domestic violence, I ask each patient whether they have been hit or threatened in a personal relationship." Victims may not be able to disclose the abuse without inquiry initiated by the medical practitioner. Pennsylvania triage nurses found that simply by asking about the history of abuse, they increased their identification of domestic violence victims by 60%. Dr. Richard Jones reports that prior to his routinizing inquiry about abuse, he identified just a few cases per year, whereas by asking directly, "Have you been hit or harmed anytime in the past year?" he now sees two or three cases per week in his practice. . . .

Document Accurately and Legibly. Since medical records assist in creating a paper trail documenting the abuse, it is particularly important that they be both accurate and legible. When some insurance companies began denying coverage to abuse victims, the concern was raised that perhaps physicians should not write a diagnosis of domestic violence in the medical record. The fear was that this information could be used as the basis for denying insurance coverage to battered women. However, substantial pressure has been brought to bear on the insurance industry, forcing them to change their policies of direct denial and replacing them with higher premiums. Although it is still a concern that documentation of domestic violence could adversely impact the victim's ability to obtain affordable insurance, the benefits of such documentation outweigh that possibility. Additionally, physicians can creatively word the medical record to reflect that the injuries were inflicted by an intimate partner, without flagging it as a "domestic violence" case.

One reason to document carefully is that medical records are readily admissible at civil and criminal trials, providing an objective diagnosis that can substantiate and bolster the victim's assertions of harm. Clear medical records can help the judge and/or jury understand the true nature and severity of the injuries, even if the victim is too terrified to testify or to fully describe the incident. Additionally, a growing number of states are following the recommendation of the National Council of Juvenile and Family Court Judge's *Model State Domestic Violence Code* that there be a rebuttable presumption against sole or joint custody being awarded to a perpetrator of domestic violence. As many victims may turn first or solely to medical providers, the medical record may be the only documented evidence of the abuse, and thus the only means for the victim to show that the perpetrator should not be given custody of the children.

A second reason to document domestic violence carefully is that such a diagnosis can trigger referrals to appropriate shelters and the development of a safety plan, as occurred in the Hedda Nussbaum case.

A third reason to fully document findings of domestic violence is that the physician can then also state the referrals and actions taken. Such information can greatly protect the physician should a malpractice claim allege failure to provide the standard of care. It is the physician's failure to act that will incur liability, not good faith efforts to assist the victim.

Domestic Violence Advocacy Programs

Ensure that Your Hospital Has a Domestic Violence Advocate or Program. Susan Hadley, a Minnesota nurse, determined to increase identification of and treatment services to battered women, started WomanKind programs [that teach health professionals how to identify abuse] at three Minneapolis area hospitals. Initially, she says they focused on emergency room interventions, assuming that most battered women would present there. However, once they began an effort to familiarize the institutions with their program, the referrals from orthopedics, mental health, obstetrics/gynecology, pediatrics, and other departments far outnumbered those from the emergency room. By having advocates on site at the hospitals, physicians and nurses were much more likely to refer victims, and victims were much more likely to avail themselves of the offered services.

"Due to the high incidence of domestic violence, I ask each patient whether they have been hit or threatened in a personal relationship."

Through Project AWAKE (Advocacy for Abused Women and Kids) at Boston Children's Hospital, the mothers of all abused children are also screened for abuse. The program was started in the mid-1980s as the hospital staff recognized that they could not protect children if they ignored the mother's abuse. By linking the mother/abuse victim with an advocate, chances greatly increase of being able to keep the nonviolent family members together. The advocate assists with court and social service advocacy, support groups, individual counseling, varied information, and referrals. To combat low birth weights and infant deaths, AWAKE recently located an advocate in a public housing project that is 25% African American and 75% Latino. The advocate was delighted to receive ten referrals just in the first week. AWAKE is sensitive to culture, race, and socioeconomic issues, with two Spanish-speaking advocates and a well-trained staff.

> *"Clear medical records can help the judge and/or jury understand the true nature and severity of the injuries."*

In addition to offering support groups for children ages 6 to 10, they provide education and support groups for the abused mothers. AWAKE staff also provide training for physicians and nurses, as well as community providers, who often are not aware of the abuse dynamics and are reluctant to ask about abuse. Most victims readily accept the help; only five or six of more than 300 women referred in 1994 refused the offered services. AWAKE director, Jennifer Robertson, asserts that, "Battered women aren't looking for counseling or advocacy services when they come to a hospital, but they are thinking about leaving their abuser. It's a good time to talk to them."

If you practice outside of a hospital, a separate unit may not be feasible, but you can ensure that all staff receive comprehensive family violence training. This will increase the likelihood that effective early identification, treatment, and referrals are made.

The Role of Medical Schools

Integrate Family Violence into the Curricula of Medical, Nursing, Social Work, and Relevant Professional Schools. The Centers for Disease Control and Prevention has documented that most medical schools spend less than 1.5 hours on family violence throughout the entire 4-year period, with most of that focused on child abuse. Most nursing and social work schools, as with other graduate and specialized programs (for example, law, religion, education, law enforcement, etc.) have also failed to provide their students with critical information regarding effective interventions, legal and ethical obligations, dynamics of family violence, and other relevant topics.

Fortunately, some institutions are taking the lead in changing that inexcusable state of affairs. For the past 6 years, Dr. Elaine Alpert at Boston University School of Medicine has been bringing in guest speakers, coordinating symposia, and requiring her students to read, discuss, and strategize about domestic violence as it will affect their patients and co-workers. Dr. Alpert also makes it clear that students cannot pass her course without substantial knowledge about family violence. Additionally, she has served as the faculty advisor for the Boston University Medical Students Against Domestic Violence, an active group that volunteers at local domestic programs and assists Dr. Alpert in her medical society efforts.

Dr. Edward Brandt is heading the AMA's committee to establish guidelines for medical schools to integrate instruction on family violence at every level of a physician's education. Both Dr. Brandt and Dr. Ronald Chez have successfully woven the topic into their course materials. Harvard Medical School has invited guest speakers to explain the dynamics of domestic violence to all first-year students and set up problem-solving sessions with more advanced literature reviews for third-year students after their clinical rotations. In the fall of 1995, domestic violence advocates and survivors were also invited to present at a day-long faculty briefing session, which included role plays and break-out groups.

In addition to changing the core curricula, existing protocols and accreditation criteria must be expanded to include, as an academic subject, the issue of family violence. Nursing, social work, and medical schools must acknowledge that their failure to provide such cutting edge information as part of the core curriculum greatly interferes with their students' ability to best serve their patients.

Reach Out to the Community

Ensure that Professional Medical Organizations Are Active in Combating Family Violence. Increasingly, national, state, and local medical associations are taking a leadership role in the efforts to eradicate family violence. In addition to those mentioned in the introduction, medical societies in California, Florida, Iowa, Minnesota, North Carolina, Oklahoma, Tulsa County (Oklahoma), Oregon, and Texas, among others, have undertaken a range of domestic violence training and education activities.

The California Medical Association sponsored a series of six public service announcements (PSAs), "Safe Choices," urging battered women to confide in their doctor or call 800-TRY-NOVA for help. In concert with medical students at the University of Texas Medical School-Houston, the Texas Medical Association set up a six-part lecture series on a wide range of topics related to family violence.

The "Stop the Violence" campaign of the Minnesota Medical Association provides PSAs, billboards, and bumper stickers, in addition to guidelines and resources to doctors. In

> *"Harvard Medical School has invited guest speakers to explain the dynamics of domestic violence to all first-year students."*

North Carolina, the state's Medical Society and medical students from East Carolina University School of Medicine sponsored community education seminars at a local mall. Additionally, they distributed wallet-sized information cards, and held a raffle to raise money for their local battered women's shelter. . . .

Sponsoring training seminars, publishing relevant articles and practice guidelines, and producing community education materials have proven to be invaluable contributions by medical groups from around the country. Formulated in collaboration with shelters and community agencies, such information has not only provided guidance to physicians, but also to victims in danger. Organized medical groups have much to offer their communities in the area of domestic violence and should not wait for future tragedies before taking action. . . .

Strive for Change

Instead of hiding behind the usual excuses, "I don't have the time or money or human resources to improve practices . . . ," we must each be willing to view the obstacles as challenges. Those medical practitioners who have dramatically improved interventions faced similar, if not the same or more awesome stumbling blocks. Yet, like Drs. Richard Jones, Elaine Alpert, Edward Brandt, and Ronald Chez, they were willing to leave defensive egos behind and ask themselves, "How can I improve what I do? How can I do an even better job at assisting patients who are victims?"

> *"Organized medical groups have much to offer their communities in the area of domestic violence and should not wait for future tragedies before taking action."*

This process involves seeking the advice and guidance of experienced domestic violence advocates who can best steer the well-intended practitioner. . . .

In summary, medical professionals should make every effort to do the following:
1) Educate yourself and colleagues about effectively combating family violence
2) Be willing to change individual and institutional practices to better protect patients who are domestic violence victims
3) Initiate comprehensive community education efforts to avail patients, co-workers, and the community of the information and safety plan available to them
4) Envision the changes needed to end family violence and by-pass the excuses obstructing reform efforts.

Having spent 19 years working with abuse victims in five states, as an advocate, survivor, and prosecutor, I can attest to the significance of health professionals' involvement in the above four areas. Certainly, these recommendations are not all-inclusive, nor are they meant to be limiting. Rather, they constitute a short list of starting points specifically designed for practitioners. The efforts of battered women's advocates have been greatly enhanced and our spirits uplifted by the involvement of the many physicians and nurses who labor tirelessly to increase victim safety and community involvement.

Therapy Can Reduce Violence Against Women

by Mary Sikes Wylie

About the author: *Mary Sikes Wylie is a senior editor of the family psychotherapy magazine* Family Therapy Networker.

It is probably fair to say that most therapists still carry in their hearts a fairly traditional idea of what therapy looks like: a confidential, very private, 50-minute hour shared by one clinician and one client, one couple or one family.

Here and there, however, other, newer visions of therapy are beginning their slow ascent into the full day of professional consciousness, modes of practice that crack the code keeping the sacrosanct space of the private therapeutic encounter segregated from the bigger, messier world of public life. A new breed of practitioners, who look less like classic therapists and more like coaches, teachers, mentors, consultants—even benign marine sergeants or openly didactic moral guides—are bridging the long-standing cultural divide in America between private therapy and public life, individual and community, personal well-being and commonweal. . . .

An example of this new wave is the work being done at the Institute for Family Services in Somerset, New Jersey, established and directed by family therapist Rhea Almeida and offering an unusual group approach to marital and family problems, particularly domestic violence. The Institute is the only domestic violence program in the state providing comprehensive and integrated services to the entire families of battering men—not just abusers, but their wives and children, as well—and the only program in the region with clinicians specifically trained and state-certified to treat violent spouses. Because of the Institute's reputation for success at reducing recidivism among batterers (75 percent of all court-mandated clients never repeat the offense, according to Institute staff), judges in the area routinely mandate violent men for treatment. Currently, a new pre-trial intervention program is underway, in which all men under restraining orders are mandated for treatment before their trials. If they

Excerpted from Mary Sikes Wylie, "It's a Community Affair." This article first appeared in the *Family Therapy Networker* (March/April 1996) and is excerpted here with permission.

make good progress in the program, they may have their charges reduced or dropped. In addition, referrals come from women's shelters and local police departments. Indeed, several of the most vocal supporters of the Institute's program are police officers who have been through it, themselves. One current client, a Newark police officer, is beginning an in-house batterers' program in the Newark Police Department.

Being Tough on Batterers

Unlike some therapeutic interventions that legal authorities and women's rights advocates alike distrust for allegedly "coddling" abusers, the Institute combines tough-minded political and social re-education with an uncompromising insistence that the mandated batterer toe the line of treatment or face expulsion from the program. "Law enforcement agencies trust Rhea because they know she supports social control to the extent that she believes the community must be protected from the violence of the individual," says Robert Jay Green, professor of family and child psychology at the California School of Professional Psychology in Berkeley. According to Monica McGoldrick, director of the Family Institute of New Jersey, the Institute saves judges from having to make Solomon-like choices about who's telling the truth in thorny battering cases when both spouses are calling each other liars or the abused woman confounds judicial authorities by refusing to press charges and taking the abuser back. "Rhea is willing to assume responsibility for a hard popu-

> *"Before coming here, I never had anybody tell me I might be wrong."*

lation that nobody likes—she makes the problem go away for judges," says McGoldrick. But what really influences law-enforcement personnel, McGoldrick suspects, is the vision of a former abuser—perhaps a repeat offender—standing before the same judge who may have sentenced him, now as a sponsor of another accused batterer, making an eloquent case for the enormous impact the program has had on his own life. "It must bowl judges over to hear guys with horrific histories as abusers talking about how much they love their children, how they have turned their lives around, and seeing that they have become totally different kinds of men."

Nontraditional Techniques

What makes the program unique—besides its singular existence in the state— is a combination of features that veer off from traditional therapeutic practice: an almost total reliance on group psychoeducation (private treatment is kept to a bare minimum), a policy of open communication and no privileged information (clients share their entire histories in the groups), a rich integration of lay people (mostly former clients) into the very weave of therapy itself, and an unabashed stance of political advocacy in its approach. Clients rarely see a thera-

195

pist individually or even as single couples. . . . All clients are given a list of sponsors or mentors—graduates of the program—any one of whom they can call at any time. Sponsors are available on a rotating schedule 24 hours a day for new clients. Beginners attend "pre-group" sessions where they are treated to a stiff dose of educational videos, articles and pointed discussions in the everyday sociology of sexism, racism and class prejudice before progressing to longer-term men's, women's and/or couple's groups (the basic program is 36 weeks long). Institute staff members make no bones about their intention to give clients a thorough political and social re-education on the conviction that "public" patterns of power, status and domination fundamentally define and color all personal relations between men and women, whites and non-whites, rich and poor, gay and straight.

> *"The [police] officers . . . provided her male clients with living, breathing examples of non-violent men."*

Contributing further to the social and political education of clients are "cultural consultants"—sponsors, or occasional lay volunteers from the community, of diverse ethnic, religious or racial backgrounds—who participate in group sessions and provide a kind of socially and politically attuned reality test about individual behavior of new clients from similar backgrounds. The Institute staff knows that a cultural consultant who happens also to be a fundamentalist Christian is in an unequalled position to challenge a male client who excuses his abusive behavior to his wife and children by saying that the Bible obliges him, as head of the household, to rigorously "discipline" members of his family. An Islamic imam (an outside lay volunteer) once helped mediate between a devout Pakistani father and his daughter who was distraught because he wouldn't allow her to go out with her head and arms uncovered. An African-American consultant knows better than the white therapist how racism hinders a black male client from getting a job, but can also challenge more credibly the latter's failure to make enough personal effort on his own behalf. On the other hand, a new client who is a well-to-do Jewish physician is less likely to dismiss questions about his own arrogance and sense of personal entitlement if they come from somebody of his own background rather than of working-class status. Gays and lesbians are regularly employed as consultants to men's and women's group on the theory that they have been forced to develop more sensitive antennae for patriarchal and heterosexist attitudes than straights.

The linchpin of the Institute's program, however, is the sponsorship system, in which new clients are immediately put in touch with sponsors of their own gender, perhaps someone of similar cultural, class or ethnic backgrounds; even children and adolescents get sponsors of their own age. A sponsor may connect with a client before the latter has even set foot in the clinic; between 30 and 40 percent of the caseload consists of court-mandated abusive spouses, and, under the Institute's new pre-trial intervention program, the new client meets the therapist and a sponsor before the court bench, almost before the signature on a restraining order is dry. Whether mandated for treatment or not, violent or nonviolent, male or female, the client is immediately embraced by a network of sponsors. . . .

Group Sessions

Once in the program, clients spend about three hours a week at these sessions, usually on the same day or evening, going first to a men's or women's group and then to a couple's group. It is in these intense group meetings that the Institute's philosophy comes vividly to life. In an early-evening session for men on one Thursday night, Frank, a powerfully built police officer who used to severely beat and kick his wife, not desisting even when she was pregnant, now, as a sponsor, tries with gentleness, humor and calm authority to break through the stubborn anger of a new member, Larry, who has raped and terrorized his own wife. Even with a restraining order forbidding him access to the family home because of his chronic violence, Larry still cannot stop trying to run his wife's life. Just the week before, he threatened her and now sullenly pursues the track of *her* inadequacies as a wife, *her* failings as a mother—she isn't paying the bills on time, he complains; she's letting house repairs go, she isn't up to being the sole parent of a son ("A boy needs his father," he says doggedly). "Let it go, man," Frank says kindly, patiently, zeroing in on Larry's refusal to take responsibility for himself or to relinquish his status as unchallenged top dog at home. "Let all this shit go—you're not going to control everything, and you're not going to have it all your own way ever again."

Later that same night, in the couples' group, Frank's wife, Liz, once as crushed and miserable as a human being can get—suicidal, terrified, hopeless, loathing herself, half zonked on psychiatric medications—confronts the same man, who is now raging about the restraining order—its unfairness, the deep wrong that has been done to him. "It's *my* house, *my* garage, *my* swimming pool—*I* built it, *I* paid for it, and now I can't even go in it!" he cries. Liz, a feisty, funny, vital woman who it is hard to imagine being intimidated by anybody, rolls her eyes. "*My* house, *my* house—*I* did this, *I* did that," she says sarcastically "*No*, you didn't! You did it *together* with your wife. She made sacrifices for you every day, which you didn't even notice, to help get that house built and make it

> "It is an axiom of the Institute's program that respect for *relationship can only be discovered* in *relationship.*"

a home. It's as much her house as it is yours!" Larry mumblingly backs down for the time being.

After the session is over, Frank sighs and tells about how typical, how invariable, is Larry's stonewalling response, his defensiveness and refusal to be accountable for his own actions, his role in the shambles of his marriage. "It's so frustrating—we're all carbon copies of each other. New guys may live in different places, come from entirely different backgrounds, but it's always the same old thing. I remember once, when Liz brought home some domestic violence literature, of course I thought it didn't pertain at all to me. Everything wrong was just her problem as far as I was concerned; I thought she was nuts if she didn't do what I told her to do. Before coming here, I never had anybody tell me I might be wrong." Indeed, one of the most important

> **"In the groups, I got the first sense I ever had of how I must sound to my wife."**

lessons the men learn in the program is that not only can they be wrong, but that their manhood, their right to respect, doesn't rest on their infallibility. This simple truth, at once terrifying and liberating, can turn the world on its axis for many male clients. One sponsor, John, says with some irony, "You must always remember that men are *never* wrong." And, if a man is never wrong, John continues, then he never has to respect anybody else whose opinion differs from his own, including his wife.

A Community of Peers

Almeida began the first program for batterers in New Jersey about 12 years ago, while teaching family therapy at Rutgers University in New Brunswick. Frustrated by the lack of success in standard marital therapy and worried for her own safety in the presence of violence-prone, intimidating men, Almeida recruited two police officers she knew to join her in therapy sessions. The officers—themselves baffled by their inability to stop abusers or protect women—not only made Almeida and the wife feel safer (this explanation for the unusual arrangement seemed to satisfy most of the couples—few left therapy), but provided her male clients with living, breathing examples of non-violent men. With the officers and others she recruited from the Lions and Rotary Club participating in sessions, she conducted mini-tutorials on the art of conflict resolution without battering.

"I would ask the police officer lots of questions in front of the couple about how *he* resolved fights in *his* home without resorting to violence, and how was it possible to have a relationship that didn't end in battering," she says. At some point, the male client would bring up some egregious act or remark made by his wife that had "provoked" and fully justified his outburst—surely, the client would challenge the officer, *your* wife would never do something like that. On the contrary, the sponsor might reply, his wife had done even worse, but that in no way, ever, under any circumstances justified violence. This was the genesis of the program to bring a community of peers—through the voices of ordinary "regular guys" who were not in therapy—into the isolated lives of batterers who had very little understanding of what is normal, appropriate behavior in an intimate relationship. . . .

Learning Respect Through Relationships

Indeed, it is an axiom of the Institute's program that respect *for* relationship can only be discovered *in* relationship, and for Institute clients who usually have had little real experience of intimacy in their personal lives, emotional re-training occurs through the intense connections they form with one another. It is hard to imagine that the didactic feminist message would have much effect on male clients, for example, if not delivered within the context of the closest, deepest and most honest relationships with other men than they have ever known. Frank says the program was the first opportunity he ever had in his life to talk honestly about himself, how he felt, what was happening in his marriage without getting in return either evasion, embarrassment or antagonism ("In my family, you avoided conflict at all costs, nobody ever challenged anybody, and if they did, the response was to 'mind your own fucking business'.") Among his police comrades, his complaints about his wife were met with knee-jerk rein-forcement for blaming her and implicit exoneration for abusing her—what Almeida and other feminists have identified as male bonding through the deval-uation of women.

About his first contact with a sponsor, Frank says that at first he didn't want to get close to another man—"When I was young, kids always said that being close to another guy meant you were gay"—and after his first session at the Institute, he walked out and stayed away for a year. "I came in there and saw the mirror and

> *"The 'communication problem,' says Almeida, begins ... with the fact that men have more power than women."*

video camera and the women therapists sitting there, and I thought this was a kind of frigging cult, with a bunch of feminazis." His wife continued in therapy, however, and Frank says he was lured back in by staff members who said they needed him there to "help" his wife; they asked him very politely if he would commit to staying three months, "for his wife's sake." In that time, he was drawn in. "Little by little, they showed me that in order to 'help my wife,' I had to help myself,"—and he found that, as his wife became stronger and more self-sufficient, he too was becoming more attached to the program, and particularly to one of the sponsors, a businessman named John. "I can talk to him about anything and not worry about how he'll react; he knows more about me than my own father—I never had that kind of trust, before."

John himself remembers how startling it was when he first started going to group sessions, to hear his own anger, righteousness, excuses, defenses, lies, posturings, fears, vulnerabilities—in short, his own story—being repeated with one variation or another over and over by other men. "I learned how to listen to myself, hear how I talked to other people. You learn how stupid you are being by watching and listening to other people being stupid in the same way. In the groups, I got the first sense I ever had of how I must sound to my wife; what I didn't understand or even see about my own behavior became clear and obvious when I saw other men doing it."

A Political Agenda

The effectiveness of mutual self-help groups for a variety of problems is well-known—Alcoholics Anonymous (AA) is a prime example. Why, one might wonder, does the Institute insist upon an explicit political and social agenda, bringing issues of power and privilege from the world way beyond home right into the center of clinical work around domestic abuse? In one answer, Almeida cites the not-uncommon case of men asking to learn how they might better "communicate" with their wives, as if they could pick up marital communications skills in a kind of neutral, all-purpose Berlitz course on spouse-speak. The "communication problem," says Almeida, begins long before the derailed marital conversation does, with the fact that men have more power than women. "I ask these men how is it different to 'communicate' with an employee versus their boss. How does the structure and context of the relationship—who has more power—transform both the message and the way it is communicated?". . .

> *"There are virtually no secrets within the walls of the Institute."*

Bringing politics into therapy is not new. Feminist therapists and clinicians who work with poor and minority populations have been doing it for years. Nonetheless, most marital therapy, notwithstanding knee-jerk homage to "changing gender roles and expectations," still seems focused on a microanalysis of marriage as a closed and private domestic circle largely untainted by external social realities. Besides giving ordinary clients more credit for social and political awareness than do most therapists, says Robert Jay Green, Almeida's use of didactic videos and reading matter is a potent therapeutic strategy. "The films and articles provide a vehicle by which men who are unable to talk about their own feelings can ask for help to talk about what is going on inside them under cover of talking about something they saw on a tape. It allows them to take part in the group without casting off their armor and feeling like naked snails."

No Secrets

If the technique of showing videos about sexism, racism and homophobia and assigning newspaper reading strikes many clinicians as an odd kind of marital intervention, the Institute's dispensal with traditional norms of therapeutic confidentiality is most likely to raise hackles in the professional therapeutic community. There are virtually no secrets within the walls of the Institute (and the therapeutic prescription to tell the truth about "private" matters to family and friends outside is not uncommon), which resembles a small village in which each individual's business is everybody's business. All the therapists know the histories of all the clients, who pretty much know one another's stories; the policy of no secrets, and the extensive participation of former clients and some community members who never were clients as sponsors, has been criticized in the profession as violating therapeutic boundaries. When Almeida first broached her ideas for the sponsorship program, critics suggested that it was unethical and possible grounds for malpractice to offer an allegedly professional service that was partly provided by rank amateurs without clinical training, who could not be held to professional standards of confidentiality. First rejected for publication by *Family Process* in 1987, Almeida's article appeared in 1991, co-written with family therapist Michele Bograd as a chapter in Bograd's book, *Feminist Approaches for Men in Family Therapy*. Traditional therapists who are seeing one of the spouses frequently object to the requirement that their clients share private details of their lives with the group. . . .

The program is also faulted by some women's shelter groups for putting women at risk for further battering by using the victim's own story as an intervention with her abuser—confronting him with what she has reported—and then treating both batterers and spouses in the same group. But, Almeida points out, they have never had an incident of severe battering (though some of verbal abuse) by a male client engaged in the program, and the women's stories, repeated in the collective presence of other clients, who have also been there, so to speak, has the effect of making the men more inclined to face their own responsibility. . . .

The Emphasis on Community

Not every case is a success story, though clients who make it through the first 90 days are a reasonably safe bet for hanging in until the end. Abusive men not mandated for treatment whose wives have finally, definitively, left them, sometimes have little motivation for remaining in the program. Obversely, the threat of losing a spouse and children can be powerful leverage for staying on. . . .

Most men deeply yearn for human connection, says Almeida, even though our culture seems to push them in the other direction, toward a posture of emotional isolationism, fear of revealing themselves, secrecy about their own needs, shame at being found out in their vulnerability. Almeida's policy of extending the conversational circle, of bringing men and women into community and making them aware of their own socialization, lightens the enormous burden of individual guilt that makes personal accountability so difficult. Says Robert Jay Green, "She helps people understand that

> *"She helps people understand that behavior is not entirely* **his** *or* **hers** *. . . but that their difficulties are part of a much larger social structure."*

behavior is not entirely *his* or *hers,* that the couple didn't create their own problems all by themselves, but that their difficulties are part of a much larger social structure." For all its apparent radicalism, there is something very old-fashioned about this approach. "It's amazing that more people haven't done what Rhea is doing," says Green. "It's very much like what the early family therapists believed: that individuals, families, communities, societies are nested together like Russian dolls. All of us know that, but Rhea makes it explicit; she is fearless, and says out loud what most of us keep safely tucked in our own little minds."

Promoting Public Awareness Can Reduce Violence Against Women

by Marissa E. Ghez

About the author: *Marissa E. Ghez is the associate director of the Family Violence Prevention Fund, a national nonprofit organization that focuses on domestic violence education, prevention, and public policy reform.*

Domestic violence continues to flourish because of silence, and the subtle but pervasive ways that American society implicitly accepts and condones disrespect of and violence against women, and the ongoing belief that domestic violence is a private, and not a public, concern. Today, the cultural climate in this country is one in which people say that domestic violence is wrong, but in which they nevertheless look the other way from the problem, subtly reinforcing its continuation through disrespect and devaluation of women. . . .

Violence Is Not Inevitable

Even though the staggering numbers of abused women indicate that progress is not being made very quickly, we know from other issues that what is learned can be unlearned. Broad cultural messages about male-female relationships can be changed; attitudes about what is acceptable behavior can be reframed; children growing up with domestic violence can be taught new behaviors. Domestic violence can be positioned as an issue that touches the lives of more than just abused women and batterers, a problem that tears families and communities apart, fills our courtrooms, hospitals and morgues. In order to galvanize Americans to take action on this issue, domestic violence must be promoted as an issue that individuals and communities alike must help address. People around the country must be educated that they have a role to play in helping battered women and their children—educated, that is, that their behavior matters, too—and shown how to get involved. The strategic use of communications

Excerpted, with permission, from Marissa E. Ghez, "Communication and Public Education: Effective Tools to Promote a Cultural Change on Domestic Violence," a Family Violence Prevention Fund position paper, available at www.igc.apc.org/fund/difference/nij.html. Portions of this paper appear in *Ending Domestic Violence*, edited by Ethel Klein (Thousand Oaks, CA: Sage Publications, 1997), and are reprinted by permission of Sage Publications. Copyright ©1997 by Sage Publications.

and public education tools can play a key role in raising public awareness, changing attitudes, and promoting personal and community involvement.

The domestic violence field is at a pivotal moment as we all begin to recognize that enacting sanctions through the justice system is essential in addressing the problem, but that it is not enough. Concomitantly, social sanctions must also be developed and woven into the everyday fabric of people's lives so that batterers know their behavior will no longer be tolerated by their friends, family and co-workers.

> *"The cultural climate in this country is one in which people say that domestic violence is wrong, but in which they nevertheless look the other way from the problem."*

To be effective, communications strategies must educate the public at large about the issue in a manner which counters the existing cultural acceptance of violence and produces public outrage about, and a commitment to stop, violence against women. We have seen this with many behavior-based health issues. In fact, addressing every significant societal health problem, especially those that involve behavior, has required changing the way people think, as well as the way they behave—whether it has been recycling, cigarette smoking, or drunk driving.

Affecting Social Change

A review of other social movements can be useful. High exposure media efforts to educate the public about the environment, for example, have brought recycling into the everyday life and habits of Americans. Attitudes about smoking have changed in this country from viewing it as glamorous, sophisticated behavior (validated by seeing our favorite movie stars lighting up on the big screen) to seeing it as dangerous (with activists boycotting movies in which smoking is glamorized); in California, where massive public education efforts have taken place to caution the public about the first- and second-hand effects of smoking, the prevalence of smokers declined from 26 percent in 1987 to 21 percent in 1990. Finally, our attitudes about drinking and driving have also been transformed by pervasive public education efforts; people have learned to watch out for potential perpetrators, and have learned to take responsibility for preventing the problem (by taking the key away from a friend too intoxicated to drive, or designating a non-drinking driver at the evening's outset).

Saturating the media with messages that promote individual involvement and action—even when the messages are unpleasant and intrusive—is an effective method for changing behavior. For example, a public service advertising campaign sponsored by the Advertising Council which urged people, particularly men, to speak to their doctors about colon cancer (not an easy or comfortable subject) was found to increase awareness about the issue from 11 percent to 29 percent after only six months of high exposure to advertising, and up to 40 percent in 12 months. The number of people who spoke to their doctors about colon cancer during the course of the education effort increased by 43 percent, with the number of men increasing by 114 percent. Because colon cancer is a disease with a good prognosis after early treatment, this public education effort presumably saved lives. . . .

This country is on the threshold of being able to effect massive social change on the issue of domestic violence because public awareness has been raised so significantly over the years. Yet if advocates want to see a lasting difference in behavior—and to ensure that domestic violence is not merely this year's fad—a concerted effort must be made to address the public's subtle acceptance of, and turning away from, the problem of domestic violence. America continues to need massive public education initiatives on the issue of domestic violence which make the issue a public one by encouraging individuals and communities to claim personal responsibility for stopping domestic violence, just as they have taken responsibility for stopping drunk driving and protecting the environment. . . .

Public Opinion Research on Domestic Violence

In 1992, the Family Violence Prevention Fund (the FUND), a national domestic violence education and policy organization, conducted pioneering market research on public opinion about domestic violence with funding from the Ford Foundation to lay the groundwork for such a campaign. Prior to this research, there had been no comprehensive, national study of public knowledge or concern about domestic violence. EDK Associates, a public opinion research firm, designed a qualitative and quantitative research effort on public attitudes toward domestic violence.

A series of 12 focus groups were conducted in five cities (Hartford, CT, Little Rock, AR, Dallas, TX, Los Angeles, CA, and San Francisco, CA). Three were comprised of white women, two of white men, two of African-American women, and one group each of Latinas, Latinos, Asian-American women and Asian-American men. The groups were led by a gender and ethnic appropriate moderator, and the Latino groups were conducted in both Spanish and English.

One of the most striking findings was that, contrary to expectations, Americans across all race and ethnic backgrounds were both ready and willing to discuss this issue. People discussed domestic violence as a real problem that they had seen in their own lives, and although not aware of the prevalence of the problem throughout society, they wanted it stopped. One man from Dallas commented, "I don't know [why my friend's boyfriend beat her], but there's no reason to hit a woman. That's absolutely wrong. . . . If she did something horrible, you can leave."

An opinion survey was then conducted which was the most comprehensive

"People around the country must be educated that they have a role to play in helping battered women."

survey on the issue to date. The survey was drawn from a national sampling of 1,000 men and women aged 18 and older who were interviewed by telephone. Three additional surveys were also conducted to oversample 300 African-Americans, 300 Latinos, and 300 Asian-Americans, with ethnic-appropriate surveyors doing the interviews.

"Saturating the media with messages that promote individual involvement and action . . . is an effective method for changing behavior."

The survey found that 87 percent of Americans felt that men beating their wives and girlfriends was a serious problem facing many families. More than one in three (34 percent) had witnessed an incident of domestic violence directly—more than had witnessed a mugging or a robbery combined (19 percent). Further, 14 percent of women indicated that they themselves had been violently abused by a husband or boyfriend, and one in two women said that battering was not uncommon in relationships.

Further, Americans of every age and racial group agreed that violence is not just a physical assault, but is also an attack on women's dignity and freedom. And, unlike a decade ago, most Americans claimed they were no longer buying the old excuses for abuse. Respondents were unwilling either to excuse him for his violent behavior ("he couldn't help it," "he was drinking") or blame her for the violence ("she provoked it," "she deserved it"). Ninety-three percent of Americans said they would talk to friends, family or clergy if someone they knew was being beaten, and 90 percent said they would call the police if they witnessed a man beating a woman.

The research also indicated that most Americans felt helpless to do anything about this widespread problem: while 81 percent said that something could be done to reduce domestic violence, more than one in four (26 percent) said they didn't know what specific action to take.

Overall, the research showed that in 1992 Americans were aware of, and concerned about, the effects of domestic violence in their lives. While unaware of the extent of the problem throughout the country, they said they no longer accepted any excuses for battering. Many people expressed willingness to become involved but said they didn't know what they should do about the problem, either in their personal lives or in general. Americans needed to be further educated about the prevalence of the problem, and given some direction for action.

National Public Education Campaign

On the basis of that information, in June 1994 the Family Violence Prevention Fund launched a national public education campaign. Called THERE'S NO EXCUSE FOR DOMESTIC VIOLENCE, the FUND's multi-year effort aims to reduce and prevent domestic violence by educating the public and creating a commitment in Americans to end the epidemic. Sponsored by the Advertising

Council and selected as its major public education and research initiative for several years, the campaign is giving unprecedented visibility to the issue.

As a part of the public education initiative, the FUND developed print, radio and television public service announcements (PSAs), as well as bus shelter and billboard displays, targeting the general public. These ads carry the campaign's key messages that "domestic violence is everybody's business" and "there's no excuse for it." In one powerful television execution called "Neighbors," viewers see a couple in their bed who hear the sounds of a man brutally beating a woman in the apartment upstairs. The couple exchange anxious looks, but when the husband reaches over to the night table, instead of picking up the phone to call the police, he turns off the light. The corresponding print execution shows a man beating a woman, and the text reads: "If the noise coming from next door were loud music, you'd do something about it." Another television ad shows wedding day images and contrasts them with the chilling fact that 42 percent of women murdered in America are killed by "someone who promised to love them.". . .

Before the launch of the campaign and the distribution of the PSAs, the Ad Council commissioned a pre-test of the 30-second television PSA, "Neighbors," to ensure that Americans would understand the strategic intentions of the ad. Overall the commercial tested extremely well, generating a recall score 15 percent above the average for other Ad Council campaigns and in-depth verbatims (many people remembered the slogan "it is your business" in particular and understood that it meant "we should all get involved").

> *"Americans of every age and racial group agreed that violence is not just a physical assault, but is also an attack on women's dignity and freedom."*

In addition, the execution appears to have a positive impact on key consumer attitudes—the commercial was found to be believable (84 percent), important (83 percent), effective (76 percent) and thought-provoking (64 percent). . . .

The Simpsons and Domestic Violence

The trial of O.J. Simpson for the murders of his ex-wife and her friend and the subsequent revelations of his violence toward her have focused national attention on the issue of domestic violence, and have served as a national "teach-in" on the subject. Many publications have dedicated prominent, in-depth feature stories and even entire issues to the subject of domestic violence, creating intense interest in the seriousness of this epidemic. What's more, because Simpson was such a beloved public figure, journalists became intrigued by the question of how such incidents can be circumvented earlier. In short, these events have prompted a public shift toward questioning how domestic violence can be stopped.

Advocates, journalists and policymakers alike have channeled renewed energies into understanding what role individuals and communities can play in addressing domestic violence, as well as how to reach women who are currently being abused before it is too late. An extraordinary, February 20, 1995, *People* cover story ran the banner headline: "Why Nobody Helped Nicole: Friends, family and police saw her bruises but failed to stop O.J.'s abuse. What went wrong?" Meanwhile, the November 1994 issue of *Self* included an article entitled "100 Things You Can Do To Prevent Domestic Violence," *Emerge* ran a piece called "The Brutal Truth: Putting domestic violence on the black agenda," and *Men's Fitness* ran a special report called "Is Someone You Know a Batterer? Domestic abuse is every man's problem. Here's how to spot it and stop it."

Public opinion polling reflects the effect this national teach-in has had on the general public's perception of the problem of domestic violence. In mid-January 1995, *Time* magazine/CNN released findings from a poll of 1,000 adults. In comparison to the Family Violence Prevention Fund's 1992 poll, which found that 87 percent of the public considered domestic violence a serious problem, this more recent study found that almost everyone in this country (96 percent) considers domestic violence a serious problem in today's society. The same poll revealed that two-thirds of men (67 percent) and 80 percent of women view domestic violence as a very serious problem; in 1991, only 57 percent of respondents in a similar poll said domestic violence was a very serious problem. . . .

Attention, Awareness, and Action

Certainly, increased media coverage about domestic violence has helped raise awareness about the issue and has helped galvanize the general public to take some action. A media audit conducted for the FUND reveals that there was a dramatic increase in both television and print coverage of domestic violence in the months following O.J. Simpson's arrest and the subsequent revelations of his abuse towards his ex-wife: During the months of April and May 1994, a total of two stories about domestic violence appeared on the three networks' evening news and a Lexis-Nexis search found 206 print stories that referred to domestic violence, spousal abuse and/or battered women; during the months of June and July 1994, however, the number of network news stories skyrocketed to 54 and the Lexis-Nexis search uncovered 454 print stories about domestic violence. This dramatic increase in coverage sustained itself until the end of 1994. Evidence suggests that battered women are more likely to seek outside intervention or leave their abusers when they perceive themselves to have resources and options for ending the violence. During the same time period when domestic abuse featured prominently in national and local media markets, including scores of articles about what to do if you are a victim, battered women across the country began seeking outside intervention in record numbers. In San Francisco alone, there was a 51 percent increase in

> *"'If the noise coming from next door were loud music, you'd do something about it.'"*

the number of people calling crisis lines in the first three months after Nicole Brown Simpson was murdered; during the same time period, 39 percent more people sought help from local domestic violence agencies.

Significantly, the same media stories that prompted battered women to come forward also seem to have had a positive effect in motivating Americans to take some action to help reduce domestic violence. Almost 50 percent reported that the stories in the media had made them more likely to do something to help reduce domestic violence (and only six percent reported that the stories had made them less likely to do something to help). . . .

> *"In San Francisco alone, there was a 51 percent increase in the number of people calling crisis lines in the first three months after Nicole Brown Simpson was murdered."*

With the public ready to take action against domestic violence, advocates and policymakers in the field must provide the public with some direction for engagement and more encouragement to do so (after all, despite an increase in the number of people getting involved, fully 79 percent of the public had not taken any action against domestic violence in the last year as of February 1995). Until recently, there has been little collective thought given to the question of how to involve and engage the general citizenry in addressing this problem. Over the next decade, advocates must identify and promote simple, safe and effective action steps that address three different, distinct levels: person-to-person contact, individual action, and community action.

Mobilizing Individuals and Communities

Person-to-Person Contact. Individuals everywhere must be educated about how to effectively talk with and give support to women they know who are currently victims of abuse so that they can help real people living with or trying to escape from violence at home. While these kinds of conversations are often emotionally difficult—and may require the commitment of the intervenor to have ongoing discussions with the victim about the situation—this kind of support is invaluable. One of the problems facing battered women is their very real sense of isolation and shame. Yet if advocates can help create a world in which battered women are surrounded by friends and relatives non-judgmentally offering support, referrals, and resources, victims will have a much easier time finding the courage to leave and the help to make it happen. Additionally, individuals must be educated about the devastating impact of spousal abuse on children living in violent homes, and encouraged to offer help and support to the youngest and most innocent victims of domestic violence whenever possible. . . .

Individual Action. Individuals who can be mobilized to take action must be provided with relatively easy action steps that allow them to be participants in the effort to end domestic violence. The Family Violence Prevention Fund's public education campaign includes a national toll-free number, publicized on each public service announcement, which provides free Action Kits to callers. These kits include specific organizing strategies that several citizens have undertaken to raise awareness about domestic violence in their communities. These strategies include getting domestic violence hotline numbers printed on milk cartons; organizing a march for women's lives to raise both awareness and funds for services; and blanketing storefronts with stickers reading "THIS IS A SAFE HAVEN," where battered women can seek refuge and know that support is available to them. . . .

Community Action. Every successful social change movement requires the commitment to get involved not just from individuals but also from the collective community of which they are a part. Orchestrated, community-wide actions and demonstrations have an awesome ability to sway public opinion, attract media support and resources, and keep community-based institutions accountable.

The AIDS movement has been particularly successful in some areas of the country at galvanizing public support, and funneling community energies into a collective project. In San Francisco, the city's annual AIDS march through the streets of the city serves as a moving reminder every year of the thousands of people who have died since the epidemic began, raising awareness about the problem and its massive effects on the lives of real people, and giving activists the opportunity to lobby publicly for increased aid for services and prevention, and other policy changes. In cities where the Names Project's travelling AIDS quilt is unravelled—in which each of the many thousands of panels that compose it represents a victim of AIDS who has died—the enormous display serves the same purpose, allowing every individual to participate in the AIDS movement (either by actually making a panel for a loved one lost to AIDS or by viewing the panel and, in so doing, experiencing the impact of AIDS on this country).

> *"Orchestrated, community-wide actions and demonstrations have an awesome ability to sway public opinion."*

The domestic violence movement must create a similar kind of public event that invites mass participation, involving all members of the community in both recognizing, remembering and mourning victims, raising awareness about the issue, and holding institutions to which battered women turn accountable for their response. Just as Mothers Against Drunk Driving instituted court monitoring to gauge the way judges handled individual drunk driving cases, activists could pack courtrooms in which domestic violence cases are being decided, and bring incidents handled poorly to the press. Just as the Ms. Foundation's "Take Our Daughters to Work Day" encouraged business communities across the country to welcome the future female workforce and give young girls a vision of possible career paths, the domestic violence movement must create a day in which the media and business communities come together to condemn abusive behavior and show young girls and boys that there is another way of life for them. Advocates must determine the most effective forum for such public events, and begin working to make them happen. . . .

Creating a Violence-Intolerant Environment

Encouraging spokespeople from many different arenas to speak out against domestic violence will create an environment in which domestic violence victims know that they are not alone and that there is help available, and in which batterers begin to recognize that their behavior will increasingly carry negative consequences. Already, such a shift has begun. On Court TV, the media outlet covering the Simpson trial most closely, a male prosecutor from New Jersey appeared and commented that "this type of activity should not be condoned. . . . If you are aware of this type of situation, by not speaking out, you in fact condone it—and something as horrendous as a death may result. So it is important that if you are aware of it, come and speak out about it."

More and more, this changed environment encourages survivors to come forward to tell their stories, and increases both public awareness about the issue and public commitment to ending the epidemic. When *Time* printed a domestic violence photograph taken by Donna Ferrato, a state legislator from Maryland saw the photo and decided to admit publicly that she herself had at one point been a victim of domestic violence. Testifying last year at a congressional subcommittee hearing, she said:

> This is the first time I've made any public statement about this issue. I'm here today because of a picture in *Time* magazine. It showed an eight-year-old boy. With his finger pointing at his father, he said, 'I hate you for beating my mother.' Another picture flashed in my mind; I saw another little boy. He was almost seven years old. His mother saw his face peering over a bannister as his father brutally beat her, and she told him, 'Go to your room.' I am that mother. That day, a little over 25 years ago, I took my children and I walked out.

The statement appeared in the national evening news around the country.

Now is the time to promote action. The same *Time* magazine/CNN poll cited earlier found that only three percent of Americans say that domestic violence is not a serious problem in our society right now. Advocates and government officials alike must seize the day with ways to galvanize the American public to address this costly and devastating epidemic.

Bibliography

Books

Vera Anderson	*A Woman Like You: The Face of Domestic Violence*. Seattle, WA: Seal Press, 1997.
Helen Benedict	*Recovery: How to Survive Sexual Assault for Women, Men, Teenagers, Their Friends and Families*. New York: Columbia University Press, 1994.
Jeff Benedict	*Athletes and Acquaintance Rape*. Thousand Oaks, CA: Sage, 1998.
Jeff Benedict	*Public Heroes, Private Felons: Athletes and Crimes Against Women*. Boston: Northeastern University Press, 1997.
Raquel Kennedy Bergen, ed.	*Issues in Intimate Violence*. Thousand Oaks, CA: Sage, 1998.
Raquel Kennedy Bergen	*Wife Rape: Understanding the Response of Survivors and Service Providers*. Thousand Oaks, CA: Sage, 1996.
Susan Brewster	*To Be an Anchor in the Storm: A Guide for Families and Friends of Abused Women*. New York: Ballantine Books, 1997.
Eve S. Buzawa and Carl G. Buzawa, eds.	*Do Arrests and Restraining Orders Really Work?* Thousand Oaks, CA: Sage, 1996.
Sandra Byers and Lucia F. O'Sullivan, eds.	*Sexual Coercion in Dating Relationships*. New York: Haworth Press, 1997.
Philip W. Cook	*Abused Men: The Hidden Side of Domestic Violence*. New York: Praeger, 1997.
Nancy A. Crowell and Ann W. Burgess	*Understanding Violence Against Women*. Washington, DC: National Academy Press, 1996.
Cynthia R. Daniels and Rachelle Brooks, eds.	*Feminists Negotiate the State: The Politics of Domestic Violence*. Lanham, MD: University Press of America, 1997.
Jill Davies et al.	*Safety Planning with Battered Women: Complex Lives, Difficult Decisions*. Thousand Oaks, CA: Sage, 1998.
Rebecca Emerson Dobash and Russell P. Dobash, eds.	*Rethinking Violence Against Women*. Thousand Oaks, CA: Sage, 1998.

Bibliography

Donald Alexander Downs	*More than Victims: Battered Women, the Syndrome Society, and the Law*. Chicago: University of Chicago Press, 1996.
Donal Dutton	*The Batterer: A Psychological Profile*. New York: Basic Books, 1995.
Andrea Dworkin	*Life and Death: Unapologetic Writings on the Continuing War Against Women*. New York: Free Press, 1997.
Raoul Felder and Barbara Victor	*Getting Away with Murder: Weapons for the War Against Domestic Violence*. New York: Simon & Schuster, 1996.
L. Kevin Hamberger and Claire Renzetti, eds.	*Domestic Partner Abuse*. New York: Springer, 1996.
Jana L. Jasinski and Linda M. Williams, eds.	*Partner Violence: A Comprehensive Review of 20 Years of Research*. Thousand Oaks, CA: Sage, 1998.
Catherine T. Kennedy and Karen R. Brown	*Report from the Front Lines: The Impact of Domestic Violence on Poor Women*. New York: NOW Legal Defense and Education Fund, 1996.
Ethel Klein et al.	*Ending Domestic Violence: Changing Public Perceptions, Halting the Epidemic*. Thousand Oaks, CA: Sage, 1997.
Mary P. Koss et al.	*No Safe Haven: Male Violence Against Women at Home, at Work, and in the Community*. Washington, DC: American Psychological Association, 1995.
Laura Lederer and Richard Delgado, eds.	*The Price We Pay: The Case Against Racist Speech, Hate Propaganda, and Pornography*. New York: Hill and Wang, 1995.
Catharine A. MacKinnon and Andrea Dworkin, eds.	*In Harm's Way: The Pornography Civil Rights Hearings*. Boston: Harvard University Press, 1998.
Esther Madriz	*Nothing Bad Happens to Good Girls: Fear of Crime in Women's Lives*. Berkeley and Los Angeles: University of California Press, 1997.
Martha McCaughey	*Real Knockouts: The Physical Feminism of Women's Self-Defense*. New York: New York University Press, 1997.
Alice Myers and Sarah Wight, eds.	*No Angels: Women Who Commit Violence*. New York: HarperCollins, 1997.
Hannah Nyala	*Point Last Seen: A Woman Tracker's Story*. Boston: Beacon Press, 1997.
Patricia Pearson	*When She Was Bad: Violent Women and the Myth of Innocence*. New York: Viking, 1997.
Claire M. Renzetti and Charles Harvey Miley, eds.	*Violence in Gay and Lesbian Domestic Partnerships*. New York: Haworth Press, 1996.
Diana Russell	*Dangerous Relationships: Pornography, Misogyny, and Rape*. Thousand Oaks, CA: Sage, 1998.

Peggy Reeves Sanday   *A Woman Scorned: Acquaintance Rape on Trial*. New York: Doubleday, 1996.

Martin D. Schwartz and   *Sexual Assault on the College Campus: The Role of Male Peer*
Walter S. DeKeseredy   *Support*. Thousand Oaks, CA: Sage, 1997.

Beth Sipe and   *I Am Not Your Victim: Anatomy of Domestic Violence*.
Evelyn J. Hall   Thousand Oaks, CA: Sage, 1996.

Nadine Strossen   *Defending Pornography: Free Speech, Sex, and the Fight for Women's Rights*. New York: Scribner, 1995.

Mollie Whalen   *Counseling to End Violence Against Women: A Subversive Model*. Thousand Oaks, CA: Sage, 1996.

Vernon R. Wiehe   *Intimate Betrayal: Understanding and Responding to the*
and Ann L. Richards   *Trauma of Acquaintance Rape*. Thousand Oaks, CA: Sage, 1995.

Periodicals

Gloria Allred   "It's Time for D.A.s to Get Tough on Domestic Violence," *Ms.*, July/August 1996.

Jeannine Amber   "Young and Abused," *Essence*, January 1997.

Vera Anderson   "Read My Face," *Utne Reader*, September/October 1997.

Malcolm Boyd   "Why Home Is Not a Haven," *Modern Maturity*, January/February 1997.

Felicia Collins Correia   "Domestic Violence Can Be Cured," *USA Today*, November 1997.

Ellis Cose   "Truths About Spouse Abuse," *Newsweek,* August 8, 1994.

Catherine Elton   "Why Batterers Get the Kids," *New Republic*, March 24, 1997.

Elizabeth Gleick   "No Way Out," *Time*, December 23, 1996.

Stephanie B. Goldberg   "Nobody's Victim," *ABA Journal*, July 1996. Available from 750 N. Lake Shore Dr., Chicago, IL 60611.

Kristen Golden   "Behind Closed Doors," *Ms.,* March/April 1997.

Jennifer Gonnerman   "Welfare's Domestic Violence," *Nation*, March 10, 1997.

Dick Haws   "Rape Victims: Papers Shouldn't Name Us," *American Journalism Review*, September 1996.

Karen Houppert   "After the Rape," *Glamour*, April 1996.

Ariella Hyman and   "Mandatory Reporting of Domestic Violence by Health
Ronal A. Chez   Care Providers: A Misguided Approach," *Women's Health Issues*, Winter 1995. Available from 409 12th St. SW, Washington, DC 20024.

Issues and   "Domestic Violence," June 12, 1998.
Controversies On File

Bibliography

John Q. Kelly	"Emerging from the Shadows: Domestic Violence as a Medical Issue," *Vital Speeches of the Day*, October 1, 1997.
John Leo	"Feminists Facilitate Rise in Female Violence," *Conservative Chronicle*, May 15, 1996. Available from PO Box 29, Hampton, IA 50441.
Linda Marsa	"The New Date-Rape Drug," *Glamour*, November 1997.
Wendy McElroy	"The New Mythology of Rape," *Liberty*, September 1994. Available from 1018 Water St., Suite 201, Port Townsend, WA 98368.
Wendy McElroy	"The Unfair Sex?" *National Review*, May 1, 1995.
Gerald McOscar	"Slap Your Spouse, Lose Your House," *Women's Quarterly,* Spring 1997.
Debra Michals	"Cyber-Rape: How Virtual Is It?" *Ms.,* March/April 1997.
Candice M. Monson et al.	"To Have and to Hold: Perceptions of Marital Rape," *Journal of Interpersonal Violence*, September 1996.
Jane O'Hara	"Rape in the Military," *Maclean's*, May 25, 1998.
Leah Rose	"Unclear and Present Danger," *On the Issues*, Summer 1995.
Robin Runge	"Double Jeopardy: Victims of Domestic Violence Face Twice the Abuse," *Human Rights*, Spring 1998.
Sally L. Satel	"Feminist Number Games," *New York Times*, September 11, 1997.
Jeffrey R. Sipe	"Is Prosecution the Best Defense Against Domestic Violence?" *Insight*, December 2, 1996. Available from 3600 New York Ave. NE, Washington, DC 20002.
Gregory L. Vistica	"Rape in the Ranks," *Newsweek*, November 25, 1996.
Barbara Vobejda	"For Battered Women, New Listeners," *Washington Post National Weekly Edition*, July 11–17, 1994.
Michael Weiss and Cathy Young	"Feminist Jurisprudence: Equal Rights or Neo-Paternalism?" *Cato Policy Analysis*, June 19, 1996. Available from Cato Institute, 1000 Massachusetts Ave. NW, Washington, DC 20001.
E. Assata Wright	"Not a Black and White Issue," *On the Issues*, Winter 1998.
Abigail Zuger	"A Fistful of Hostility Is Found in Women," *New York Times*, July 28, 1998.

Organizations to Contact

The editors have compiled the following list of organizations concerned with the issues debated in this book. The descriptions are derived from materials provided by the organizations. All have publications or information available for interested readers. The list was compiled on the date of publication of the present volume; the information provided here may change. Be aware that many organizations take several weeks or longer to respond to inquiries, so allow as much time as possible.

Advocates for Abused and Battered Lesbians (AABL)
PO Box 85596, Seattle, WA 98105-9998
(206) 547-8191
e-mail: aabl@isomedia.com • website: http://www.isomedia.com/homes/AABL

AABL provides services for lesbians and their children who are or have been victims of domestic violence. Through community education and outreach, its members encourage communities to recognize and eliminate lesbian battering, homophobia, and misogyny. AABL provides information on intimate abuse, and its website includes stories from survivors of domestic violence.

American Bar Association Commission on Domestic Violence
740 15th St. NW, Washington, DC 20005-1022
(202) 662-1737 • (202) 662-1744 • fax: (202) 662-1594
e-mail: abacdv@abanet.org • website: http://www.abanet.org/domviol/home.html

The commission researches model domestic violence programs in an effort to develop a blueprint for a national multidisciplinary domestic violence program. The commission provides information on domestic violence law and publishes several books, including *Stopping Violence Against Women: Using New Federal Laws* and *The Impact of Domestic Violence on Your Legal Practice: A Lawyer's Handbook.*

Center for the Prevention of Sexual and Domestic Violence
936 N. 34th St., Suite 200, Seattle, WA 98013
(206) 634-1903 • fax: (206) 634-0115
e-mail: cpsdv@cpsdv.org • website: http://www.cpsdv.org

The center is an interreligious ministry addressing issues of sexual and domestic violence. Its goal is to engage religious leaders in the task of ending abuse through institutional and social change. The center publishes educational videos, the quarterly newsletter *Working Together,* and many books, including *Violence Against Women and Children: A Christian Theological Sourcebook* and *Sexual Violence: The Unmentionable Sin—An Ethical and Pastoral Perspective.*

Concerned Women for America (CWA)
1015 15th St. NW, Suite 1100, Washington, DC 20024
(202) 488-7000 • fax: (202) 488-0806
website: http://www.cwfa.org

CWA seeks to protect the interests of American families, promote biblical values, and provide a voice for women throughout the United States who believe in Judeo-Christian values. CWA believes pornography contributes to abusive behavior in men and publishes the monthly magazine *Family Voice*.

Family Research Laboratory (FRL)
University of New Hampshire
126 Horton Social Science Center, Durham, NH 03824-3586
fax: (603) 862-1122
website: http://www.unh.edu/frl

FRL is an independent research unit devoted to the study of the causes and consequences of family violence, and it also works to dispel myths about family violence through public education. It publishes numerous books and articles on violence between men and women, marital rape, and verbal aggression. FRL's website offers a complete listing of available materials, such as the article "Stress and Rape in the Context of American Society," and the book *Understanding Partner Violence: Prevalence, Causes, Consequences, and Solutions*. However, many of the publications are intended for research scholars rather than the general public.

Feminist Majority Foundation
National Center for Women and Policing
8105 W. Third St., Suite 1, Los Angeles, CA 90048
(213) 651-2532 • fax: (213) 653-2689
e-mail: womencops@aol.com • website: http://www.feminist.org/police/ncwp.html

The center is a division of the Feminist Majority Foundation, an activist organization that works to eliminate sex discrimination and social and economic injustice. The center's members believe that female police officers respond more effectively to incidents of violence against women than do their male counterparts. It acts as a nationwide resource for law enforcement agencies and community leaders seeking to increase the number of female police officers in their communities and improve police response to family violence. Its publications include *Equality Denied: The Status of Women in Policing, 1997* and "Police Family Violence Fact Sheet." The Feminist Majority Foundation also publishes the quarterly *Feminist Majority Report*.

Independent Women's Forum
(800) 224-6000
e-mail: info@iwf.org • website: http://www.iwf.org

The forum is a conservative women's advocacy group that believes in individual freedom and personal responsibility and promotes common sense over feminist ideology. The forum believes that the incidence of domestic violence is exaggerated and that the Violence Against Women Act is ineffective and unjust. It publishes the *Women's Quarterly*.

National Clearinghouse on Marital and Date Rape
website: http://members.aol.com/ncmdr/index.html

The clearinghouse operates as a consulting firm on issues of marital, cohabitant, and date rape. It attempts to educate the public and to establish social and political equality in intimate relationships. Its publications include *Marital Rape Victims Fight Back, Prosecution Statistics on Marital Rape*, and the pamphlet *State Law Chart on Marital Rape*.

National Criminal Justice Reference Service (NCJRS)
PO Box 6000, Rockville, MD 20850
(800) 851-3420 • (301) 519-5500
e-mail: askncjrs@ncjrs.org • website: http://www.ojp.usdoj.gov/nij

A component of the Office of Justice Programs of the U.S. Department of Justice, NCJRS supports and conducts research on crime, criminal behavior, and crime prevention. It also acts as a clearinghouse for criminal justice information. Many reports are available from the clearinghouse, including *Domestic Violence, Stalking, and Antistalking* and *Civil Protection Orders: Victims' Views on Effectiveness.*

NOW Legal Defense and Education Fund (NOW LDEF)
99 Hudson St., New York, NY 10013-2871
(212) 925-6635 • fax: (212) 226-1066
website: http://www.nowldef.org

NOW LDEF is a branch of the National Organization for Women (NOW). It is dedicated to the eradication of sex discrimination through litigation and public education. The organization's publications include several legal resource kits on rape, stalking, and domestic violence, as well as information on the Violence Against Women Act.

U.S. Department of Justice Violence Against Women Office
10th & Constitution Ave. NW, Room 5302, Washington, DC 20530
National Domestic Violence Hotline: (800) 799-SAFE
fax: (202) 307-3911
website: http://www.usdoj.gov/vawo

The office is responsible for the overall coordination and focus of Department of Justice efforts to combat violence against women. It maintains the National Domestic Violence Hotline and publishes a monthly newsletter. An on-line domestic violence awareness manual is available at the office's website along with press releases, speeches, and the full text of and news about the Violence Against Women Act.

Women's Educational Equity Act Equity Resource Center
55 Chapel St., Newton, MA 02158-1060
(617) 969-7100
e-mail: weeactr@edc.org • website: http://www.edc.org/womensequity

The Women's Educational Equity Act is a U.S. Department of Education program dedicated to reducing the educational disparity between men and women. The Equity Resource Center works to improve educational, social, and economic outcomes for women and girls and believes that schools can educate against the behaviors that lead to violence against women. The center publishes the *WEEA Digest.*

Women's Freedom Network (WFN)
4410 Massachusetts Ave. NW, Suite 179, Washington, DC 20016
(202) 885-6245
e-mail: wfn@american.edu • website: http://www.womensfreedom.org

The network was founded in 1993 by a group of women who were seeking alternatives to both extremist ideological feminism and antifeminist traditionalism. It opposes gender bias in the sentencing of spouse abusers and believes acts of violence against women should be considered individually rather than stereotyped as gender-based hate crimes. WFN publishes a newsletter and the book *Neither Victim Nor Enemy: Women's Freedom Network Looks at Gender in America.*

Index

Index